P9-AGP-782

DATE DUE

DE 8 '95			
AG 8 '9			
DE 11 97			
OC 10 88			
DE 20 99			
NO 29 '01			
DE 19 01			
JE 10 02			
DE 11 '92			
NO 10 03			
DE 8 05			
AP 4 '07			
DE 21 '07			

ISRAEL

OPPOSING VIEWPOINTS®

Other Books of Related Interest in the Opposing Viewpoints Series:

Africa
American Foreign Policy
America's Defense
The Breakup of the Soviet Union
Central America
China
Eastern Europe
Japan
The Middle East
The New World Order
Nuclear Proliferation
The Third World
The Vietnam War

ISRAEL

OPPOSING VIEWPOINTS®

David Bender & Bruno Leone, *Series Editors*

Charles P. Cozic, *Book Editor*

OPPOSING VIEWPOINTS SERIES®

Greenhaven Press, Inc.   PO Box 289009   San Diego, CA 92198-9009

Library of Congress Cataloging-in-Publication Data

Israel : opposing viewpoints / Charles P. Cozic, book editor. — [Rev. ed.]
        p.   cm. — (Opposing viewpoints series)
    Includes bibliographical references and index.
    ISBN 1-56510-133-2 (lib.) — ISBN 1-56510-132-4 (pbk.)
    1. Israel. 2. Zionism. 3. Palestinian Arabs—Israel. 4. Israel—Ethnic relations. 5. West Bank. [1. Israel. 2. Zionism. 3. Palestinian Arabs—Israel. 4. Israel-Arab conflicts.] I. Cozic, Charles P., 1957–   . II. Series: Opposing viewpoints series (Unnumbered)
    DS126.5.I793 1994
    956.94—dc20   93-30964
                                                                        CIP
                                                                        AC

"Congress shall make no law . . . abridging the freedom of speech, or of the press."

First Amendment to the U.S. Constitution

The basic foundation of our democracy is the first amendment guarantee of freedom of expression. The Opposing Viewpoints Series is dedicated to the concept of this basic freedom and the idea that it is more important to practice it than to enshrine it.

Contents

Page

Why Consider Opposing Viewpoints? 9

Introduction 12

Chapter 1: Historical Debate: Is a Homeland for the Jews Necessary?
Chapter Preface 16
1. A Separate Jewish State Is Necessary 17
   Theodor Herzl
2. A Separate Jewish State Is Not Necessary 25
   Ahad Ha'am
3. Palestine Is the Jewish Birthright 32
   David Ben-Gurion
4. Palestine Is the Arab Birthright 37
   George Antonius
5. Palestine Should Be a Binational State 43
   Judah L. Magnes

Chapter 2: Does Israel Need Zionism?
Chapter Preface 51
1. Israel Should Promote Zionism 52
   Meir Kahane
2. Israel Should Reject Zionism 60
   Uri Avnery
3. Zionism Strengthens Israel 69
   Simon N. Herman
4. Zionism Weakens Israel 76
   Leon T. Hadar
5. Zionism Equals Racism 82
   Sami Hadawi
6. Zionism Is Not Racism 88
   Benjamin Netanyahu
Periodical Bibliography 94

Chapter 3: What Are the Prospects for Arab-Israeli Peace?
Chapter Preface 96
1. Israel Is Committed to Peace 97
   Yitzhak Rabin
2. Israel Is Not Committed to Peace 102
   Yeshayahu Leibowitz, interviewed by Chaim Shur

3. The Israel-PLO Accord Is a Prelude to Peace 106
   Khalil E. Jahshan
4. The Israel-PLO Accord Is a Prelude to Violence 111
   Ze'ev Benjamin Begin
5. Hamas Terrorists Are a Growing Threat to Peace 117
   Lamia Lahoud
6. Violence from Jewish Settlers Is a Growing Threat to Peace 122
   Marguerite Michaels & Graham Usher
7. Syria Is Committed to Peace 127
   Hafez al-Assad, interviewed by Patrick Seale
8. Syria Is Not Committed to Peace 132
   Zalman Shoval
Periodical Bibliography 136

Chapter 4: Should Israel Give Up Land for Peace?
Chapter Preface 138
1. Palestinians Should Have Their Own Nation 139
   Haydar 'Abd al-Shafi
2. Palestinians Should Not Have Their Own Nation 147
   Benjamin Netanyahu
3. An Independent Palestine Would Threaten Israel's Security 154
   Yohanan Ramati & Shlomo Baum
4. An Independent Palestine Would Not Threaten Israel's Security 162
   Walid Khalidi
5. Israel Should Share Control of Jerusalem 168
   Adnan Abu Odeh
6. Israel Should Control All of Jerusalem 174
   Ehud Olmert & Bernard I. Lindner
7. Israel Must Return the Golan Heights to Syria 180
   Laura Drake
8. Israel Must Retain the Golan Heights 187
   Eliav Shochetman
Periodical Bibliography 195

Chapter 5: Are Palestinian Rights Being Violated?
Chapter Preface 197
1. Israel Violates Palestinian Civil Rights 198
   Arab Association for Human Rights
2. Israel Does Not Violate Palestinian Civil Rights 204
   Peter Schwartz
3. Israel Abuses Palestinian Prisoners 210
   Graham Usher

4. Israel Does Not Abuse Palestinian Prisoners 216
   Judith D. Simon & Rita J. Simon
Periodical Bibliography 223

Chapter 6: Should the United States Support Israel?
Chapter Preface 225
1. The United States Should Strengthen Relations
   with Israel 226
   Charles Brooks
2. The United States Should Not Support an
   Oppressive Israel 233
   Anne Marie Baylouny
3. The United States Should Maintain Aid to Israel 241
   Thomas A. Dine
4. The United States Should Eliminate Aid to Israel 249
   George W. Ball & Douglas B. Ball
Periodical Bibliography 258

For Further Discussion 259
Map of Israel and Occupied Territories 261
Chronology of Events 262
Text of the Israeli-Palestinian
   Declaration of Principles 267
Organizations to Contact 275
Bibliography of Books 279
Index 282

Why Consider Opposing Viewpoints?

"The only way in which a human being can make some approach to knowing the whole of a subject is by hearing what can be said about it by persons of every variety of opinion and studying all modes in which it can be looked at by every character of mind. No wise man ever acquired his wisdom in any mode but this."

John Stuart Mill

In our media-intensive culture it is not difficult to find differing opinions. Thousands of newspapers and magazines and dozens of radio and television talk shows resound with differing points of view. The difficulty lies in deciding which opinion to agree with and which "experts" seem the most credible. The more inundated we become with differing opinions and claims, the more essential it is to hone critical reading and thinking skills to evaluate these ideas. Opposing Viewpoints books address this problem directly by presenting stimulating debates that can be used to enhance and teach these skills. The varied opinions contained in each book examine many different aspects of a single issue. While examining these conveniently edited opposing views, readers can develop critical thinking skills such as the ability to compare and contrast authors' credibility, facts, argumentation styles, use of persuasive techniques, and other stylistic tools. In short, the Opposing Viewpoints Series is an ideal way to attain the higher-level thinking and reading skills so essential in a culture of diverse and contradictory opinions.

In addition to providing a tool for critical thinking, Opposing Viewpoints books challenge readers to question their own strongly held opinions and assumptions. Most people form their opinions on the basis of upbringing, peer pressure, and personal, cultural, or professional bias. By reading carefully balanced opposing views, readers must directly confront new ideas as well as the opinions of those with whom they disagree. This is not to simplistically argue that everyone who reads opposing views will—or should—change his or her opinion. Instead, the series enhances readers' depth of understanding of their own views by encouraging confrontation with opposing ideas. Careful examination of others' views can lead to the readers' understanding of the logical inconsistencies in their own opinions, perspective on why they hold an opinion, and the consideration of the possibility that their opinion requires further evaluation.

Evaluating Other Opinions

To ensure that this type of examination occurs, Opposing Viewpoints books present all types of opinions. Prominent spokespeople on different sides of each issue as well as well-known professionals from many disciplines challenge the reader. An additional goal of the series is to provide a forum for other, less known, or even unpopular viewpoints. The opinion of an ordinary person who has had to make the decision to cut off life support from a terminally ill relative, for example, may be just as valuable and provide just as much insight as a medical ethicist's professional opinion. The editors have two additional purposes in including these less known views. One, the editors encourage readers to respect others' opinions—even when not enhanced by professional credibility. It is only by reading or listening to and objectively evaluating others' ideas that one can determine whether they are worthy of consideration. Two, the inclusion of such viewpoints encourages the important critical thinking skill of objectively evaluating an author's credentials and bias. This evaluation will illuminate an author's reasons for taking a particular stance on an issue and will aid in readers' evaluation of the author's ideas.

As series editors of the Opposing Viewpoints Series, it is our hope that these books will give readers a deeper understanding of the issues debated and an appreciation of the complexity of even seemingly simple issues when good and honest people disagree. This awareness is particularly important in a democratic society such as ours in which people enter into public debate to determine the common good. Those with whom one disagrees should not be regarded as enemies but rather as people whose views deserve careful examination and may shed light on one's own.

Thomas Jefferson once said that "difference of opinion leads to inquiry, and inquiry to truth." Jefferson, a broadly educated man, argued that "if a nation expects to be ignorant and free . . . it expects what never was and never will be." As individuals and as a nation, it is imperative that we consider the opinions of others and examine them with skill and discernment. The Opposing Viewpoints Series is intended to help readers achieve this goal.

David L. Bender & Bruno Leone,
Series Editors

Introduction

"The crux of the Palestine problem is the struggle between two national movements."

Walid Khalidi, Palestinian scholar, 1991

For decades, independence has been as vital a cause and objective for Palestinian Arabs as it had been for the Jewish settlers of Palestine, the land that is today Israel and its occupied territories. Although both independence movements began with the common goal of nation-building, the Palestinian movement lags behind the Jewish movement. In 1948, Jews declared and immediately won their independent state, an accomplishment Palestinians continue to strive for today.

In the early twentieth century, Palestine was an undeveloped land inhabited by Arabs and a scattering of European Jewish settlers. After Allied forces liberated Palestine and much of the Middle East from Turkish rule during World War I, the League of Nations, under the British Mandate, granted Britain control of what is today Israel and Jordan. After the liberation, both Arabs and Jews in the Middle East eagerly anticipated gaining independent states. Indeed, British statesmen such as Henry McMahon and Arthur Balfour openly supported the establishment of homelands in Palestine for both peoples.

However, according to Bernard Reich, an international affairs professor at George Washington University, "Britain promised independence to various Arab groups in the Middle East. . . . The promises were vague, but Arab leaders assumed they included Palestine." When the British eventually denied such a specific promise, the denial fueled Arab resentment toward the British as well as toward Jewish settlers. In 1920 and 1921, Arab riots in Jerusalem and Jaffa took the lives of more than fifty Jews and left hundreds more wounded or homeless. These riots marked the beginning of decades of Arab-Jewish conflict and violence.

Such attacks forced Jewish settlers to defend themselves. As Israeli research fellow Shabtai Teveth reports, "The Arabs posed a problem of security to Jewish settlements; the response was to establish the Haganah (self-defense)." As Arab enmity grew in the 1920s and 1930s, so too did the effectiveness of the Jewish defense groups, later praised by Israeli president Chaim Herzog as "a motivated, idealistic, and effective fighting force."

Despite Arab-Jewish tension, Jewish immigration increased and Jews continued to hope that Britain would fulfill its promise of independence. But in 1939, the British began to restrict both Jewish immigration and land purchases. The Jewish defense groups reacted by waging an underground revolt against the British to win their independence. In the 1940s, successful raids led by future Israeli prime ministers Menachem Begin and Yitzhak Shamir, among others Jews, pressured Britain to relinquish control of Palestine.

In 1947, the United Nations voted to partition Palestine into two states for Arabs and Jews. Jews accepted the decision and, just six months later, Israel declared independence. While the United States, the Soviet Union, and the UN immediately recognized the move, it also prompted Arab nations, who rejected the partition, to declare war the very next day.

Like the Jewish underground, Palestinian Arabs also engaged in violence to spur nationalist aspirations, but with far less success. According to author David K. Shipler, a 1936-39 revolt amounted to "a futile series of riots and killings . . . to block the coming to Israel." Ultimately, the Palestinian independence movement stalled. In the opinion of experts, several key reasons explain why.

The first reason involved a lack of Arab unity. As early Jewish political leader David Ben-Gurion stated, "The Arabs are not organized as a nation. They do not have one national party but many parties." Palestinian journalist Daoud Kuttab agrees and blames Arab leadership, writing that "the Arab world gave lip service to Palestinians but rarely came through."

Experts pinpoint the lack of a national identity as a second reason the movement faltered. To Great Britain and the United States, who held great influence in the region, Palestinian Arabs were largely an anonymous group, not differentiated from the rest of the Arab world. As writer Donald Neff explains, "Not until 1969 did the Palestinians receive official [UN] recognition as a separate people with 'inalienable rights.' Up to that time, Palestinians were lumped with other Arabs." Thus, the plight of Palestinian Arabs could not compare to that of the Jews, who stood out in Europe and elsewhere as a long-persecuted people without a homeland.

Finally, the influence of Great Britain and the United States played a major role. After World War I, for example, Britain, then in control of Palestine, supported Jewish independence but not that of Arabs in Palestine. As the UN Special Committee on Palestine stated in 1947, "The principle of self-determination was not applied to [Arabs in] Palestine, obviously because of [Britain's] intention to make possible the creation of the Jewish National Home." Moreover, experts such as Palestinian scholar Sami Hadawi note that America's strong foreign influence has benefited Israel at the expense of the Palestinian movement. In Hadawi's words, "Had it not been for the active part played by the White House in 1947 and 1948, the Jewish state would never have come into existence." Hadawi and other critics blame the United States and other nations for continuing to oppose the creation of an independent Palestinian state.

Nevertheless, the Palestinian movement has made progress. In 1988, the Palestine Liberation Organization (PLO) declared Palestinians an independent people and renounced PLO violence, a gesture that many nations welcomed. Although the UN and much of the world do not recognize Palestinian independence, the PLO today enjoys diplomatic relations with many countries who accept it as the legitimate representative of Palestinians. Furthermore, Israel and the PLO negotiated a breakthrough agreement in 1993 granting Palestinians limited autonomy in the Gaza Strip and the town of Jericho. Though Palestinians are divided as to whether the agreement furthers their movement, they continue to work toward full independence.

Mindful of the past—and evolving—relationship between Jews and Palestinians, the authors in *Israel: Opposing Viewpoints* debate issues critical not only to Arabs and Jews, but to much of the world as well in these chapters: Historical Debate: Is a Homeland for the Jews Necessary? Does Israel Need Zionism? What Are the Prospects for Arab-Israeli Peace? Should Israel Give Up Land for Peace? Are Palestinian Rights Being Violated? Should the United States Support Israel? Working together in a new partnership, Israeli and Palestinian leaders have committed themselves to usher in an era of peace, and perhaps one of greater freedom, for Arabs and Jews alike.

Historical Debate: Is a Homeland for the Jews Necessary?

Chapter Preface

The year 135 A.D. marked the defeat of the last Jewish nation in the Holy Land. Jews then began a thousand-year period of diaspora; they resided in other countries and frequently suffered persecution. How this millennium of exile affected the Jewish people and their culture is one basis of an important question that early twentieth-century Zionists faced—must a homeland for the Jewish people be predominantly Jewish?

Most Zionist leaders looked back on this diaspora and concluded that Jews must be a majority in their own state. Despite being a productive and highly literate populace, Jews had been victims of the medieval Crusades, the notorious Spanish Inquisition, pogroms in late nineteenth-century Russia, and many other devastating anti-Semitic episodes. Zionists concluded that Jews would be truly safe only when they were a majority in their own country.

A small dissident group of Jews held a different view of the diaspora and the question of a Jewish state. While acknowledging the persecution Jews had experienced, they argued that as the Old Testament prophesied, suffering had uplifted the Jews. As an oppressed people, Jews had developed an empathic sense of justice. To become a majority in a Jewish state in Palestine, these dissidents argued, would require displacing or establishing dominion over the Arabs already living there. Either course of action would corrupt Jewish ethics and turn Jews into oppressors, a people no better than the Gentiles who had persecuted them for centuries.

The viewpoints in the following chapter present both responses to Jewish history as they examine the question, is a homeland for the Jews necessary?

"The Jews who will it shall achieve their State."

A Separate Jewish State Is Necessary

Theodor Herzl

Theodor Herzl (1860-1904) is considered the founder of modern Zionism. He was instrumental in convening the first Zionist Congress, in Basle, Switzerland, in August 1897, where it was declared that Palestine should be a homeland for the Jews. The following viewpoint is an excerpt from *The Jewish State*, a pamphlet Herzl wrote in Vienna in 1895. In it, he argues that Jews remain a persecuted minority in most countries. By designating territory as a Jewish homeland, Herzl believed, Jews could protect their rights and maintain their cultural identity.

As you read, consider the following questions:

1. In Herzl's opinion, why would it be dangerous for Jews to remain exiled from their homeland?
2. What steps should Jewish emigrants take in developing their homeland, according to the author?
3. How does Herzl argue that a Jewish state will benefit its Arab neighbors?

From *The Jewish State* by Theodor Herzl, written in Vienna in 1895.

The idea which I have developed in this viewpoint is an ancient one: It is the restoration of the Jewish State.

The world resounds with clamor against the Jews, and this has revived the dormant idea. . . .

The Jewish question still exists. It would be foolish to deny it. It is a misplaced piece of medievalism which civilized nations do not even yet seem able to shake off, try as they will. They proved they had this high-minded desire when they emancipated us. The Jewish question persists wherever Jews live in appreciable numbers. Wherever it does not exist, it is brought in together with Jewish immigrants. We are naturally drawn into those places where we are not persecuted, and our appearance there gives rise to persecution. This is the case, and will inevitably be so, everywhere, even in highly civilized countries—see, for instance, France—so long as the Jewish question is not solved on the political level. The unfortunate Jews are now carrying the seeds of anti-Semitism into England; they have already introduced it into America.

One People

Anti-Semitism is a highly complex movement, which I think I understand. I approach this movement as a Jew, yet without fear or hatred. I believe that I can see in it the elements of cruel sport, of common commercial rivalry, of inherited prejudice, of religious intolerance—but also of a supposed need for self-defense. I consider the Jewish question neither a social nor a religious one, even though it sometimes takes these and other forms. It is a national question, and to solve it we must first of all establish it as an international political problem to be discussed and settled by the civilized nations of the world in council.

We are a people—*one* people.

We have sincerely tried everywhere to merge with the national communities in which we live, seeking only to preserve the faith of our fathers. It is not permitted us. In vain are we loyal patriots, sometimes superloyal; in vain do we make the same sacrifices of life and property as our fellow citizens; in vain do we strive to enhance the fame of our native lands in the arts and sciences, or her wealth by trade and commerce. In our native lands where we have lived for centuries we are still decried as aliens, often by men whose ancestors had not yet come at a time when Jewish sighs had long been heard in the country. The majority decide who the "alien" is; this, and all else in the relations between peoples, is a matter of power. I do not surrender any part of our prescriptive right when I make this statement merely in my own name, as an individual. In the world as it now is and will probably remain, for an indefinite period, might takes precedence over right. It is without avail, therefore, for us to be loyal patriots, as were the Huguenots, who were forced to emigrate. If we were left in peace. . . .

But I think we shall not be left in peace.

Oppression and persecution cannot exterminate us. No nation on earth has endured such struggles and sufferings as we have. Jew-baiting has merely winnowed out our weaklings; the strong among us defiantly return to their own whenever persecution breaks out. This was most clearly apparent in the period immediately following the emancipation of the Jews. Those Jews who rose highest intellectually and materially entirely lost the sense of unity with their people. Wherever we remain politically secure for any length of time, we assimilate. I think this is not praiseworthy. . . .

The Power of the State Idea

No human being is wealthy or powerful enough to transplant a people from one place of residence to another. Only an idea can achieve that. The State idea surely has that power. The Jews have dreamed this princely dream throughout the long night of their history. "Next year in Jerusalem" is our age-old motto. It is now a matter of showing that the vague dream can be transformed into a clear and glowing idea.

Viewed with Favour

His Majesty's Government view with favour the establishment in Palestine of a national home for the Jewish people, and will use their best endeavours to facilitate the achievement of this object, it being clearly understood that nothing shall be done which may prejudice the civil and religious rights of existing non-Jewish communities in Palestine, or the rights and political status enjoyed by Jews in any other country.

Arthur James Lord Balfour, letter to Lord Rothschild, November 2, 1917.

For this, our minds must first be thoroughly cleansed of many old, outworn, muddled, and shortsighted notions. The unthinking might, for example, imagine that this exodus would have to take its way from civilization into the desert. That is not so! It will be carried out entirely in the framework of civilization. We shall not revert to a lower stage; we shall rise to a higher one. We shall not dwell in mud huts; we shall build new, more beautiful, and more modern houses, and possess them in safety. We shall not lose our acquired possessions; we shall realize them. We shall surrender our well-earned rights for better ones. We shall relinquish none of our cherished customs; we shall find

19

them again. We shall not leave our old home until the new one is available. Those only will depart who are sure thereby to improve their lot; those who are now desperate will go first, after them the poor, next the well to do, and last of all the wealthy. Those who go first will raise themselves to a higher grade, on a level with that whose representatives will shortly follow. The exodus will thus at the same time be an ascent in class. . . .

No one can deny the gravity of the Jewish situation. Wherever they live in appreciable number, Jews are persecuted in greater or lesser measure. Their equality before the law, granted by statute, has become practically a dead letter. They are debarred from filling even moderately high offices in the army, or in any public or private institutions. And attempts are being made to thrust them out of business also: "Don't buy from Jews!"

Attacks in parliaments, in assemblies, in the press, in the pulpit, in the street, on journeys—for example, their exclusion from certain hotels—even in places of recreation are increasing from day to day. The forms of persecutions vary according to country and social circle. In Russia, special taxes are levied on Jewish villages; in Romania, a few persons are put to death; in Germany, they get a good beating occasionally; in Austria, anti-Semites exercise their terrorism over all public life; in Algeria, there are traveling agitators; in Paris, the Jews are shut out of the so-called best social circles and excluded from clubs. The varieties of anti-Jewish expression are innumerable. But this is not the occasion to attempt the sorry catalogue of Jewish hardships. We shall not dwell on particular cases, however painful.

A Model State

I do not aim to arouse sympathy on our behalf. All that is nonsense, as futile as it is dishonorable. I shall content myself with putting the following questions to the Jews: Is it not true that, in countries where we live in appreciable numbers, the position of Jewish lawyers, doctors, technicians, teachers, and employees of every description becomes daily more intolerable? Is it not true that the Jewish middle classes are seriously threatened? Is it not true that the passions of the mob are incited against our wealthy? Is it not true that our poor endure greater suffering than any other proletariat? I think that this pressure is everywhere present. In our upper economic classes it causes discomfort, in our middle classes utter despair.

The fact of the matter is, everything tends to one and the same conclusion, which is expressed in the classic Berlin cry: *"Juden 'raus!"* ("Out with the Jews!").

I shall now put the question in the briefest possible form: Shouldn't we "get out" at once, and if so, whither?

Or, may we remain, and if so, how long?

Let us first settle the point of remaining. Can we hope for better days, can we possess our souls in patience, can we wait in pious resignation till the princes and peoples of this earth are more mercifully disposed toward us? I say that we cannot hope for the current to shift. And why not? Even if we were as near to the hearts of princes as are their other subjects, they could not protect us. They would only incur popular hatred by showing us too much favor. And this "too much" implies less than is claimed as a right by any ordinary citizen or ethnic group. The nations in whose midst Jews live are all covertly or openly anti-Semitic. . . .

Nazi Germany, 1933: Persecution of the Jews. Jewish boy is forced to cut his father's beard while German soldiers watch jeeringly.

The Bettmann Archive

We are one people—our enemies have made us one whether we will or not, as has repeatedly happened in history. Affliction binds us together, and thus united, we suddenly discover our strength. Yes, we are strong enough to form a State, and, indeed, a model State. We possess all the requisite human and material resources.

This would, accordingly, be the appropriate place to give an account of what has been somewhat crudely termed our "human material." But it would not be appreciated till the broad outlines of the plan, on which everything depends, have first been marked out.

The whole plan is essentially quite simple, as it must necessarily be if it is to be comprehensible to all.

Let sovereignty be granted us over a portion of the globe adequate to meet our rightful national requirements; we will attend to the rest.

To create a new State is neither ridiculous nor impossible. Haven't we witnessed the process in our own day, among nations which were not largely middle class as we are, but poorer, less educated, and consequently weaker than ourselves? The governments of all countries scourged by anti-Semitism will be keenly interested in obtaining sovereignty for us.

The plan, simple in design but complicated in execution, will be executed by two agencies: the Society of Jews and the Jewish Company. . . .

We must not visualize the exodus of the Jews as a sudden one. It will be gradual, proceeding over a period of decades. The poorest will go first and cultivate the soil. They will construct roads, bridges, railways, and telegraph installations, regulate rivers, and provide themselves with homesteads, all according to predetermined plans. Their labor will create trade, trade will create markets, and markets will attract new settlers—for every man will go voluntarily, at his own expense and his own risk. The labor invested in the soil will enhance its value. The Jews will soon perceive that a new and permanent frontier has been opened up for that spirit of enterprise which has heretofore brought them only hatred and obloquy.

The founding of a State today is not to be accomplished in the manner that a thousand years ago would have been the only possible one. It is silly to revert to older levels of civilization, as many Zionists propose. Supposing, for example, we were obliged to clear a country of wild beasts, we should not set about it in the fashion of the fifth-century Europeans. We should not take spear and lance and go out individually in pursuit of bears; we would organize a grand and glorious hunting party, drive the animals together, and throw a melinite bomb into their midst.

If we planned to erect buildings, we should not drive a few shaky piles in a marsh like the lake dwellers, but should build as men build now. Indeed, we shall build in bolder and more stately style than has ever been done before; for we now possess means which heretofore did not exist.

Emigrants

The emigrants standing lowest in the economic scale will be gradually followed by those of the next grade. Those now in desperate straits will go first. They will be led by the intellectual mediocrities whom we produce so abundantly and who are oppressed everywhere. . . .

Who would go with us, let him fall in behind our banner and fight for the cause with word and pen and deed.

Those Jews who agree with our State idea will rally around the Society. Thereby they will give it the authority in the eyes of governments to confer and treat on behalf of our people. The Society will be recognized as, to put it in terminology of international law, a State-creating power. And this recognition will, in effect, mean the creation of the State.

A Work of Wisdom

The Zionists know that they have undertaken a work of unparalleled difficulty. . . .

What gives Zionists the courage to begin this labor of Hercules is the conviction that they are performing a necessary and useful task, a work of love and civilization, a work of justice and wisdom. They wish to save eight to ten million of their kin from intolerable suffering. They desire to relieve the nations among whom they now vegetate of a presence which is considered disagreeable. They wish to deprive anti-Semitism, which lowers the morals of the community everywhere and develops the very worst instincts, of its victim. They wish to make the Jews, who are nowadays reproached with being parasites, into an undeniably productive people. They desire to irrigate with their sweat and to till with their hands a country that is today a desert, until it again becomes the blooming garden it once was. Zionism will thus equally serve the unhappy Jews and the Christian peoples, civilization and the economy of the world.

Max Nordau, *Zionism*, 1902.

Should the powers show themselves willing to grant us sovereignty over a neutral land, then the Society will enter into negotiations for the possession of this land. Here two regions come to mind: Palestine and Argentina. Significant experiments in colonization have been made in both countries, though on the mistaken principle of gradual infiltration of Jews. Infiltration is bound to end badly. For there comes the inevitable moment when the government in question, under pressure of the native populace—which feels itself threatened—puts a stop to further influx of Jews. Immigration, therefore, is futile unless it is based on our guaranteed autonomy.

The Society of Jews will treat with the present authorities in the land, under the sponsorship of the European powers, if they prove friendly to the plan. We could offer the present authorities enormous advantages, assume part of the public debt, build new thoroughfares, which we ourselves would also require, and do many other things. The very creation of the Jewish State would be beneficial to neighboring lands, since the cultivation of a strip of land increases the value of its surrounding districts.

Is Palestine or Argentina preferable? The Society will take whatever it is given and whatever Jewish public opinion favors. The Society will determine both these points. . . .

Palestine is our unforgettable historic homeland. The very name would be a marvelously effective rallying cry. If His Majesty the Sultan were to give us Palestine, we could in return undertake the complete management of the finances of Turkey. We should there form a part of a wall of defense for Europe in Asia, an outpost of civilization against barbarism. We should as a neutral state remain in contact with all Europe, which would have to guarantee our existence. . . .

Let me repeat once more my opening words: The Jews who will it shall achieve their State.

We shall live at last as free men on our own soil, and in our own homes peacefully die.

The world will be liberated by our freedom, enriched by our wealth, magnified by our greatness.

And whatever we attempt there for our own benefit will redound mightily and beneficially to the good of all mankind.

"Judaism . . . does not need an independent State."

A Separate Jewish State Is Not Necessary

Ahad Ha'am

Rabbi Ahad Ha'am (1856-1927) was the pen name of Asher Zvi Ginsberg, an author and agnostic. Born in Ukraine, Ha'am supported the Hibbat Zion movement, founded in 1881, which advocated sending Jews to Palestine. Unlike Theodor Herzl, the author of the opposing viewpoint, Ha'am believed that Jewish culture and teachings must be revived before a state was created. Without this revival, a Jewish state would have little meaning. The following viewpoint is Ha'am's response to the August 1897 Zionist Congress meeting in Basle, Switzerland, which had advocated establishing a Jewish state in Palestine.

As you read, consider the following questions:

1. According to the author, what was the motivation behind the Zionist Congress's call for a Jewish state?
2. What does Ha'am mean when he draws a distinction between "political Zionists" and Zionists inspired by the "spiritual problem"?
3. Why does Ha'am think it would be dangerous to create a Jewish state prematurely?

From *The Jewish State and the Jewish Problem* by Ahad Ha'am, written in 1897.

Some months have passed since the Zionist Congress, but its echoes are still reverberating in daily life and in the press. All kinds of gatherings—small and large, local and regional—are taking place. Since the delegates returned home, they have been calling public meetings and repeatedly regaling us with tales of the wonders that were enacted before their very eyes. The wretched, hungry public is listening, becoming ecstatic, and hoping for salvation. It is inconceivable to them that "they"—the Jews of the West—can fail to succeed in what they propose. Heads grow hot and hearts beat fast, and many "leaders" who had for years—until [the Congress]—lived only for Palestinian settlement, and for whom a penny donation in aid of Jewish labor in Palestine or the Jaffa School was worth the world, have now lost their bearings and ask one another: "What's the good of this sort of work? The days of the Messiah are near at hand, and we busy ourselves with trifles! The time has come for great deeds, for great men, men of the West, have enlisted in the cause and march before us."

A Name from the West

There has been a revolution in their world, and, to emphasize it, they have given the cause itself a new name: It is no longer "Love of Zion," but "Zionism" (Zioniyuth). Indeed, there are even "precisionists" who, being determined to leave no loophole for error, use only the European form of the name ("Zionismus")—thus announcing to all and sundry that they are not talking about anything so antiquated as Hibbat Zion, but about a new, up-to-date movement, which comes, like its name, from the West, where people are innocent of the Hebrew language. . . .

There is no doubt that, even when the Jewish State is established, Jewish settlement will be able to advance only by small degrees, as permitted by the resources of the people themselves and by the progress of the economic development of the country. Meanwhile the natural increase of Jewish population both within the Palestinian settlement and in the Diaspora, will continue, with the inevitable result that, on the one hand, Palestine will have less and less room for the new immigrants, and, on the other hand, despite continual emigration, the number of those remaining outside Palestine will not be appreciably diminished. In his opening speech at the Congress, Dr. Theodor Herzl, wishing to demonstrate the superiority of his State idea to the previous form of Palestinian colonization, calculated that by the latter method it would take nine hundred years before all the Jews could be settled in their land. The members of the Congress applauded this as a conclusive argument. But this was a cheap victory. The Jewish State itself, do what it will, will find no way to make a more favorable calculation.

The truth is bitter, but with all its bitterness it is better than illusion. We must admit to ourselves that the "ingathering of the exiles" is unattainable by natural means. We may, by natural means, someday establish a Jewish State; it is possible that the Jews may increase and multiply within it until the "land is filled with them"—but even then the greater part of our people will remain scattered on foreign soils. "To gather our scattered ones from the four corners of the earth" (in the words of the Prayer Book) is impossible. Only religion, with its belief in a miraculous redemption, can promise such a consummation.

But if this is so, if the Jewish State, too, means not an "ingathering of the exiles" but the settlement of a small part of our people in Palestine, then how will this solve the material problem of the Jewish masses in the lands of the Diaspora?

Freeing the Jewish Soul

We must revitalize the idea of the national renascence, and use every possible means to strengthen its hold and deepen its roots, until it becomes an organic element in the Jewish consciousness and an independent dynamic force. Only in that way, as it seems to me, can the Jewish soul be freed from its shackles and regain contact with the broad stream of human life without having to pay for its freedom by the sacrifice of its individuality.

Ahad Ha'am, *The Law of the Heart*, 1894.

The material problem will not be ended by the establishment of a Jewish State, and it is, indeed, beyond our power to solve it once and for all. (Even now there are various means at our disposal to alleviate this problem to a greater or lesser degree, e.g., by increasing the proportion of farmers and artisans among our people *in all lands*, etc.) Whether or not we create a Jewish State, the material situation of the Jews will always basically depend on the economic condition and the cultural level of the various nations among which we are dispersed.

Zionism's Real Basis

Thus we are driven to the conclusion that the real and only basis of Zionism is to be found in another problem, the spiritual one.

But the spiritual problem appears in two differing forms, one in the West and one in the East, which explains the fundamental difference between western "Zionism" and eastern "Hibbat Zion." Nordau dealt only with the western form of the problem, apparently knowing nothing about the eastern; and the Congress as a whole concentrated on the first, and paid little attention to the second.

The western Jew, having left the ghetto and having sought acceptance by the gentile majority, is unhappy because his hope of an open-armed welcome has been disappointed. Perforce he returns to his own people and tries to find within the Jewish community that life for which he yearns—but in vain. The life and horizon of the Jewish community no longer satisfy him. He has already grown accustomed to a broader social and political life, and on the intellectual side the work to be done for our Jewish national culture does not attract him, because that culture has played no part in his earliest education and is a closed book to him. In this dilemma he therefore turns to the land of his ancestors and imagines how good it would be if a Jewish State were re-established there—a State and society organized exactly after the pattern of other States. Then he could live a full, complete life within his own people, and he could find at home all that he now sees outside, dangled before his eyes but out of reach. Of course, not all the Jews will be able to take wing and go to their State; but the very existence of the Jewish State will also raise the prestige of those who remain in exile, and their fellow citizens will no longer despise them and keep them at arm's length, as though they were base slaves, dependent entirely on the hospitality of others. As he further contemplates this fascinating vision, it suddenly dawns on his inner consciousness that even now, before the Jewish State is established, the mere idea of it gives him almost complete relief. It provides an opportunity for communal work and political excitement; his emotions find an outlet in a field of activity which is not subservient to non-Jews; and he feels that, thanks to this ideal, he stands once more spiritually erect and has regained his personal dignity, without overmuch trouble and purely by his own efforts. So he devotes himself to the ideal with all the ardor of which he is capable; he gives rein to his fancy and lets it soar as it will, beyond reality and the limitations of human power. For it is not the attainment of the ideal that he needs; its pursuit alone is sufficient to cure him of his spiritual disease, which is that of an inferiority complex, and the loftier and more distant the ideal, the greater its power to exalt.

Eastern Zionism

This is the basis of western Zionism and the secret of its attraction. But eastern Hibbat Zion originated and developed in a different setting. It, too, began as a political movement; but, being a result of material evils, it could not be content with an "activity" consisting only of outbursts of feeling and fine phrases, which may satisfy the heart but not the stomach. Hibbat Zion began at once to express itself in concrete activities—in the establishment of colonies in Palestine. This practical work soon clipped the wings of fancy and demonstrated conclusively that Hibbat Zion could not lessen the material woe of the Jews by one iota. One might, therefore, have thought that, when this fact became patent, the Hovevei Zion would give up their effort and cease wasting time and energy on work which brought them no nearer their goal. But, no: they remained true to their flag and went on working with the old enthusiasm, though most of them did not understand, even in their own minds, why they did so. . . .

The eastern form of the spiritual problem is absolutely different from the western. In the West it is the problem of the Jews; in the East, the *problem of Judaism*. The first weighs on the individual; the second, on the nation. The one is felt by Jews who have had a European education; the other, by Jews whose education has been Jewish. The one is a product of anti-Semitism, and is dependent on anti-Semitism for its existence; the other is a natural product of a real link with a millennial culture, and it will remain unsolved and unaffected even if the troubled of the Jews all over the world attain comfortable economic positions, are on the best possible terms with their neighbors, and are admitted to the fullest social and political equality. . . .

The Biblical Palestine

A word to the Jews in Palestine. I have no doubt that they are going about it in the wrong way. The Palestine of the Biblical conception is not a geographical tract. It is in their hearts. . . .

Let the Jews who claim to be the chosen race prove their title by choosing the way of non-violence for vindicating their position on earth. Every country is their home including Palestine not by aggression but by loving service.

Mohandas K. Gandhi, *My Non-Violence*, 1960.

Judaism is, therefore, in a quandary: It can no longer tolerate the *Galut* form which it had to take on, in obedience to its will-to-live, when it was exiled from its own country; but, without that form, its life is in danger. So it seeks to return to its historic center, where it will be able to live a life developing in a natural way, to bring its powers into play in every department of human culture, to broaden and perfect those national possessions which it has acquired up to now, and thus to contribute to the common stock of humanity, in the future as it has in the past, a great national culture, the fruit of the unhampered activity of a people living by the light of its own spirit. For this purpose

29

Judaism can, for the present, content itself with little. It does not need an independent State, but only the creation in its native land of conditions favorable to its development: a good-sized settlement of Jews working without hindrance in every branch of civilization, from agriculture and handicrafts to science and literature. This Jewish settlement, which will be a gradual growth, will become in course of time the center of the nation, wherein its spirit will find pure expression and develop in all its aspects to the highest degree of perfection of which it is capable. Then, from this center, the spirit of Judaism will radiate to the great circumference, to all the communities of the Diaspora, to inspire them with new life and to preserve the over-all unity of our people. When our national culture in Palestine has attained that level, we may be confident that it will produce men in the Land of Israel itself who will be able, at a favorable moment, to establish a State there—one which will be not merely a State of Jews but a really Jewish State.

This Hibbat Zion, which concerns itself with the preservation of Judaism at a time when Jewry is suffering so much, is something odd and unintelligible to the "political" Zionists of the West. . . . And so political Zionism cannot satisfy those Jews who care for Judaism; its growth seems to them to be fraught with danger to the object of their own aspiration.

The Secret of Our People

The secret of our people's persistence is that at a very early period the Prophets taught it to respect only the power of the spirit and not to worship material power. Therefore, unlike the other nations of antiquity, the Jewish people never reached the point of losing its self-respect in the face of more powerful enemies. As long as we remain faithful to this principle, our existence has a secure basis, and we shall not lose our self-respect, for we are not spiritually inferior to any nation. But a political ideal which is not grounded in our national culture is apt to seduce us from loyalty to our own inner spirit and to beget in us a tendency to find the path of glory in the attainment of material power and political dominion, thus breaking the thread that unites us with the past and undermining our historical foundation. Needless to say, if the political ideal is not attained, it will have disastrous consequences, because we shall have lost the old basis without finding a new one. But even if it is attained under present conditions, when we are a scattered people not only in the physical but also in the spiritual sense—even then, Judaism will be in great danger. Almost all our great men—those, that is, whose education and social position have prepared them to be at the head of a Jewish State—are spiritually far removed from Judaism and have no true conception of its nature and its value. Such men, however loyal to their State and devoted to its interests, will necessarily envisage those interests by the standards of the foreign culture which they themselves have imbibed; and they will endeavor, by moral persuasion or even by force, to implant that culture in the Jewish State, so that in the end the Jewish State will be a State of Germans or Frenchmen of the Jewish race. We have even now a small example of this process in Palestine.

History teaches us that in the days of the Herodian house Palestine was indeed a Jewish State, but the national culture was despised and persecuted. The ruling house did everything in its power to implant Roman culture in the country and frittered away the resources of the nation in the building of heathen temples, amphitheaters, and so forth. Such a Jewish State would spell death and utter degradation for our people. Such a State would never achieve sufficient political power to deserve respect, while it would be estranged from the living inner spiritual force of Judaism. The puny State, being "tossed about like a ball between its powerful neighbors, and maintaining its existence only by diplomatic shifts and continual truckling to the favored of fortune," would not be able to give us a feeling of national glory; the national culture, in which we might have sought and found our glory, would not have been implanted in our State and would not be the principle of its life. So we should really be then—much more than we are now—"a small and insignificant nation," enslaved in spirit to "the favored of fortune," turning an envious and covetous eye on the armed force of our "powerful neighbors"; our existence in such terms, as a sovereign State would not add a glorious chapter to our national history. . . .

Jewish National Culture

In sum: Hibbat Zion, no less than "Zionism," wants a Jewish State and believes in the possibility of the establishment of a Jewish State in the future. But while "Zionism" looks to the Jewish State to furnish a remedy for poverty and to provide complete tranquillity and national glory, Hibbat Zion knows that our State will not give us all these things until "universal Righteousness is enthroned and holds sway over nations and States"—it looks to a Jewish State to provide only a "secure refuge" for Judaism and a cultural bond to unite our nation. "Zionism," therefore, begins its work with political propaganda; Hibbat Zion begins with national culture, because only *through* the national culture and *for its sake* can a Jewish State be established in such a way as to correspond with the will and the needs of the Jewish people.

"For our future's sake, let us put forth the will, the faith and power to reconstruct the basis of our existence and establish a sovereign, self-governing Jewry in Israel. "

Palestine Is the Jewish Birthright

David Ben-Gurion

The following viewpoint is an excerpt from a speech David Ben-Gurion (1886-1973) made before a Zionist meeting in Basle, Switzerland, in 1931. In 1929 Palestinian Arabs had rioted against Jewish settlements. Ben-Gurion's speech is a response to the fighting. He maintains that only when Jews are a majority in a Jewish state will they be truly safe and free from discrimination. Ben-Gurion was born in Poland and emigrated to Palestine in 1906. Long an important figure in Israeli politics, he founded the national labor union, Histadrut, and was its general secretary from 1921 to 1935. In 1948, he became the first prime minister of the newly created state of Israel.

As you read, consider the following questions:

1. Why does hostility toward the idea of a Jewish state persist, according to Ben-Gurion?
2. Why does the author argue that Jews must not be a minority in their homeland?
3. According to Ben-Gurion, what rights do Arabs have in the Jewish homeland?

We appear from the battlefront of "Zionism on the way," sent to you by the Army of Fulfillment, linked in destiny, for life or death, with the realization of Zionism. For more than twenty-five years, first a tiny platoon, then in companies and battalions, and now in brigades and divisions, that Army stands guard, firm and fast, over our agricultural development, our educational advances, our political progress in the Land. It is as such that we face you here, swayed by a profound sense of responsibility and solicitude for the position of the Zionist Movement and all its works. . . .

We were murderously attacked, we are exposed to systematic and continuous incitement, to the libels and provocation of effendis [upper-class Arabs] of the Comintern's agents, of Government officers. The essence of our right to be in Palestine is wantonly assailed, and not just by this officer or that but by a Great Britain governed today by the British Labor party. Even our civic status is disputed at every turn. . . .

Persistent Gentile Hostility

We saw that international testimony and recognition did not dispel the universal unfriendliness, the atmosphere of hostility, suspicion and misunderstanding, which surround our eternal people. The Gentiles cannot yet stomach our strangeness, nor comprehend our longings and lament, cannot register consciously our basic, natural right to be independent again in our Homeland. In the global upset of a World War the foundations of all the earth are shaken, the great Powers fight for their lives and the least external succor is worthwhile. That succor our small nation gave, and, in return, a right was given it. But to the public opinion of Great Britain and the world it is not yet an ironclad, unappealable right. Unpleasant, perhaps, to say so, but we should be purblind, playing ostrich-politics, not to see exactly where we stand with the nations. The Balfour Declaration, the Mandate and fifty years of proudest construction in Palestine are behind us, and still it is gallingly necessary to tell an incredulous world of our rights and works, to make it see we come neither to extort nor exploit, but in equity to remodel our lives. It is the worst kind of self-deception to preach that if we possess a scrap of paper furbished with the seals of Britain and the League, a Jewish State on both banks of Jordan is safe in our hands and all we need do is elect a new leader and all will be well. . . .

Avoiding Further Exile

If we are to be few amongst many in Palestine, as in every other land we are, trusting to the magic of superior intellect unsupported by moil and toil, or by husbandry and independent living, and if you think that the air of Israel and its ancient memories will then spare us an exilic fate, you will be tragically

Jewish immigrants from war-ravaged Europe are shown at the port of Tel Aviv. They disembarked from ships which had been waiting for the British Mandate to expire.

mistaken. If we are a minority, out of touch with creativity and labor, landless and denied all earthy livelihoods, in short—unless we become an autonomous nation, the Galuth [exile] malady, the plague of cultural assimilation and physical decline, will never quit us, not even in Palestine. For our future's sake, let us put forth the will, the faith and power to reconstruct the basis of our existence and establish a sovereign, self-governing Jewry in Israel. If we do not, we only make a second Galuth.

Achad Ha'am once dreamed of a new Jewish type in Palestine, a pattern to pilgrims who would enjoy the brilliance of this invention and tell the Diaspora of the marvels it did. Except we are a working people, that lovely dream will not come true.

What he saw in Palestine twenty years ago led him to conclude that the only invention was an upper-class of precocious Jewish landowners employing Arab labor. He did not then believe that the great proletariat that would do the rough chores of colonization would be Jews. He made two mistakes. First, a Jewish landowner without Jewish labor would be not a pattern but a pest. Second, lacking faith in the possibility of undiluted Jewish labor, Achad Ha'am could not grasp that, adrift in a great non-Jewish sea, we can create nothing, and that it will not take long in present circumstances of Palestine to turn a Jewish minority into what we were in Galuth: middlemen of foreign cultures and economies. On the fringes of our intelligentsia in Palestine signs of British coloring already emerge; if we continue a negligible minority, there will be Arab assimilation as well. Freedom and nationhood alone are the antidote.

As one who has lived and worked in Palestine many years, who came as a Zionist, I want to say that my faith in its promise was never so buoyant. Mine own eyes have seen the unfolding of infinite, hidden riches of dunes, of swamps and boulders. They saw the greater miracle, the creativeness of young workers aflame with vision and burning to resurrect Land and folk—in the Emek, in Sharon and Tel Aviv, in the trenches of Haganah, in industry and in organized labor. Labor and soul—if they bind the Jew in faith to his Land, then assuredly there is room in Palestine, there are prospect and capacity yet unrevealed. All we need is that the will of a few should grow into the will of a whole people. . . .

Arab Rights

We are not blind, withal, to the fact that Palestine is no void. Some million Arabs inhabit both sides of Jordan, and not since yesterday. Their right to live in Palestine, develop it and win national autonomy is as incontrovertible as is ours to return and, by our own means and merit, uplift ourselves to independence. The two can be realized. We must, in our work in Palestine, respect Arab rights, and if our first contact was unhappy, we were not in the wrong. Nor, perhaps, were the Arabs, for there are historic imponderables. We knew we lived at the edge of the desert, that our neighbors still kept largely to its ways; so we quickly raised a posse for self-protection, and many of our finest men paid the price of insecurity with their lives. Before the World War, and after, we declared roundly that we should always be unsafe, till we were so numerous that we could defend ourselves. . . .

The moral content of Zionism and its necessary practical objects demand a policy of rapprochement and mutual under-standing towards the Palestinian Arabs, in economics, enlighten-ment and politics.

We endorse constitutional changes designed to give the inhabi-tants a share in administration. . . . Here, to Jewry, to Labor, and to the Arab nation, we vow that we shall never agree to one na-tional group in Palestine dominating the other, now or evermore. If we do not accept the idea of a Jewish State wherein Jews rule over Arabs, neither do we accept bi-nationalism as in Switzerland or Canada. The political problem of Israel is sui generis. The rights to Palestine do not, as in those countries they do, belong to the existing settlers, whether it be Jews or Arabs. The crux is the Right of Return of Jewry dispersed, a prerogative of rebuilding and development, of freedom and sovereignty, yet not to infringe the prerogatives of others or hold sway over them. To be impervi-ous to that conception, is to vitiate our title to Israel. . . .

We dissent from dominion of present majority over present minority, for that minority is but the nucleus of a returning na-tion. So, too, shall we dissent from Jewish dominion over Arabs when the dynamism of Aliyah [immigration] alters the balance of power in our favor. We scorn the plea that, while we are a minority, a British High Commissioner be empowered to pre-vent majority domination, but, as soon as we reverse the roles, he hand authority to us. It is playing with political fire to inter-pret messianic redemption and liberation as a lust to govern be-hind the bayonets of imperial Britain, condemning the right of those who are citizens of Palestine as much as we are.

A Free Nation

In our view, the form of government should be so modified as to associate both national groups in it, together with Britain, on a basis of parity and without regard to numbers. But we shall never let ourselves become 'protected Jews' in Palestine, and never a ruling race. We shall be a free and self-sufficing nation, honoring Arab rights in an accord of equality, and living in peace with neighbor countries.

"The rights of the Arabs are derived from actual and long-standing possession. . . . Their connexion with Palestine goes back uninterruptedly to the earliest historic times."

Palestine Is the Arab Birthright

George Antonius

In a 1915 letter to the Arab leader Sharif Husain, British official Sir Henry McMahon promised that Palestine would become an independent Arab state. In the following viewpoint, written in 1939, George Antonius argues that the British should fulfill this promise. He maintains that Palestine should be an Arab state because Arabs are the indigenous population and have a long heritage in Palestine. Antonius was an Arab historian and a senior civil servant in the Palestine Mandate government.

As you read, consider the following questions:

1. What two reasons does Antonius offer for his argument that Palestine should be an Arab state?
2. How does Antonius respond to the issue of Arabs using violent tactics against Jews?
3. What will be the role of Jews in an Arab state, according to the author?

From *The Arab Awakening: The Story of the Arab National Movement* by George Antonius. Philadelphia: J.B. Lippincott, 1939. Copyright 1939 by George Antonius.

There is in existence already a considerable body of literature in English and other European languages on the history of the British mandate in Palestine. But it has to be used with care, partly because of the high percentage of open or veiled propaganda, and partly because the remoteness of the indispensable Arabic sources has militated against real fairness, even in the works of neutral and fair-minded historians. A similar inequality vitiates the stream of day-to-day information. Zionist propaganda is active, highly organised and widespread; the world Press, at any rate in the democracies of the West, is largely amenable to it; it commands many of the available channels for the dissemination of news, and more particularly those of the English-speaking world. Arab propaganda is, in comparison, primitive and infinitely less successful: the Arabs have little of the skill, polyglottic ubiquity or financial resources which make Jewish propaganda so effective. The result is, that for a score of years or so, the world has been looking at Palestine mainly through Zionist spectacles and has unconsciously acquired the habit of reasoning on Zionist premises. . . .

Perhaps the best approach to the problem is to begin with a review of the rights, claims and motives of each of the three parties concerned, as they stood at the end of the [First World] War.

The Rights of the Arabs

The rights of the Arabs are derived from actual and long-standing possession, and rest upon the strongest human foundation. Their connexion with Palestine goes back uninterruptedly to the earliest historic times, for the term 'Arab' denotes nowadays not merely the incomers from the Arabian Peninsula who occupied the country in the seventh century, but also the older populations who intermarried with their conquerors, acquired their speech, customs and ways of thought and became permanently arabised. The traditions of the present inhabitants are as deeply rooted in their geographical surroundings as in their adoptive culture, and it is a fallacy to imagine that they could be induced to transplant themselves, even to other Arab surroundings, any more than the farmers of Kent or Yorkshire could be induced to go and settle in Ireland. It may seem superfluous to point this out, but the fallacy is one on which the Palestine Royal Commission have raised a new edifice of false hopes; and the fact needs stressing, therefore, that any solution based on the forcible expulsion of the peasantry from the countryside in which they have their homesteads and their trees, their shrines and graveyards, and all the memories and affections that go with life on the soil, is bound to be forcibly resisted.

In addition to those natural rights, the Arabs had acquired specific political rights derived from the Sharif Husain's compact with Great Britain and the help they gave her, in Palestine amongst other theatres. The thesis that Palestine west of the Jordan was excluded from the British pledges can no longer be maintained. The texts now available show that the Sharif Husain was given a general promise relating to its independence in the McMahon Correspondence and a specific promise securing the political and economic freedom of its Arab population in the message conveyed to him by the late Commander Hogarth. There is also the pledge contained in the Declaration to the Seven. Taken together, these undertakings amount to a binding recognition of Arab political rights. . . .

An Alien State

The whole Arab people is unalterably opposed to the attempt to impose Jewish immigration and settlement upon it, and ultimately to establish a Jewish State in Palestine. Its opposition is based primarily upon right. The Arabs of Palestine are descendants of the indigenous inhabitants of the country, who have been in occupation of it since the beginning of history; they cannot agree that it is right to subject an indigenous population against its will to alien immigrants, whose claim is based upon a historical connection which ceased effectively many centuries ago. Moreover they form the majority of the population; as such they cannot submit to a policy of immigration which if pursued for long will turn them from a majority into a minority in an alien state; and they claim the democratic right of a majority to make its own decisions in matters of urgent national concern.

The Arab Office, evidence submitted to the Anglo-American Committee of Inquiry, March 1946.

In other words, the Arab claims rest on two distinct foundations: the natural right of a settled population, in great majority agricultural, to remain in possession of the land of its birthright; and the acquired political rights which followed from the disappearance of Turkish sovereignty and from the Arab share in its overthrow, and which Great Britain is under a contractual obligation to recognise and uphold.

Respect for Jewish Minorities

Thus in their opposition to the British mandate, the Arabs are animated by the motive of self-preservation as well as that of self-determination. Their attitude is not dictated by any hostility to the Jewish race. Both in the Middle Ages and in modern times, and thanks mainly to the civilising influence of Islam, Arab history remained remarkably free from instances of deliberate persecution and shows that some of the greatest achievements of the Jewish race were accomplished in the days of Arab power, under the aegis of Arab rulers, and with the help of their enlightened patronage. Even to-day, in spite of the animosity aroused by the conflict in Palestine, the treatment of Jewish minorities settled in the surrounding Arab countries continues to be not less friendly and humane than in England or the United States, and is in some ways a good deal more tolerant. . . .

The rights of the Jews are of a different order. In the minds of many people in the West, and more particularly in the Protestant countries, Zionism appears as a new embodiment of the old Jewish yearning for the Holy Land, and one that is destined to bring about the fulfillment of the Biblical prophecies. That is only one more of the prevalent misconceptions. There does exist a school of 'spiritual' Zionists, sponsored by some of the most eminent names in Jewry, whose aims are primarily cultural and whose mainsprings are to be found in the idealistic and religious sentiments which had hitherto inspired Judaism in its affection for Palestine. But their influence in international politics has become relatively insignificant. The real power is wielded by the exponents of 'political' Zionism which is not a religious but a nationalist movement aiming at the establishment of a Jewish state in Palestine on a basis of temporal power backed by the usual attributes of possession and sovereignty. It is against that school of Zionism that the Arab resistance in Palestine is directed. . . .

The Zionists base their claims on the historic connexion of Jewry with Palestine, which they represent as entitling the Jews to return to their ancient homeland. The connexion is too well-known to need recapitulation; but what does need stressing, in view of the widespread misconceptions that prevail, is that an historic connexion is not necessarily synonymous with a title to possession, more particularly when it relates to an inhabited country whose population claims, in addition to an ancient historic connexion of their own, the natural rights inherent in actual possession. Ever since the Dispersion, the Jews have been a minority—and most of the time a very small minority—in Palestine, living mainly in the cities sacred to Judaism and enjoying no distinctive rights other than those enjoyed from time to time by the other minorities. At the end of the War, they numbered barely 55,000 souls, that is to say less than 8% of the total population of which the Arabs formed over 90%. . . .

Moral Violence

No lasting solution of the Palestine problem is to be hoped for until the injustice is removed. Violence, whether physical or moral, cannot provide a solution. It is not only reprehensible in itself: it also renders an understanding between Arabs, British and

Jews increasingly difficult of attainment. By resorting to it, the Arabs have certainly attracted an earnest attention to their grievances, which all their peaceful representations in Jerusalem, in London and in Geneva had for twenty years failed to do. But violence defeats its own ends; and such immediate gains as it may score are invariably discounted by the harm which is inseparable from it. Nothing but harm can come of the terror raging in Palestine; but the wise way to put an end to it is to remove the causes which have brought it about. The fact must be faced that the violence of the Arabs is the inevitable corollary of the moral violence done to them, and that it is not likely to cease, whatever the brutality of the repression, unless the moral violence itself were to cease.

A Sacred Right

I am an Arab, and I believe that the Arabs constitute one nation. The sacred right of this nation is to be sovereign in her own affairs. Her ardent nationalism drives her to liberate the Arab homeland, to unite all its parts, and to found political, economic, and social institutions more sound and more compatible than the existing ones.

Manifesto of the First Arab Students' Congress, December 1938.

To those who look ahead, beyond the smoke-screen of legend and propaganda, the way to a solution is clear: it lies along the path of ordinary common sense and justice. There is no room for a second nation in a country which is already inhabited, and inhabited by a people whose national consciousness is fully awakened and whose affection for their homes and countryside is obviously unconquerable. The lesson to be drawn from the efforts hitherto made to lay the foundations of a Jewish state in Palestine is that they have turned the country into a shambles—not because of any inherent Arab hatred of Jews or lack of feeling for their plight, but because it is not possible to establish a Jewish state in Palestine without the forcible dislodgement of a peasantry who seem readier to face death than give up their land. On that ground alone, and without taking the political issues into account, the attempt to carry the Zionist dream into execution is doomed to failure; and the first step along the road to a solution is to face that fact objectively and realise its implications.

An Arab State

Once the fact is faced that the establishment of a Jewish state in Palestine, or of a national home based on territorial sovereignty, cannot be accomplished without forcibly displacing the Arabs, the way to a solution becomes clearer. It is not beyond the capacity of British, Jewish and Arab statesmanship to devise one. There seems to be no valid reason why Palestine should not be constituted into an independent Arab state in which as many Jews as the country can hold without prejudice to its political and economic freedom would live in peace, security and dignity, and enjoy full rights of citizenship. Such an Arab state would naturally be tied to Great Britain by a freely-negotiated treaty which should contain provisions for the safeguarding of British strategic and economic interests, for ensuring the safety and the inviolability of the Holy Places of all faiths, for the protection of all minorities and minority rights, and for affording the Jewish community the widest freedom in the pursuit of their spiritual and cultural ideals.

A solution on those lines would be both fair and practicable. It would protect the natural rights of the Arabs in Palestine and satisfy their legitimate national aspirations. It would enable the Jews to have a national home in the spiritual and cultural sense, in which Jewish values could flourish and the Jewish genius have the freest play to seek inspiration in the land of its ancient connexion. It would secure Great Britain's interests on a firm basis of consent. And it would restore Palestine to its proper place, as a symbol of peace in the hearts of Judaism, Christianity and Islam.

"It is possible to say that the Jews are right and that the Arabs are right."

Palestine Should Be a Binational State

Judah L. Magnes

Judah L. Magnes was a San Francisco native who went to Palestine in 1922. He founded Hebrew University in Jerusalem and became its chancellor in 1925. Part I of the following viewpoint is an excerpt from a pamphlet he published in 1930, after serious fighting had broken out between Arabs and Jews. Magnes believed the fighting showed that trying to establish Jewish dominion over Arabs was futile and violated Jewish ethics. He advocated a binational state in which both groups shared power. Part II is an addendum to the pamphlet, written in 1937.

As you read, consider the following questions:

1. Why is Magnes willing to give up a Jewish majority in Palestine?
2. How has the dispersion of Jews throughout the world benefited Judaism, according to the author?
3. Why does Magnes believe that even a small, poor Jewish community in Palestine is better than a community which rules over a hostile Arab population?

From "Like All the Nations?" by Judah L. Magnes. In *The Zionist Idea*, edited by Arthur Hertzberg. Copyright © 1959 by Arthur Hertzberg. Used by permission of Doubleday, a division of Bantam Doubleday Dell Publishing Group, Inc. Excerpted by permission of the publishers from *Dissenter in Zion: From the Writings of Judah L. Magnes*, edited by Arthur Goren. Cambridge: Harvard University Press. Copyright © 1982 by the President and Fellows of Harvard College.

The discussion concerning the future political regime in Palestine is now happily beginning to take on a more or less objective character and the searching question is being asked as to what we want here. What is our Zionism? What does Palestine mean for us?

As to what we should want here I can answer for myself in almost the same terms that I have been in the habit of using many years:

Immigration.

Settlement on the land.

Hebrew life and culture.

If you can guarantee these for me, I should be willing to yield the Jewish state, and the Jewish majority; and on the other hand I would agree to a legislative assembly together with a democratic political regime so carefully planned and worked out that the above three fundamentals could not be infringed. Indeed, I should be willing to pay almost any price for these three, especially since this price would in my opinion also secure tranquillity and mutual understanding. If the Jews really have an historical connection with Palestine, and what student of history will deny it, and if the Jewish people is to be in Palestine not on sufferance (as during the days of the Turks) but as of right—a right solemnly recognized by most governments and by the League of Nations, and also by thinking Arabs—then surely these three rights are elemental and hardly to be contested.

Without Palestine

Whether through temperament or other circumstances I do not at all believe, and I think the facts are against believing, that without Palestine the Jewish people is dying out or is doomed to destruction. On the contrary it is growing stronger; and what is more, it should grow stronger, for Palestine without communities in the dispersion would be bereft of much of its significance as a spiritual center for the Judaism of the world. To me it seems that there are three chief elements in Jewish life, in the following order of importance: the living Jewish people—now some sixteen million; the Torah, in the broadest sense of this term, i.e., all our literature and documents and history, as also the great religious and ethical and social ideals the Torah contains for use and development in the present and the future; and third, the Land of Israel. My view is that the people and the Torah can exist and be creative as they have existed and have been creative without the Land; that, however, the Land is one of the chief means, if not the chief means, of revivifying and deepening the people and the Torah.

The living Jewish people is primary. It is the living carrier and vessel of Judaism, the Jewish spirit. It has used even its Exile for spreading light and learning. Palestine can help this people to understand itself, to give an account of itself, to an intensification of its culture, a deepening of its philosophy, a renewal of its religion. Palestine can help this people perform its great ethical mission as a national-international entity. But this eternal and far-flung people does not need a Jewish state for the purpose of maintaining its very existence. The Jewish community throughout the world is a wondrous and paradoxical organism. It participates in the life of many nations, yet in spite of numberless predictions in the past and the present, it is not absorbed by them. It is patriotic in every land, yet it is international, cosmopolitan. Palestine cannot solve the Jewish problem of the Jewish people. Wherever there are Jews there is the Jewish problem. It is part of the Jewish destiny to face this problem and make it mean something of good for mankind.

Both Sides Love the Land

We could not and cannot renounce the Jewish claim; something even higher than the life of our people is bound up with this land, namely its work, its divine mission. But we have been and still are convinced that it must be possible to find some compromise between this claim and the other, for we love this land and we believe in its future; since such love and such faith are surely present on the other side as well, a union in the common service of the land must be within the range of possibility.

Martin Buber, letter to Mahatma Gandhi, 1939.

Nor are the Jews dying out, despite their weaknesses, their mixed marriages, their ignorance of Judaism, and the deterioration that has laid hold of many a limb. I see them in America growing healthier and stronger in numbers and intellectual power. Their hearts respond generously to every Jewish call. They are multiplying their communities, their synagogues, schools, societies, libraries, unions. They are acquiring economic independence, and their sons and daughters are getting what the universities and colleges can give them. They are ignorant of Judaism. But they are asking eagerly, mostly in vain, to know what Judaism is. Perhaps it is not the fault of the teachers that the answers take so long in coming. Judaism is a complex phenomenon. It is and it is not religion, philosophy, ethics, politics, ceremonies, life. The answer as to what it is and may mean to a new generation cannot come overnight. . . .

But if I have thus exalted the Diaspora, what is Palestine to us? It is the Land of Israel, our Holy Land. It is holy for us in a practical and a mystic sense. . . .

Three great things this poor little land has already given Israel in two generations. Hebrew has become a living possession and has thus restored to us and our children the sources of our history and our mind, and has thus given us the medium again for classic, permanent Jewish expression. The second great thing is the return of Jews to the soil, not only for the sake of a living from the soil but also for the sake of their love of this particular soil and its indissoluble connection with the body of the Jewish people. Third, the brave attempt on the part of city-bred, school-bred young Jews—moderns of the modern—to work out in life, in the cities and on the land, a synthesis between the radicalism of their social outlook and their ancestral Judaism. It is problems of the same nature that a whole world in travail is laboring to solve; and among Jewry no more splendid attempt at a synthesis has been made than here, in everyday life and not in theory alone.

The beginnings of all this, and much more than the beginnings, were made under the Turks; and Palestine is of such moment to us that it is capable of giving us much even though our community here be poor and small. I have indicated above that I do not want it to be poor and small. But poor and small and faithful to Judaism, rather than large and powerful like all the nations. . . .

Our theories may differ as to the purposes Palestine may or may not serve. But there is no question that it is now serving as a testing ground, a dangerous frontier land for the lovers of peace in Israel. Much of the theory of Zionism has been concerned with making the Jews into a normal nation in Palestine like the gentiles of the lands and the families of the earth. The desire for power and conquest seems to be normal to many human beings and groups, and we, being the ruled everywhere, must here rule; being the minority everywhere, we must here be in the majority. There is the *Wille zur Macht* [Will through power], the state, the army, the frontiers. We have been in exile; now we are to be masters in our own Home. We are to have a Fatherland, and we are to encourage the feelings of pride, honor, glory that are part of the paraphernalia of the ordinary nationalistic patriotism. In the face of such danger one thinks of the dignity and originality of that passage in the liturgy which praises the Lord of all things that our portion is not like theirs and our lot not like that of all the multitude.

The Danger of Seeking Power

We are told that when we become the majority we shall then show how just and generous a people in power can be. That is like the man who says that he will do anything and everything to get rich, so that he may do good with the money thus accumulated. Sometimes he never grows rich—he fails. And if he does grow rich under those circumstances his power of doing good has been atrophied from long lack of use. In other words, it is not only the end which for Israel must be desirable, but what is of equal importance, the means must be conceived and brought forth in cleanliness. If as a minority we insist upon keeping the other man from achieving just aims, and if we keep him from this with the aid of bayonets, we must not be surprised if we are attacked and, what is worse, if moral degeneration sets in among us. . . .

What I am driving at is to distinguish between two policies. The one maintains that we can establish a Jewish Home here through the suppression of the political aspirations of the Arabs, and therefore a Home necessarily established on bayonets over a long period—a policy which I think bound to fail because of the violence against us it would occasion, and because good opinion in Britain and the conscience of the Jewish people itself would revolt against it. The other policy holds that we can establish a Home here only if we are true to ourselves as democrats and internationalists, thus being just and helpful to others, and that we ask for the protection of life and property the while we are eagerly and intelligently and sincerely at work to find a *modus vivendi et operandi* [method of living and operating] with our neighbors. The world—not in Palestine alone—may be bent upon violence and bloodshed. But will not my opponent agree that there is a better chance of averting this tendency to bloodshed if we make every possible effort politically as well as in other ways to work hand in hand—as teachers, helpers, friends—with this awakening Arab world?

Arab and Jewish Rights

We have the Arab natural rights, on the one hand, and the Jewish historical rights on the other. The question therefore is, "How can an honourable and reasonable compromise be found?" There are those, we know, who reject the very idea of compromise. But no answer can be found for this complicated situation, except through compromise, that may be reasonable and feasible.

Judah L. Magnes, speech delivered to the United Nations Special Committee on Palestine, Jerusalem, July 14, 1947.

You ask me, Do I want to quit? No, I do not. The Jew will not abandon the Land of Israel. He cannot abandon it. Palestine is of value by and of itself—its rocks, its hills, its ruins, its beauty— and that it is of value to Judaism even if our community here be small and poor. I am afraid the first of the quitters will be those who say it is useless except we be in the majority. But I also know that we cannot establish our work as it should be established if it be against the determined will of the Arab world, and if we have not the good will of the good European world on our side. . . .

Palestine is holy to the Jew in that his attitude toward this Land is necessarily different from his attitude toward any other land. He may have to live in other lands upon the support of bayonets, but that may well be something which he, as a Jew, cannot help. But when he goes voluntarily as a Jew to repeople his own Jewish Homeland, it is by an act of will, of faith, of free choice, and he should not either will or believe in or want a Jewish Home that can be maintained in the long run only against the violent opposition of the Arab and Moslem peoples. The fact is that they are here in their overwhelming numbers in this part of the world, and whereas it may have been in accord with Israelitic needs in the time of Joshua to conquer the land and maintain their position in it with the sword, that is not in accord with the desire of plain Jews or with the long ethical tradition of Judaism that has not ceased developing to this day.

II

Not nearly enough stress has been laid upon the fact that Palestine is a Holy Land for three great religions.

No one should expect to have his maximalist aspirations fulfilled in such a land. The presence here of so many differing sects and peoples requires moderation, concession, compromise, so that they may live together in peace without at the same time giving up their peculiarities and the differentiae to safeguard which they may have come here. . . .

Palestine is no place for maximalist Jewish aspirations. That this is so, is also part of the Jewish tragedy. There are those who speak of a Jewish National Home containing many millions of Jews—present-day Palestine, Transjordan, the Hauran, and Sinai as far as the Suez Canal. Such aspirations are due in large measure to the pressure of Jewish life, the persecution to which Jews are being subjected in all too many parts of the world. When Israel Zangwill said: "Give the land without a people to the people without a land," neither he nor many other Jews realized that there was a people here. The Jews are justified in seeking the active support of Government for settlement possibilities for as large a number of Jews as is in any way possible; but this must always be compatible with the natural rights of the Arabs. If the Jews could come to a political understanding with the Arabs as to Palestine, there would doubtless be an opportunity for the settlement of a large number of oppressed Jews in other Arab lands. These would not, to be sure, be part of the Jewish National

Home, but they would be contiguous and helpful to it.

Palestine is no place for maximalist Arab aspirations. The whole world knows that Palestine is not just an Arab land. It belongs in the spiritual sense to millions of people scattered throughout the world; and in a real sense not only to the Arabs but also to those Jews and Christians who, coming here and living here, are trying through their devotion to make of it a land worthy of being called holy. Palestine may some day become a member of an Arab federation and/or of the League of Nations, but not just as an Arab land. Rather as a bi-national land, entrusted to the two peoples who are the sole actual descendants of the Semites of antiquity; a Holy Land, entrusted to these two peoples, from whom these religions are derived, and entrusted also to the League of Nations and to Great Britain, the representatives of the European mind and the Christian conscience. . . .

A Tragic History

It is possible to say that the Jews are right and that the Arabs are right. Such a situation has within it the elements of tragedy. The whole history of Palestine has been one of tragedy. But the question is, must the tragedy again march to its appointed end? Is there perhaps no solution to the problem?

Yet those of us who are not willing to accept fate without an effort to influence it, must make our choice. There are those on all sides who say that there is no way out of the impasse except through sword and blood, because that is the history of conquest and that the history of Palestine. Yet there is another way that must be tried: through a moderation of ambitions, through concession and compromise, to find the way of life.

Does Israel Need Zionism?

Chapter Preface

Zionism is an ideology and movement that grew in Europe during the 1800s, proclaiming that all Jewish people have the right to exist in a safe homeland of their own. As stated by the World Zionist Congress, the aims of Zionism include "the unity of the Jewish people and the centrality of Israel in Jewish life; the ingathering of the Jewish people in its historic homeland from all countries; [and] the preservation of the identity of the Jewish people through the fostering of Jewish and Hebrew education and of Jewish spiritual and cultural values."

Since the creation of Israel in 1948, Zionism has exerted great influence on the nation's culture, laws, and policies. But while the goal of creating a Jewish homeland has been achieved, many Arabs, Jews, and others disagree on Zionism's present role and effect on Israel.

Many Jews and other supporters of Israel maintain that Zionism remains vital in keeping Israel and Jewish culture thriving. Conservative Jews, for example, embrace the Zionist notion of Israel as a distinctly Jewish state, one that must promote the interests of Jews and safeguard them from widespread anti-Semitism and what writer Marie Syrkin describes as "the Arab lust for the 'extinction' of the Jewish state."

Other Jews, however, argue that Zionism—its mission of creating a Jewish homeland completed—has lost its relevance and divides the nation rather than strengthens it. Israeli writer Michael Warschawski, for example, calls Zionism "a classic, colonialist ideology. It is a *utopia*, more suited to the 19th century than to present-day reality." Moreover, many Arabs and liberal Jews charge Zionism and Israel's Zionist government with unbridled racism toward Arabs. To these critics, Zionism and its effects are the primary obstacles to peace between Arabs and Jews.

Such differences of opinion reflect decades of Zionism's influence on the lives of Arabs and Jews. The authors in this chapter examine the past effects of Zionism and debate its future role in Israel.

"There is a Chosen People, a chosen land, a chosen state, and a chosen destiny, and the conduct of the Jew and his state must be directed toward that destiny."

Israel Should Promote Zionism

Meir Kahane

Meir Kahane (1932-1990) was an American-born rabbi and founder of the militant Jewish Defense League who later served in the Knesset, Israel's parliament. First published in 1974, the following viewpoint reflects the views that Kahane espoused until his assassination in New York City and the views of many Jews today. In this excerpt from his book *Our Challenge: The Chosen Land*, Kahane argues that Israel must preach the ideas and truths of Judaism and Zionism in order for Israel and the Jewish people to succeed. Kahane urges Israel to reform its schools so that their primary mission becomes the indoctrination of Jewish youths with traditional Jewish values. Kahane asserts that by promoting such values, Israel defines itself as a distinctly Jewish state and helps fulfill its divine purpose. Failure to do so, Kahane contends, aids enemies that seek Israel's destruction.

As you read, consider the following questions:

1. How is the creation of the state of Israel part of Jews' divine purpose, according to Kahane?
2. In the author's opinion, why is secular nationalism an insufficient ideology for Jews?
3. Why does Kahane believe that Israel belongs only to Jews?

There is a Jewish destiny. That which happened to the Jewish people in the past, that which occurs in our times, that which will happen in the days and years to come, is not haphazard, a game of chance. The Jewish people plays its role in history within the limits of divine ordinance.

We stand today, all of us—leaders, captains, elders, men, women, and little ones—before a great moment in history. Those of us who have been chosen, for some inexplicable reason, to live in these times of unparalleled disasters and unequaled miracles of triumph must surely sense in every fiber of our being that the things that we have seen and experienced are not mere chance.

The soul-shattering Holocaust that ripped away a third of our people, followed immediately by the incredible ending of the incredible Exile, the creation of the third Jewish commonwealth, the Ingathering of the Exiles from the four corners of the earth, the smashing of the enemy in Six Days [Israel's 1967 defeat of Egypt, Jordan, and Syria] and the return to [Jerusalem's Western, or Wailing] Wall and the liberated lands of Judea and Samaria [West Bank]—all are parts of the great moment in history before which we stand.

It is clear that the Almighty is prepared to bring us into the final deliverance and that the beginning of the redemption is under way. We stand at a historic moment of deliverance.

Facing Great Moments

But great moments must be seized. They wait to be grasped. They always join together the ultimate deliverance with a potential for preceding disaster. Salvation is invariably coupled with a possible attendant tragedy that wipes away the human blemish with the terrible scourge of pain and suffering.

It need not be. The great moments that proclaim oncoming deliverance wait for an instant to be understood and grasped. If we recognize them and respond to them, we are blessed. If we do not, they disappear from view and make us pay a tragic and terrible price before the advent of the deliverance.

And the most terrible part of the price is its *avoidability:* the fact that it need not have been paid had we understood and acted.

The great tasks of our day are to clearly and boldly define, teach, and implement.

To define clearly and precisely the purpose and destiny of the Jewish people; the purpose and reason for the Land of Israel and the state therein; the relationship between the Jew and the state; the relationship between the Jew of the state and the Jew in the Exile; the total aim and destiny of the Jew, his people, land, and state.

To teach and implement that definition boldly and relentlessly;

to create the kind of Jew and the kind of Jewish people that is their sole reason for being; to create the uniquely Jewish kind of state and policy within the Land of Israel that is the sole reason for having one; to create the kind of relationship between Jew and Jew and Jew and state that is the only true and honest one in terms of Jewishness.

A Jewish People and State

In a word, our people must be a Jewish people, not a pale replica of others. Our state must not seek merely to be like all the rest, but a distinctively Jewish one.

The Jewish people stands or falls on the knowledge that it is *not* like all other people. The foundation of foundations and the raison d'être of the Jewish people is that it is the Chosen People, a godly people—the people chosen by the Almighty to do his will. It is a people that was called into being by G-d [spelling reflects author's religious beliefs] and whose existence and fate are decreed by him. And from this chosenness, this call to holiness and challenge to greatness, flow certain absolute and necessary axioms. If we are chosen, then we are a certain kind of people with a certain kind of role and a certain kind of state. There is a Chosen People, a chosen land, a chosen state, and a chosen destiny, and the conduct of the Jew and his state must be directed toward that destiny. The normal rules of nationhood and statehood do not apply to us; the normal logic of foreign policy is not ours. If we obey the call of the Jewish destiny and the command of the Almighty we shall endure and live, both in this world and the next. If we do not return to the Jewish role, we will pay a terrible price before the ultimate redemption comes, wiping away our sins with the suffering of pain and war.

The creation of the Jewish people and its survival has a divine purpose. The rebirth of the State of Israel and the miracles that have accompanied that rebirth are part of that purpose. It has been ordained that the Jewish people return home and rebuild their Jewish lives in their land—all of it. Are we capable of understanding this and the fact that only a truly *Jewish* state is the aim of the divine decree? If we do, we will hasten the advent of the redemption; if we do not, we will not only lengthen it but we will pay a terrible price in the form of our own sufferings and the soul-sufferings of our youth.

Giving Youth the Jewish Idea

Today our youth, many of them, stand confused. Tomorrow there will be more of them and the ideas that to their elders seem basic and easy to understand will not be obvious or clearly understood. We have taken these ideas as well as our youth for granted, and we stand to lose them both. That will be the price of our neglect and mistaken self-assurance. We have not given our youth the most basic of human needs, the idea—the *Jewish* idea. Our youth wait for it, as a hungry man for bread. They wait and are prepared to accept—if we give it.

Rabin Addresses the World Zionist Congress

All the statistics show that the Jewish people is slowly disappearing, that Jewish education is no longer part and parcel of every Jewish home. The link to Israel is weakening. In the Diaspora, the Zionist idea is rapidly losing ground. We are very worried.

We call upon you to do everything possible to strengthen the ties with the State of Israel. We are proud of our relationship in troubled times, in days of war. We are proud of our partnership in fateful days and in dangerous hours. Your readiness to stand by us warms our hearts. . . .

The ties between us must be cemented and must not be based only on the dangers facing Israel. Our shared Jewish destiny is forever.

Yitzhak Rabin, *Jewish Frontier*, September/October 1992.

The idea is the weapon. If you have it and believe in it, if you teach it and spread it, if you organize pupils who will teach it and spread it to others, you can change a world. For actions and reactions are predicated upon ideas, and depending on the idea we will act and react in a certain way—correctly or wrongly, with truth or with falsehood.

We in the State of Israel are in a struggle for the souls of the generation that is growing into manhood. If we wish to win them—and not lose them either to the enemy or to the well-meaning fools who would destroy us just as effectively—we must have the *idea*, believe in it completely and teach it unceasingly. We must fill the minds and hearts and souls of our youth with it daily. . . .

A Decline in Jewish Values

Unless the Jew is special, chosen, and different we will continue to have results such as those revealed in the careful and brilliant study made of the attitudes of Israeli high school children by Professor Simon Herman.

That survey showed a shocking lack of interest in and a deep negativism concerning Jewish values. Thus, in response to the question, "Does the fact that you are Jewish play an important part in your life?" some 25 percent replied that it was of little importance, while no fewer than 7 percent said none.

"If you were to be born again would you wish to be born a Jew?" brought a response by fully 28 percent that it was a matter of indifference to them, with 2 percent flatly admitting that they would not. When the same question was posed as, "If you were to live outside of Israel, would you wish to be born a Jew?" a staggering 21 percent said no, with 25 percent saying it made no difference to them. The negativists become a majority when one eliminates the many Orthodox students who took part in the survey—all of whom responded affirmatively. One need hardly add that on the question of personal intermarriage 27 percent declared that they would marry a non-Jew if the occasion arose. It is important to quote Professor Herman's gloomy conclusion:

"Significant differences consistently appear on Jewish-identity items between religious, traditionalist, and nonreligious students. The Jewish identity of the religious student is much stronger than that of the traditionalist and nonreligious student; the Jewish identity of the traditionalist is stronger than that of the nonreligious student. . . . Not only do the religious students feel more Jewish and value their Jewishness more under all circumstances, but they feel closer to, and have a greater identification with, Jews everywhere." Bear in mind that this survey was taken in 1964; since then the identity problem has grown significantly worse.

It may be most unpleasant for some but at least honest to recognize that unless *Judaism* is brought into the schools (and by this I do not mean the bland Bible class that is taught by disbelievers as an exercise in futile hypocrisy), then *Jewishness* will also begin to disappear. Unless an immediate effort is made to introduce into the schools religious subjects taught by trained religious teachers with the point of emphasizing that element of the Jewish people that makes them different, there will be no point to being different. . . .

Teach Zionism and Jewish Pride

Overhaul the schools, I say. Make them places of Jewish indoctrination, instilling Jewish values from the youngest age. From the time the Jew enters his school at kindergarten, let the aim be to instill in him the knowledge and belief that the Jewish people and tradition are divinely chosen, unique and true. Let the knowledge of his glorious history, taught in a prideful way, flow over him. Let him open a traditional Jewish book and, under the guidance of sympathetic, believing teachers, let him begin to understand the warmth and beauty of its substance and why, for books like these, his great-grandparents were prepared to make the ultimate sacrifice.

Let the pride of the Revolt, of the Irgun and Lechi and Palmach and Haganah [Jewish freedom fighters] fill his mind at an early age. Let him know of the heroes of the nation who went to the gallows and let him mark their passing with bowed head and their exploits with joy. What normal nation hides its heroes from its youth? Only the abnormal one that is in the hands of politicians.

Liberation and Expansion

The Jew is forbidden to give up any part of the land of Israel. The land belongs to the G-d of Israel and the Jew, given it by G-d, has no right to give away any part of it. All the areas past liberated, or areas which may be liberated in the future, must be annexed, made part of the State of Israel, and populated by Jews as rapidly as possible. Jewish settlement in every part of Eretz-Yisrael, including cities that today, sadly, are *Judenrein* (Jewish excluded), must be unlimited. Maximum continuous expansion of Jewish settlement must be encouraged by well-coordinated national policies binding upon all agencies of the State of Israel and all related Jewish institutions with authority or influence over urban and rural development, housing, agriculture, transportation and industrial investment.

Meir Kahane, *"Kahane" The Magazine of the Authentic Jewish Idea*, March/April 1988.

Let Zionism be taught and Zionist history—in detail and with positive pride. Let the story of the Jewish communities in the Galut [Exile] be taught so that the ties between Jews here and there are strengthened. Let the names of Jewish heroes throughout the ages be learned and known in depth, and not superficially. Let the Holocaust be a meaningful thing for the young Israeli from earliest childhood and let it be taught with pride in that which once was sadness for that which disappeared. Let the exploits of Jewish partisans and freedom fighters of Eastern Europe be known. In short, let Jewish nationalism infuse the mind and the spirit of the Jewish youngster in Eretz Yisroel [Land of Israel] from the day that he enters the Jewish school.

Jewish Identity Must Be Defined

Yet, let us remember that while it is vital to begin immediately to strengthen, reinforce, and add to the nationalist indoctrination of our young children, to overhaul the sterility and empty national education of our schools, in the end it is not in mere secular nationalism, like that of other nations, that we will find the real answer to the salvation of our national soul and the redemption of our confused children. It is not secular education and not secular movements or parties that hold the key. For

57

while energetic nationalist education will halt the tide temporarily and save not a few from the purposelessness of their lives, the secular nationalist can never succeed in giving an honest answer to the question: Why be a Jew? And if there is one thing that youth both in Israel and outside demands, it is honesty. . . .

The struggle for the souls and minds of our youth is the greatest problem facing the State of Israel today. Before it, all other problems fade into insignificance, for their solutions depend largely on whether our Jewish youth will be proud Jews, good Jews, sacrificing Jews, Jews who conceive of themselves as uniquely different, hence bound together in one common ideal. Without this, he will see the constant wars with the Arabs and scream in frustration: who needs a new state if there is no end to the wars? He will either leave the country or turn his back on Zionism and the great dream for him will have the taste of ashes.

We ignore the problem or belittle it or underestimate it at our own peril. The jackals, the demagogues, the wreckers are already at work and we must meet them and give our youth the Idea. We must give them a reason for being Jews, a reason for holding on to the traditional and ancient Jewish values. We must define our youth; we must tell them who they are. We must answer their questions: What and why is a Jew? What and why am I? . . .

The Truths of Zionism

We must instill in our youth, and in ourselves, deep national pride, but we must realize, too, that all the secular nationalism in the world will not suffice to justify Jewish exclusiveness. It is only religion that justifies nationalism and, indeed, it is impossible to speak of Judaism without connecting the two. Judaism is religio-nationalism. . . .

The time has come to express firmly and loudly the religio-national truths:

The Jewish nation, formed at Sinai as a divine religio-nation; chosen, special, hallowed, and set apart with an eternal mission to study, practice, and model themselves by the Torah.

A nation that is bound by eternal and unbreakable bonds; whose every Jew is brother and sister to every other Jew; whose obligation of Ahavat Yisroel [love of all Jews] demands the utmost love and sacrifice on behalf of a suffering Jew; whose unity is clear and is not divided by false and artificial boundaries of class struggle; and whose Jewish interests take precedence over those of others.

A land that is hallowed and given to us by the Creator and Possessor of all the earth; which is not given over to partition; which is not the property or right of any other people.

A state which is the trustee of all the Jewish people, which has the right to demand support from them and which has, in return, the obligation to protect them; which must work to bring them home from the four corners of the earth.

A state that must teach its own citizens the meaning of Ahavat Yisroel so as to overcome the evils of poverty, social injustice, and anarchy of values; that must learn to bridge the chasm of hate between differing groups.

A state that must teach its youth that they are part of the Jewish people *before* they are part of the Israeli state or of themselves: that must teach its youth the beauties of its heritage and Judaism from childhood on.

A state that must be *Jewish*—not western or secular or like the other nations—in its character and personality and behavior.

A people, land, and state with a destiny that is sure and unchangeable.

We live, today, in the dawn of the final redemption, and the footsteps of the Messiah can be clearly heard. The Jewish Destiny is determined and no force on earth can prevent its coming.

"Only the repudiation of [Zionism] . . . will eventually lead to Israel's becoming a normal secular state."

Israel Should Reject Zionism

Uri Avnery

Uri Avnery, a former Jewish freedom fighter and soldier, is a peace activist and writer in Israel. In the following viewpoint, excerpted from his 1968 book, *Israel Without Zionists*, Avnery argues that Zionism has achieved its goal of the creation of a nation for Jews. Its purpose realized (although not as it was originally envisioned), Zionism is now obsolete. Avnery maintains that the "concept of oneness of religion and nation" has created paradoxical laws that irritate the vast majority of Israelis. But perhaps the most dangerous legacy that Zionism has bequeathed to Israel, Avnery contends, is the government's serious neglect of Israeli-Arab affairs, which he states is a great obstacle to peace. Although the author writes about Israel from his perspective in the late 1960s, the circumstances he discusses remain largely unchanged in present-day Israel.

As you read, consider the following questions:

1. According to Avnery, how is the relationship between Israelis and Jews similar to that between Australians and the British?
2. Why does Zionism continue to exert a strong influence on Israel, according to Avnery?
3. In the author's opinion, why can Jews only be defined in a religious sense?

On October 12, 1492, Columbus landed on a Bahama island called Guanahani by the Indians—and discovered the New World.

But Columbus did not have the slightest idea what he'd done. Nothing was farther from his mind than discovering new worlds; it was the oldest of worlds he was looking for—India and the spice islands. A new world was not an economic proposition, and one may wonder whether the whole expedition would have come about if the result had been foreseen.

Yet, using only the crudest of instruments, knowing very little about geography, his head crammed with false ideas, Columbus bravely sailed forth into the unknown and inadvertently changed the shape of the world.

Something like this happened to Zionism, and therein lie the causes of all its inner conflicts, as well as the solutions to its problems.

Zionism's False Theory

Zionism set out with the idea that the Jews of the world constitute a nation—a nation in the European sense, a group of people who identify themselves with a political state, either an existing one or one to be established. Starting from this assumption, the problem was one of transportation, in the widest sense: once a Jewish homeland in Palestine was created, all Jews, or at least most of them, would go there to live in [Zionist pioneer] Theodor Herzl's *Judenstaat*.

History has proved this theory false. A Jewish state was indeed set up in Palestine, but the great majority of Jews has not shown any undue inclination to go there. Two and a half million, most acting under diverse forms of duress, have indeed settled in what is now Israel. But several million others, who were not subject to physical persecution, stayed where they were. . . .

It seems, therefore, that world Jewry is not a nation, in the Zionist sense. This would have spelled the failure of the Zionist experiment, if something quite unforeseen had not happened in the meantime: A new nation was, indeed, born in Palestine.

Looking back today, this seems to have been as inevitable as the discovery of the New World, once Columbus and his little fleet left the shores of Europe on a westward course. If you transfer hundreds of thousands of people to a foreign land—a new climate and landscape—in which they speak a newly resurrected language and respond to different physical and political challenges, the stage is set for the emergence of a new society. If this society has a sense of political destiny and unity, it becomes a new nation. This has happened in the United States, in Australia, in Brazil, in many other countries. It has happened in Palestine.

We, the sons and daughters of Zionism, are indeed a new nation, not just another part of world Jewry that happens to live in Palestine. This is the central fact of our life, obscured by obsolete ideas and slogans, a truth that must be grasped if anything about our existence, our problems, and our future is to be understood.

© Goldberg/*People's Weekly World*. Reprinted with permission.

What is a nation? Many answers have been given to this question, each influenced by the particular ideology of its proponent. Some put the emphasis on a common territory, others on a common culture or economy. I don't believe in abstract formulas to which life has to be somehow adapted. To me the answer seems simple and pragmatic: A nation is a group of people who believe that they are a nation, who want to live as a nation, have a common political destiny, identify themselves with a political state, pay its taxes, serve in its army, work for its future, share its fate—and, if necessary, die for it.

In this sense, we in Israel are a nation, unmistakably and irrevocably, for better or for worse. Our nation comprises all of us, from [cities] Dan to Elat, but it does not include a Jew in Brooklyn, Paris or Bucharest, much as he may sympathize with our country and feel an affinity for it. . . .

We are a new nation, the Hebrew nation, whose homeland is Palestine (which we call Eretz-Israel) and whose political creation is the State of Israel.

This does not mean, except for a small lunatic fringe, that we want to turn our backs on world Jewry and cut ourselves off from it. As the period of the [1967] Six-Day War has clearly demonstrated, there is a very real and profound feeling of solidarity between Jews all over the world and Israel. We are grateful for this and reciprocate it. Solidarity there is. Affinity there is. But world Jewry is not a nation, while the Hebrew Israelis are.

It is never quite accurate to draw an analogy between different peoples, because there are no two quite alike. Yet, to illustrate a point, one could say that the relationship between Israelis and Jews is like that between Australians and Englishmen. Australia has a deep sense of affinity for Great Britain; in two world wars, Australia rushed to the defense of England long before it was threatened itself. Some Australians, even today, say "home" when they mean England. Yet there can be no doubt that Australia is a nation by itself, with its own special interests, trying to respond to its own particular challenges, conducting a national policy suited to its own geo-political circumstances (as its participation in the war in Viet Nam showed).

Thus, Zionism created something which it never consciously intended, a new nation. And by its very success, Zionism has become obsolete; by attaining its goals, Zionism provided for its own negation.

A Lingering Ideology

The existence of a new nation, Middle Eastern by birth, makes an entirely different approach to the Israeli-Arab problem possible. Unfortunately, this has yet to become clear to both Arab and Israeli. It is a common historical phenomenon that the ideological superstructure of a society, what the French call *mystique*, may linger on long after the reality upon which it was based has disappeared and made a new approach necessary.

An ideology is not just a set of ideas which can be changed easily. It is bound up with vested interests on many different levels. It exists in the textbooks of schools and in the mental set of generations of teachers, thereby molding the minds of boys and girls born into a new reality. Social institutions, with their hosts of functionaries and economic enterprises, are based upon ideology. Political parties fighting for the advantages of political power perpetuate the philosophies imprinted on them since their inception; this is particularly true in Israel, all of whose political parties were founded in Europe before their leaders even came to the country. It is natural that a political regime which led Zionism to its heroic period is not one to relinquish power voluntarily and easily. The Zionist ideological and political superstructure, therefore, still exerts an immense influence in Israel. The establishment of the state has not changed this; indeed, it has changed very little in the personal and political composition of the leading class in the country. Therefore it is very difficult to answer a question like: "Is Israel a Zionist state?"

For many young people in Israel, the word *Zionism* is derogatory. In *sabra* [native Israeli] slang, "to talk Zionism" means to talk nonsense, to use highfaluting slogans devoid of concrete meaning. To the practical *sabra* mind, pragmatic by nature, it has long been obvious that some fundamental tenets of Zionism have not stood the test of time; yet these same *sabras* may unconsciously cling to Zionist ideas which they know to have been proved false.

The Fundamentals of Zionism

The fundamental tenets of Zionism can be defined as follows: (a) all the Jews in the world are one nation; (b) Israel is a Jewish state, created by the Jews and for the Jews all over the world; (c) the Jewish dispersal is a temporary situation, and sooner or later all Jews will have to come to Israel, driven, if by nothing else, by inevitable anti-Semitic persecution; (d) the Ingathering of these Exiles is the *raison d'être* of Israel, the primary purpose to which all other aims have to be subservient. This line is taught in Israeli schools, propounded in political speeches, written in the press. It is the essence of the existing regime.

Yet nothing could be further from what young Israelis believe in. Theirs is a different outlook, an Israeli nationalism pure and simple, sometimes moderate and sometimes extreme, but a nationalism very similar to any other one, bound up with the fortunes of the State of Israel, its territory, its language, its culture and its army.

The two different sets of ideals can co-exist only because the gap between them seldom becomes obvious. Yet it is real and has a profound, if hidden, influence on the day-to-day conduct of affairs.

Let's take, for example, the question of religion.

Few people are as non-religious, even anti-religious, as the great majority of Israelis, but in few countries has organized religion such a stranglehold on life. While Jews in America are the most extreme defenders of the principle of the separation of church and state, this idea is considered heresy in Israel, for a very elementary reason: The Declaration of Independence, promulgated on May 14, 1948, proclaims Israel to be a Jewish state, and this is embedded in the legal structure of Israel. The Law of Return gives every Jew the automatic right to come and settle in Israel. A second law confers Israeli citizenship upon every Jewish immigrant the minute he enters the country, unless he undergoes a specific procedure waiving his right; if he happens to be married to a Christian, this right is not conferred on his spouse, who must acquire citizenship by the normal process of naturalization.

Zionism Denies Jewish Rights

Far from being, as the Zionists claim, a Jewish liberation movement, Zionism is a movement of Jewish reaction bent on restricting Jewish freedoms. Thanks to the U.S. Constitution and Bill of Rights, which a "Jewish state" cannot by its very nature replicate, a Jew in the United States is freer than a Jew in Israel. Not only as an individual, but also as a Jew. For example, he can get married in any Jewish ceremony of his choice whereas in Israel he cannot. In Israel he can only get married in a ceremony prescribed by the laws of the state. Not by chance, all segments of the Zionist movement, the extreme "left" included, have been forcing their members, including atheists, to get married only according to prescribed religious rites. Zionism's reactionary character can be shown even without referring to the Palestinians and to the denial of their rights. For Zionism has denied the rights of the Jews as well, with the help of religious coercion deliberately instituted for the sake of "nation-building," according to the pattern all reactionary movements advocate.

Israel Shahak, *Journal of Palestine Studies*, Spring 1993.

Yet what is a Jew? Who is a Jew? No clear-cut legal definition exists. Nor can there exist any definition but a religious one. Throughout the ages, Jews were a religious community. In fact, the courts of Israel have decided that a person ceases to be a Jew if he adopts another religion—a decision which makes it clear that being Jewish is basically a religious thing. If so, the argument runs, how can there be a separation between synagogue and state? If Israel exists for world Jewry, if its main aim is to ingather these Jews who are organized as a religious community, how can the concept of a Jewish nation be separated from the Jewish religion? Indeed, those of us in Israel who fight for the separation of synagogue and state are constantly accused of trying to sever Israel from world Jewry, turning it into just another small Levantine [eastern Mediterranean] state. Thus, not one of the big, old Zionist parties advocates such a separation. All of them declare state and religion, nation and religion, to be one in the unique case of the Jews.

Paradoxes of Religion and State

The minority in Israel who are religious, therefore, have a power quite disproportionate to their numerical strength. Only about fifteen per cent of the population voted for the three religious parties represented in the *Knesset* [Israel's parliament], giving them seventeen out of 120 seats in the 1965 elections [religious parties won one less seat in 1992]. But by Israeli law there is neither civil marriage nor civil divorce, these affairs being within the sole dominion of the Rabbinate (and the functionaries of other religious groups, as far as their people are concerned). A Jew cannot marry a Christian or a Moslem, nor can a Jew named Cohen marry a divorced woman. Cohens or those with similar names are assumed to belong to the ancient families of priests, who are forbidden by Jewish law to marry anyone but a virgin: in theory, they might be called upon someday to officiate again in a new Temple. One cannot abdicate this right even if one wishes to—once a Cohen, always a Cohen. (In fact, a justice of the Israeli Supreme Court, a sophisticated man named Chaim Cohen, had to go to the United States in order to marry a divorced woman; and the validity of this marriage is extremely doubtful under the laws which he himself has to administer!) Neither busses nor the railway operates in Israel from sundown Friday until the first three stars appear in the sky on Saturday evening (but everyone can travel, in private cars and via a highly organized taxi service, along the exact routes of the busses). The law forbids the raising of pigs in all parts of the country except those where Christian Arabs constitute a local majority (yet one can easily buy pork anywhere in Israel, and pork steaks—euphemistically called "White steaks" or "French steaks"—can be clandestinely obtained at Tel Aviv steak-stands).

It is a situation of many paradoxes, with controversy and clashes, extremely irritating to the vast majority of the people. Yet these same people accept the situation as natural and inevitable, forced to this conclusion by the concept of oneness of religion and nation. Only the repudiation of this concept by Israeli nationalism, an ever-growing factor in Israeli life, will eventually lead to Israel's becoming a normal secular state. . . .

The idea of a homogeneous Jewish state is inherent in Zionism.

A state which exists for the solution of the Jewish problem should be populated, so the Zionists feel, by Jews. Any non-Jew is really a foreign element in the present Israeli regime. Non-Jewish immigrants, even non-Jewish spouses of Jewish immigrants, find great obstacles to their absorption into Israeli society. Here, Zionist religionism and Israeli nationalism part. In modern times it should be easy to join a nation, the average Israeli feels: if you want to be a part of Hebrew society, speak its language, bring up your children in its culture, support its state, and serve in its army, you should be welcome. For a Zionist, this idea is unacceptable. You can become a Jew only by undergoing a religious ritual—circumcision for men, immersion in water in a religious bathhouse for women, with all the accompanying religious ritual.

While this question may only be important to the few non-Jewish immigrants, the idea of a homogeneous Jewish state has grave consequences for Arabs. It was not only a question of security and political allegiance which made it impossible for Israel to integrate the 300,000 Arabs living in it before the 1967 war. Far more operative, though seldom mentioned, was the instinctive conviction of old-time Zionists that Arabs could never really be a part of a state which was Jewish. For anyone entertaining this conviction, the idea of repatriating Arab refugees and increasing the Arab minority was positively obnoxious. . . .

Arabs Feel Threatened

Nothing frightens the Arabs more than the idea of the Ingathering of the Exiles. There arises before Arab eyes the spectre of a wave of Jewish immigration, bringing to Israel another ten million Jews, overflowing its narrow frontiers and conquering Arab states, evicting the inhabitants and grabbing land for innumerable new *kibbutzim* [communes]. There is something ludicrous in the present situation. Zionist leaders . . . make visionary speeches about millions of Jews who will soon arrive on the shores of Israel, fulfilling the prophecy of Zionism. To an Israeli audience, knowing the reality, this is the sort of wishful thinking by which an antiquated regime tries desperately to preserve its obsolete slogans. Yet, to millions of Arabs these speeches sound like definite threats to Arab existence, threats made even more terrible by Israel's manifest military superiority.

Thus an empty slogan can become a political factor in the most negative sense.

But the Zionist philosophy has a more destructive influence on Israel's own mentality. Because a Zionist considers Israel the beachhead of world Jewry, world Jewry is seen as an inexhaustible reservoir of manpower and money; thus, the relationship between Israel and the Jews, mainly in the West, seems of primary importance, while that between Israel and the Arab world automatically, therefore, takes a back seat. The location of Israel in the Middle East seems a geographical accident, to be disregarded whenever possible, dealt with by military means if necessary. The ideal solution for a Zionist would be to saw off Israel from the Middle East and tow it away to a more congenial environment, somewhere opposite the French Riviera—if not off Long Island or near Miami Beach.

Israel Ignores Arab Concerns

How else can one explain the most astonishing fact in Israeli public life. After a Zionist-Arab conflict which has gone on for three generations, and the actual state of war between Israel and the Arab states, there does not exist an effective government department for Arab affairs. While we have a Ministry for Posts and a Ministry for Transportation, to say nothing of a Ministry for Tourism and a Ministry for Police, we don't have a Ministry for Middle Eastern Affairs. These are relegated to the Foreign Ministry, whose primary job is to defend Israel in the international arena from the political onslaught of the Arabs and, therefore, has nothing much to do with making contact with the Arab world and creating an atmosphere of peace. Indeed, such a task requires quite different approaches and talents. All the dealings between Israel and the Arab countries, all political initiatives from Israel toward the Arab world, are the proper province of the department for Middle Eastern affairs in the Foreign Ministry. But this department employs only thirty out of 900 officials in the Foreign Office, out of a total number of government employees well over 50,000, excluding policemen and teachers. Even this figure of thirty is misleading. If we deduct from it the personnel dealing with non-Arab Middle Eastern countries, such as Iran, and the purely clerical jobs, there are but three or four officials left to deal with what obviously is the main problem of Israel. . . .

Such a neglect of Israeli-Arab affairs would be impossible, after all that has happened, were it not for the Zionist image of an Israel oriented toward Western Jewry and the West in general. Of all the legacies Zionism bequeathed to the State of Israel, this is perhaps the most dangerous.

"Zionism in Israel . . . has to be based on a recognition of the unity of the Jewish people and of the central role of Israel as the Jewish state."

Zionism Strengthens Israel

Simon N. Herman

Israeli Jews should embrace Zionism, Simon N. Herman argues in the following viewpoint, because the movement strengthens Israel by uniting Jews and working for their survival as a national entity. Herman contends that the vast majority of Israelis regard themselves as Zionists and that they view Israel as "part of the Jewish historical continuity [and] as the homeland of the entire Jewish people." Herman is a professor of social psychology at Hebrew University in Jerusalem and the author of *The Reaction of Jews to Anti-Semitism* and *Jewish Identity*, from which this viewpoint is excerpted.

As you read, consider the following questions:

1. In Herman's opinion, how does Zionism stress unity among Jews?
2. Why does Herman believe that Zionism benefits youths?
3. According to the author, how have Zionist views differed among younger and older Jews?

69

In recent years social scientists have given increased attention in their studies to the place of Israel in Jewish life, but there has been little reference to the role of a Zionist ideology, actual or potential. And so the social psychological analysis we undertake moves in what is largely an uncharted field.

The essential constituents of a Zionist program are contained to a large extent, although not in completeness, in the resolutions of the twenty-seventh Zionist congress held in Jerusalem in 1968. These resolutions, termed the Jerusalem Program, state the aims of Zionism as follows:

> The unity of the Jewish people and the centrality of Israel in Jewish life;
>
> The ingathering of the Jewish people in its historic homeland, the Land of Israel, through aliya [immigration to Israel] from all countries;
>
> The strengthening of the State of Israel which is based on the prophetic vision of justice and peace;
>
> The preservation of the identity of the Jewish people through the fostering of Jewish and Hebrew education and of Jewish spiritual and cultural values;
>
> The protection of Jewish rights everywhere.

The propositions stated in this form are likely to be acceptable to a large section of the Jewish people. There is need, however, to spell out and amplify the ideological implications of these elements as part of an overall approach to contemporary Jewry. Indeed, it is necessary to stress that what characterizes Zionist ideology is not any one of the elements in isolation but the combination of these elements integrated into a comprehensive view of Jewish life. Such elaboration and amplification would reveal that there are ideological issues in regard to which both confusion of thought and differences of opinion exist.

The Essence of Zionism

The Zionist movement allows for the different religious, social, and political emphases reflected in the programs of the political parties which function within its framework. We shall seek to distill out what seems to us to be the essence of a Zionist approach without entering into the various emphases, however important they may be. . . .

(1) One people with common history and destiny. Basic to a Zionist view is the affirmation of Jewish peoplehood; it sees Jews as one people, bound together by a common history and a common destiny.

The recognition of the unity of the Jewish people engenders a sense of mutual responsibility and paves the way for an understanding by Jews of the need for united action. It becomes the task of Zionists to show that the Zionist program represents the most effective form of such concerted action for the creative survival of Jews as a national entity.

(2) Israel as the Jewish national center. Zionism has differed from other movements (such as Diaspora [Jewish communities outside the Holy Land] nationalism) affirming Jewish peoplehood in that it regards Israel as the homeland of the Jewish people, as the Jewish national center. It seeks equality of national status for the Jew through the establishment of Israel as the Jewish State. (The antisemitic part of the world denies to the Jewish collective in Israel the equality which it formerly denied the individual Jew.) . . .

The Aims of Zionism

The aims of Zionism are:

The unity of the Jewish people and the centrality of Israel in Jewish life;

The ingathering of the Jewish people in its historic homeland Eretz Yisrael through Aliyah [immigration] from all countries;

The strengthening of the State of Israel, founded on the Prophetic ideals of justice and peace;

The preservation of the identity of the Jewish people through the fostering of Jewish and Hebrew education and of Jewish spiritual and cultural values;

The protection of Jewish rights everywhere.

Adopted by the 27th World Zionist Congress, Jerusalem, June 1968.

Just as in the Diaspora no clear distinction is drawn between Zionism and support for Israel, so in Israel the term Zionism is often used to include all that relates to the upbuilding of the country. The Zionist outlook of the founders of the state bore the imprint of the ideologies they had brought with them from the countries of their origin and the pioneering ("halutzic") immigration from Eastern Europe in particular had a formative influence on the Zionism which developed in Israel. The years following the establishment of the State were years of immersion in the tasks of immigrant absorption, land settlement, and defense, and little attention was given to the ideological implications of Zionism. The Zionism of the generation born in Israel still has a vague, amorphous character, and it becomes necessary to consider what elements enter into it.

It was natural that a people returning to a homeland from

which it had been exiled for centuries should place the emphasis on the love of the land in the education of the younger generation. A popular form of such education were the "tiyulim," the excursions into the countryside, exploring every nook and cranny, often with Bible in hand. There is, however, a growing recognition that it is necessary to foster a love not only for the land but for the Jewish people in the countries of the dispersion. The Hebrew literature which had negated the galut [exile] has also impaired for the young generation the image of the Jew who remained in what was regarded as a degrading condition. Eloquent expression was given to this problem by the third president of the State of Israel, Zalman Shazar, on the occasion of his inauguration. In the Diaspora, he observed, a people yearned through the centuries for its distant homeland; the young generation of Israelis who have grown up in that homeland are now required to define their relationship to a people in the far-flung lands of the Diaspora.

The feeling of Jewish interdependence which exists among a large section of Israeli youth provides a foundation on which the school, the youth movements, and other educational agencies can proceed to build further. The Ministry of Education is indeed revising curricula to allow for a fuller attention to the study of Zionism and of contemporary Jewry. The extensive educational services of the Israel army are placing special emphasis on the subject of Zionism; their publications, their training courses, their seminars for soldiers of all ranks have Zionism as a key topic. The climate of opinion that now prevails in Israel—further stimulated by the reaction to the U.N. resolution of November 1975 stigmatizing Zionism—constitutes a favorable background for these educational efforts.

Zionism Among Youths

The great majority of Israelis regard themselves as Zionists. In a survey conducted during July-September, 1973, by the Israel Institute of Applied Social Research, 82 percent of the urban population over the age of twenty declared themselves Zionists. When the survey was replicated in October, after the outbreak of the Yom Kippur War, 90 percent so declared themselves.

In our 1974 study of a countrywide sample of 1,875 eleventh graders 80 percent declared themselves Zionists. It may be assumed that if the study was carried out after the U.N. resolution of November, 1975, the percentage defining themselves as Zionists would have been even higher. . . .

The Zionism of the young Israelis differs from that of their parents or grandparents, many of whom know the galut from personal experience with it. The "revolt against the galut," the desire to terminate their condition of dependence on the goodwill of the non-Jewish majority, was a significant element in the Zionist outlook of the older Zionists. The Zionism of the younger generation is largely Israel-centered. When asked in what way they were Zionists, some of the young Israelis we interviewed in our study replied that they were such by virtue of the fact that they were living in Israel, were ready to serve in the army and fulfill all the duties of citizenship. They were equating Zionism with Israeli patriotism. Others did indeed go beyond this and declared that their Zionism found expression in their desire to see more Jews immigrate to Israel and in their readiness to do what they could to aid in the process of "klita," the integration of the new immigrants. Still others came closer to a more comprehensive definition when they stated that their Zionism was reflected in their conception of Israel as a Jewish state designed to serve as the homeland of all Jews. When asked what Zionism meant in the case of Jews abroad, the majority equated Zionism with aliya and a minority with support for Israel.

What Is Zionism?

Zionism is the modern expression of the ancient Jewish heritage.

Zionism is the national liberation movement of a people exiled from its historic homeland and dispersed among the nations of the world. . . .

Zionism is creating a society, however imperfect it may still be, which tries to implement the highest ideals of democracy—political, social and cultural—for all the inhabitants of Israel, irrespective of religious belief, race or sex.

Zionism is, in sum, the constant and unrelenting effort to realize the national and universal vision of the prophets of Israel.

Yigal Allon, *Zionism—A Basic Reader*, 1975.

The popular impression existed some years ago that Zionism had become a term of derision among Israel's youth. While this impression was an exaggeration of the situation, it did derive from the fact that a number of young Israelis tended to label as "Zionist" any excessively declamatory statement about patriotic intention. There is little trace of this derision at the present time. Zionism has a variety of meanings for Israeli youth but the connotation is generally positive. At times, indeed, the connotation is too broad. It embraces all that is idealistic and patriotic and deprives Zionism of its particular meaning.

While significance attaches to the declaration of the majority of the young Israelis that they are Zionists, their Zionism generally lacks a clearly defined content and a proper orientation to the Jewish people in the Diaspora. In terms of the analysis we have developed, we would submit that what distinguishes a Zionist whose Zionism has this content from a non-Zionist in Israel is the perspective in which the Zionist views the Jewish state; he sees it as part of the Jewish historical continuity, as the homeland of the entire Jewish people, and as having as its primary function the redemption of that people. Nathan Rotenstreich has expressed this view of Zionism in the following words: "Zionism is not the state itself nor even what is done inside its borders, but the historic meaning the state has for Jews."

In recent years Israel's foes have launched a vehement propaganda campaign disputing the right of the Jewish people to its land. By way of reaction, increased attention is being given in the education of the young Israeli to the exposition of the Jewish historical association with the land of Israel. But this has to be seen as only one item in a Zionist education and not as its full substance.

Inside Israeli circles an intense debate is proceeding as to what parts of the land presently under Israel's control should constitute its inalienable possession and what parts, if any, may be ceded as part of a future peace settlement. Without detracting from the importance of this issue or entering into the merits of the arguments advanced by the contending parties, we would state that it does not appear to us to relate, as some maintain, to the essence of the Zionist perspective. Zionists may, and do, range themselves on either side of the debate for reasons which are not incompatible with the Zionist perspective.

The Central Role of Israel

What has been said about the elements of a Zionist ideology in the Diaspora applies *mutatis mutandis* [necessary changes being made] to Zionism in Israel. Zionism in Israel, like Zionism in the Diaspora, has to be based on a recognition of the unity of the Jewish people and of the central role of Israel as the Jewish state in the life of all sections of that people. The propositions which follow are a restatement of what is in essence contained in the Jerusalem Program as it would apply to the Zionism of a Jew located in Israel.

(a) The Jews of Israel and the Jews of all countries of the Diaspora belong to one interdependent Jewish people and share the responsibility for their common future.

(b) Israel is the homeland not only of the Jews already resident in it but of the entire Jewish people, and the right inheres in every Jew to come to settle in this homeland.

(c) A primary responsibility of Israel as the Jewish state is "the ingathering of the exiles" ("kibbutz galuyot").

(d) Israel represents the continuity in the present and into the future of the Jewish historical tradition and is called upon to develop a Jewish culture which is in accord with that tradition and which should be a source of inspiration to Jews throughout the world.

(e) It is Israel's duty to aid in the preservation of the Jewish identity of communities everywhere and to extend them whatever assistance it can in the development of Jewish education and cultural life.

(f) Israel represents not only its own citizens but the Jewish people in the councils of nations. A threat to the security and welfare of any community is a matter of direct concern to it.

The test of a Zionist in Israel would be the acceptance of, and action in accordance with, these propositions.

The Ideology of Zionism

In his essay on "Ideology as a Cultural System," Clifford Geertz has properly criticized the tendency of social scientists to adopt an a priori [presumptively] pejorative view of "ideology." It should be the task of the social scientist to subject to scientific examination the function of ideologies as "maps of problematic social reality and matrices for the creation of collective conscience." Instead of projecting a blanket aversion to all ideologies, he should evaluate each ideology on its merits. He may then find—in the light of the value premises which underlie his examination— that while there are some ideologies which are morally repugnant, there are others deserving his commendation.

In our view Zionism is an ideology based on liberal, humanistic principles. Its analysis of the Jewish condition and the course of action it proposed have, moreover, stood the test of historical experience. Geertz has referred to the attempt of ideologies "to render otherwise incomprehensible social situations meaningful, to so construe them as to make it possible to act purposefully within them." We have sought to sketch the contours of a Zionist ideology which we believe can provide this purposeful direction in the complex, changing situations which face a Jewish people located in a world in turmoil.

"The idea of a non-Zionist and secular alternative for Israel . . . can become in the long run an important vision."

Zionism Weakens Israel

Leon T. Hadar

Many Jews and others believe Israel should reject Zionism and build a more secular society. In the following viewpoint, Leon T. Hadar agrees and argues that Zionism harms Israel because it officially distinguishes its citizens as either "Jewish" or "Arab." Hadar contends that this distinction discriminates against Arabs and favors Jews in many aspects of life. Hadar maintains that a non-Zionist society would reduce discrimination, improve Israel's relations with Palestinian Arabs and Middle East nations, and integrate Israel within the global economy. Hadar, a former United Nations (UN) bureau chief for the *Jerusalem Post*, teaches international relations at American University and is an adjunct scholar at the Cato Institute in Washington, D.C.

As you read, consider the following questions:

1. According to Hadar, how has Zionism turned Israel into "a new Jewish Ghetto"?
2. Why does the author believe that Israel should keep religion and state separate?
3. In Hadar's opinion, why does Israel need a constitution?

From "A Non-Zionist Israel: A Contradiction in Terms or a Realistic Option?" by Leon T. Hadar. Reprinted from *Issues of the American Council for Judaism*, Winter/Spring 1991, by permission of the American Council for Judaism, PO Box 9009, Alexandria, VA 22304.

Until the establishment of Israel in 1948, opposition to Zionism and to the idea of an exclusive Jewish state in which all members of the Hebrew faith will eventually settle had enjoyed strong support among members of Jewish communities around the world who refused to subscribe to the notion of Jewish nationalism. After 1948, "anti-Zionism" has been identified in many quarters with pro-Arab and anti-Israeli positions and with few exceptions, such as the American Council for Judaism, ceased to be a powerful political force. "Zionism," at the same time, has been used by the popular Western media to refer in general terms to political and public support for Israel.

Very little attention has been paid, however, to important political ideologies and movements inside Israel, and before 1948 in the Jewish community in Palestine, which have been strongly opposed to the tenets of Zionism and have proposed alternative secular and territorial concepts of national identity to replace it. These groups, which were not confined to the extreme left but were actually closely linked to Israel's political right, have enjoyed for many years popular support especially among young native Israelis, and although they have been unable to form a viable political force they still retain a major influence on Israeli political and intellectual life.

A Non-Zionist Alternative

The idea of a non-Zionist and secular alternative for Israel, including the possibility of separating religion and state and creating an independent Israeli nationalism that will not be identified with Judaism, can become in the long run an important vision, strongly rivaling that of militant and messianic Zionism that is dominating Israel today. A non-Zionist Israel can establish a federation with an independent Palestinian state, a new entity that can, in turn, become a nucleus of a new political realignment in the region. . . .

A non-Zionist group that emerged in the early forties was led by a colorful Palestinian-Jew, Hillel Kook, the son of a well-known Rabbi, who was very active among the right-wing Revisionist party. Kook arrived in the U.S. at the beginning of World War II, changed his name to Peter Bergson, and formed an organization, the Palestine National Committee, which was very active in efforts to save European-Jews during the Holocaust. Among other things, Bergson and his groups accused the Zionist leadership of concentrating its lobbying efforts in the U.S. on trying to gain political victories in Palestine instead of trying to pressure Washington to get out as many Jews as possible from Europe, even if that would mean settling them in the U.S. and not in Palestine.

After Israel was established in 1948, Bergson returned to the country and was elected as a member of the Knesset [Israel's parliament] on a small independent list that proposed what amounted to a revolutionary agenda. Zionism, he suggested, ended its mission after 1948. Israel should now become a "normal" state, a secular constitutional Republic, whose main obligation is to its citizens, Jews and non-Jews. Instead, he argued, Israel's Zionist founders have turned it into a new Jewish Ghetto, which maintains "special ties" to Jews who are citizens of other countries and discriminates against its own Arab citizens. "Israel belongs to its citizens and not to citizens of other nations," he emphasized, "while Jews who live in the U.S. are part of that nation and are not quasi-Israelis."

Zionism Will Destroy Israel

As an Israeli child, I was taught in school that the Arabs were not human beings like us, that they didn't need to eat more than a few olives a day, and that they would stab you in the back no matter how friendly they might seem.

This Zionist ideology also governs the justice system. The Israeli Supreme Court declared the deportations [of more than four hundred suspected Islamic militants in 1992] to be legal and usually allows Jewish rightwing fundamentalists to go unpunished when they murder innocent Palestinians.

The Palestinian uprisings (Intifada) of the last several years clearly show that faced with continuing oppression, resistance ever intensifies.

And Zionism, born out of the desire for a secure Jewish homeland, will inevitably lead to destruction of that very Home.

Raya Fidel, *The Freedom Socialist*, July/September 1993.

Bergson was in particular opposed to the "Law of Return" which, he contended, assigns to Jews who live abroad the status of potential Israeli citizens, one which creates dilemmas of dual loyalty for them and which they reject. If Israel would continue to demand from Jewish citizens of foreign countries special commitment to its security and prosperity, it would create growing tensions between Israel and the Jewish communities of the West, which, in turn, would produce eventually a "rebellion" against Israel on their part.

Israel is a "Jewish state" in the same way that Italy is a Catholic state or the U.S. is a Christian state. That is, the majority of its citizens belong to the Jewish faith and maintain religious and cultural affinity with Jews in other countries, explained Bergson. However, he argued that Israel should separate state and synagogue and should not force Israeli citizens to identify their religion in the state's identity cards.

As far as nationality is concerned, Israel should welcome Arab Christians and Moslems as members of the new Israeli nation, and should not make the distinction between members of the "Jewish" and "Arab" nations. Bergson was involved in a major case that was presented before the Israeli supreme court in which he asked the judges to force the Israeli government to recognize "Israeli" as a legitimate national identity. The judges rejected the case and argued that "Israeli," "Jewish" and "Hebrew" are synonyms.

Although Bergson had a small following in Israel and was the driving force behind several groups that emerged in the new state, such as the "Movement for Separating Religion and State," he became very frustrated in his effort to change Israel's policy and immigrated to the U.S. . . . .

Mixed Success

Israel's record of achievements remain[s] mixed. While establishing a relatively modern political and economic system and providing a home to Jewish refugees, Israel failed in its efforts to fulfill the grand Zionist plan. It did not attract [an expected] 12 million to immigrate to the new Jewish state and created major political dilemmas for Jewish citizens of other countries. Actually, thousands of young professional Israelis immigrate to the West, and most of the "miracle" of Soviet-Jewish immigration to Israel was a result of a decision by the American administration and Israeli government to force those Jews to move to Israel, despite the fact that most of them have expressed an interest to immigrate to the U.S.

Moreover, the idea of Jewish nationalism did not even succeed in establishing a secular identity for the Jewish citizens of Israel. Israel is today a theocracy in which state and religion are linked and in which the orthodox definition of Judaism is gaining political influence. The absorption into Israel of hundreds of thousands of Jews from Islamic countries, whose own sources of Jewish life and culture were traditional and religious, weakened the power of the more secular and Western European elite that established the state. Their vision of a liberal and open commonwealth in the East was gradually replaced by a vision of a new Jewish Ghetto on the Mediterranean.

More important, Israel's definition of an exclusive Jewish state made it impossible for it to absorb politically and economically the Palestinian-Arabs living inside its borders and in the territories it occupied in 1967, while the more militant version of Zionism that came to power in that country in 1977 refused to recognize the rights of those Palestinian-Arabs for self-determination while calling to maintain Israel's political and ideological control and eventual annexation of the West Bank and Gaza. The militant religious-orthodox and anti-Western groups that lead the Jewish settlement movement in the West Bank represent this extreme wing of Zionism that is gaining more and more power in Israel today.

Israel and the Cold War

A lack of a solution to the Palestinian-Israeli conflict makes it difficult for Israel to solve its problems with the surrounding Arab states and to integrate itself in the region. The Zionist elites that dominated Israel since its establishment were able to take advantage of the Cold War in order to advance Israel's security interests and to perpetuate the country's bankrupt socialist economy. Serving the interests of British and French imperialism in the Middle East in the 1950's and later, after 1967, that of America's Cold War policies, saved the Israeli elite from the need to face the economic and diplomatic music.

Three Zionist Myths

Limiting Israel's territorial claims and allowing it to redevelop its culture and institutions means giving up three cherished Zionist myths: (1) that Jews have an a priori right to the whole of Palestine, (2) that the other people resident there historically, the Arab Palestinians, do not have a parallel claim on the land as a national community, and (3) that Israel must be an outpost of European people and culture, not a part of the "Levant" [eastern Mediterranean]. It is these three Zionist myths that have walled Israel into a segregated, hostile, and violent relationship to the rest of the communities that live around it.

Rosemary Radford Ruether and Herman J. Ruether, *The Witness*, May 1989.

In exchange for its services as a "strategic asset," helping to defend American interests in the region and in other parts of the Third World as part of the Cold War strategy, Israel could maintain and expand its national security and welfare state and after 1967 continue to suppress the alienated Arab population and deny its political rights. Ironically, American and European Jews who were supposed to immigrate to Israel, as well as other supporters of the Jewish State in the West, became a source of political and economic survival of Israel, and helped to construct the Cold War ideology, in which Moscow's hostility towards Israel and its refusal to allow Jews to leave the Soviet Union became an important component. American neoconservatism became the intellectual link between militant Israel and American Cold Warriors.

Israel's Future: Two Visions

Israel . . . is divided today between the forces of progress and reaction. There is the vision of Israel, symbolized by the Mediterranean city of Tel Aviv and the other coastal urban centers where Israel's academic institutions, high tech industry, art and literary life are located. This is a dynamic commercial center, dominated by a secular population oriented towards a modern life style, whose intellectual currents, popular music and women's fashion imitate those of London, Paris and New York. This is a Western Israel, which hopes to reach a solution with the Palestinian population, to integrate the state in the region and to make it part of the forward global economy. It is an Israel which wants to reform the country's economy, to separate state and religion and to legislate a constitution.

And there is the vision of Israel symbolized by Jerusalem and its militant Zionist leadership. It is an Israel that looks to the past, whose vision of the country is of "us," the Jewish people, against "them," the "Goyim": the murderous Palestinians and hostile Arabs, the unreliable and wimpy U.S. and the anti-Semitic and decadent West. It is a Ghettoized Israel, a theocracy whose identity is religious, mystical and messianic, which hopes to "Judaize" "Judea and Samaria," annex those territories and eventually force the Palestinian-Arabs to leave the country or to remain there in an Apartheid-like system. It sees Israel engaged in a never-ending, all-out war with the Arab World and Islam, a war that will end only when one side wins.

It is in this coming struggle between the "two Israels" that non-Zionist . . . movements could serve as a source for a new ideological revival in Israel, around which liberal and secular citizens could develop an alternative agenda. . . . Creating the basis for a new secular Israeli nationalism, decoupled from its diplomatic and financial dependency on the U.S. and its lobby there, living in peace with Palestinian nationalism, with a constitution that guarantees rights to all citizens, will be on the top of this new agenda.

Unfortunately, one of the major obstacles to such a development is the power of the Israeli lobby and its neoconservative intellectual supporters whose efforts to prevent any American pressure on Israel to change its diplomatic posture as well as its economic system, such as cutting U.S. aid that goes into building new Jewish settlements in the West Bank and to support a socialist economy, plays into the hands of the Likud [party] and weakens those in Israel who call for peace with the Palestinians and for economic reform.

> "All the evidence . . . prove[s] the racist and
> racial discriminatory policies, laws, and
> practices of the Zionist-Israeli hierarchy."

Zionism Equals Racism

Sami Hadawi

Sami Hadawi is a Palestinian scholar and author of *Bitter
Harvest: A Modern History of Palestine*, from which this viewpoint is excerpted. In the following viewpoint, Hadawi argues
that Zionism is a racist belief practiced by Israel, whose laws
and policies unjustly grant privileges to Jews and discriminate
against non-Jews. Hadawi contends, for example, that Israel's
Law of Return automatically and unconditionally confers nationality and residency rights on any Jew who emigrates to
Israel, but denies the same rights to both Arabs and Christians
who were born and raised in Israel or its occupied territories.
The author concludes that a nation that enforces such a law
cannot be considered a democracy.

As you read, consider the following questions:

1. In Hadawi's opinion, how did Israel long avoid being
   penalized by the United Nations for practicing racism?
2. According to the author, why are Israel's supporters unable
   to refute the charge that Zionism equals racism?
3. Why does Hadawi believe that Zionism is a political ideology
   with no religious significance?

From *Bitter Harvest: A Modern History of Palestine* by Sami Hadawi. Revised and updated
edition Brooklyn: Olive Branch Press, 1990. Copyright © 1989 by Sami Hadawi. Reprinted
with permission of Olive Branch Press, an imprint of Interlink Publishing Group, Inc.

In 1945, the major powers, with representatives of the smaller nations, gathered in San Francisco and drafted the Charter for the proposed United Nations Organization which was to replace the defunct League of Nations; in 1948, the United Nations adopted the Universal Declaration of Human Rights; and in 1949, the Fourth Geneva Convention Relative to the Protection of Civilian Persons in Times of War came into effect. But notwithstanding these international agreements, the scourge of racism and racial discrimination continued to be practised in certain countries.

On November 20, 1963, the UN General Assembly proclaimed the Declaration on the Elimination of All Forms of Racial Discrimination, which provides in Article 1: "Discrimination between human beings on the ground of race, color, or ethnic origin is an offence to human dignity and shall be condemned." The resolution went on to affirm that "any doctrine of racial discrimination or superiority is scientifically false, morally condemnable, socially unjust and dangerous." It expressed its alarm at the manifestations of racial discrimination still in evidence in some areas of the world, some of which are imposed by certain governments by means of legislative, administrative or other measures.

In 1965, the International Convention on the Elimination of All Forms of Racial Discrimination went a step further by proclaiming in Article 1: "In this convention, the term racial discrimination shall mean any distinction, exclusion, restriction or preference based on race, color, descent, or national or ethnic origin.". . .

In the case of Israel, the Jewish state managed during many years—through the power and influence of Zionism in the capitals of the western world—to remain clear of the arm of the United Nations. However, this could not go on forever as more and more injustices of a racist character were being inflicted with impunity against the Palestinian people and could no longer be ignored.

Equating Zionism with Racism

In 1975, the case against Israel was brought before the UN General Assembly. Dr. Fayez Sayegh, delegate of Kuwait, arguing in favor of the draft resolution, said: "The Zionism of which the draft resolution speaks, is a concrete political ideology, articulated by a concrete political organization which launched a concrete political movement at a precise moment in time, which created political institutions, and which manifested itself in concrete practices which had the effect of excluding some people on the basis of their being non-Jews and including others on the basis of their being Jews—Jewishness being defined officially by Zionism as an ethnic and not strictly a religious definition."

The Israeli representative, in an attempt to confuse the issue

83

and to inject an accusation of anti-Semitism, equated the attack on Zionism as an attack on Judaism, and alleged that it was "born of a deep, pervading feeling of anti-Semitism."

On November 10, 1975, the General Assembly, by a vote of 72 in favor, 35 against, and 27 abstentions, adopted a resolution which "determines that Zionism is a form of racism and racial discrimination."

A Racist Ideology

Either Zionism equates with racism, or it does not. Judging from the passage of UN General Assembly Resolution 37/40 of 3 December 1982, in which 122 out of the then 156 member states condemned the racism pursued in the occupied Arab territories by the Israeli government, a large part of the world believes that in practice, if not in theory, Zionism as pursued by Israel is indeed a racist ideology.

Emma Murphy, *Middle East International*, August 30, 1991.

After the passage of the resolution, attacks appeared in the press of the United States and Canada against the United Nations describing it as an impotent organization, and against the nations which voted in favor of the resolution accusing them of being stooges of the oil-rich Arab States.

To understand the resolution, a student of Middle East affairs put it this way:

The resolution is not:

an attack against world Jewry by a mass of anti-Semitic people or governments;

an attempt by communist and Third World nations to take over or wreck the United Nations;

the result of a vast purchase of votes by oil-rich Arab states.

The resolution is:

an expression of resistance to Israeli intransigence in their refusal to deal with the Palestinian people;

an attempt to isolate Israel in the United Nations for her disregard of numerous UN resolutions and appeals to respect the human rights of Palestinians in the territories occupied in 1967;

an attempt to isolate Israel for her refusal to withdraw from those territories;

a criticism of Israel as a Jewish state, i.e., a state founded on principles according to which Jews enjoy privileges not shared by non-Jewish citizens;

84

a reaction against policies pursued by western nations—especially the United States—which ignore the plight of the Palestinian people and attempt to reach a solution to the Middle East problem through exclusion of the Palestine Liberation Organization from negotiations;

an attempt to show solidarity with the Palestine struggle subsequent to the Sinai Agreement in regard to which Egypt pursued national, as opposed to regional interests.

The nations which supported the resolution actually did so as a matter of principle and on the basis of the evidence presented. They categorically opposed the apartheid policies and practices of South Africa and as such, they could not very well remain indifferent to the racist policies and practices of Zionism and its off-spring Israel.

Rejecting the Resolution

Speaking in the General Assembly after the vote, the Israeli representative said: "For us, the Jewish people, this is no more than a piece of paper, and we shall treat it as such." He was later reported to have angrily torn up a copy of the resolution in the presence of the UN membership. He made no effort, however, to defend the principles of Zionism by rebutting the evidence presented.

The U.S. representative, on the other hand, joined the Israeli bandwagon. Ambassador Daniel Moynihan vehemently attacked the resolution and told the General Assembly: "There appears to have developed in the United Nations the practice for a number of countries to combine for the purpose of doing something outrageous." He added: "The United States rises to declare before the General Assembly, and before the world, that it does not acknowledge, it will not abide by, and will never acquiesce in the infamous act." Moynihan then referred to the description made by the U.S. representative on the Social, Humanitarian and Cultural Committee to the effect that "it was obscene," and he continued to declare that "the abomination of anti-Semitism . . . has been given the appearance of international sanction," alleging that "the General Assembly today grants sympathetic amnesty—and more—to the murderers of the six million Jews." He went on to describe the findings of the General Assembly as "a lie which the United Nations has now declared to be a truth."

Two pertinent points arise out of this erratic outburst by Moynihan: The first, he proved it to be a lie that the United States is the champion of the United Nations. It appears that the U.S. government will support the world organization only if it follows United States policy. The second, the representative of the United States has given the Israelis support for their disrespect and non-compliance with resolutions of the United Nations.

Had United States opposition to the resolution been based on arguments capable of refuting the substance of the evidence which brought about its passage, one would perhaps feel sympathy for the logic of the United States position; but for the representative of a great power to make attacks of a general character and fail to prove that the majority of nations was wrong indicates bias, and reflects adversely on the government of the United States.

Apart from the denunciations of the equation between Zionism and racism in general terms, the only argument that appeared in print was the usual claim that Zionism is synonymous with Judaism. The Canadian Zionist Federation, for example, argued that "the separation of Zionism from Judaism is like separating Muhammad from Islam and Christ from Christianity."

The analogy is as preposterous as it is absurd. Judaism is based on the Five Books of Moses; Christianity on the Teachings of Christ; and Islam on the Revelations made to the Prophet Muhammad. In essence, the three faiths are identical in their religious and human values of love, humanity, humility, tolerance and equality, and none justify a political movement based on occupation and oppression.

Grounds Supporting the Resolution

Zionism—unlike Judaism—lacks any religious significance, and uses Judaism as a means to further its political objectives. Furthermore, it has capitalized on the persecution and oppression of Jews in Christian Europe down through the ages, and on what the Nazis did to the Jews during World War II—neither of which calamities exists anywhere in the world today.

It would be too lengthy a process to enumerate all the evidence and arguments to prove the racist and racial discriminatory policies, laws, and practices of the Zionist-Israeli hierarchy. Suffice it to [analyze] one example. The Israeli Law of Return confers the [nationality and residency] rights of entry automatically and unconditionally upon any Jew, of whatever nationality, the moment he steps on Israeli soil, even though he may never before have set foot in Palestine. This same right is denied to a Palestinian Arab who was born, raised, owns property in Palestine, and lived there all his life, as well as his ancestors before him. How can a country that enacts such a law be described as a democracy? And how can the label of racism and racial discrimination against such a country be questioned or defended? This law is unique in its principles, and did not exist even in South Africa's apartheid.

Article 13(2) of the Universal Declaration of Human Rights gives "everyone the right to leave any country, including his own, and to return to his country"; and while the Israeli government is a signatory to this universal declaration and insisted that its provisions should be applied to Soviet Jews, it has flouted its provisions with impunity where the Palestinian Moslems and Christians are concerned.

Even Arabs who have at no time left the territory that came under Israeli jurisdiction were denied the same rights as alien Jews. To become an Israeli citizen, an Arab must be naturalized under the provisions of the Nationality Law. This is only possible by proving that he was born in the country; that he lived in Israeli-occupied territory three out of five years preceding the date of his application for citizenship; that he is entitled to permanent residence; and that he has a sufficient knowledge of the Hebrew language. Even if the Arab met all these requirements, it was still up to the discretion of the Minister of the Interior to grant or refuse the application.

Admitting Discrimination

The Israeli Minister of the Interior admitted in parliament that racial discrimination did exist in Israel. But he pointed out that this stemmed not from the Nationality Law but from the Law of Return, which endowed only Jews with the right of return.

Israeli Professor M.R. Konvitz expressed fears that such a law might be unfavorably compared with Nazi legislation, since it embodied "a principle of exclusion which constitutes religious discrimination." He argued that though the law might offer temporary advantages at a time when large numbers of displaced persons have to be settled, thereafter it would undoubtedly be considered discriminatory.

After the Bill became law in 1950, the Jewish Newsletter warned that the Law of Return revives a dangerous racist theory that smacks of the slogan of a previous generation: "A German is a German wherever he is"; while Rueven Grass, a religious immigrant from the United States, compared the law to the Nazi laws because "it gives immigration privileges to anyone who is Jewish under the Nuremberg Laws' definition, i.e., having a Jewish grandparent."

"Zionism is a unique moral phenomenon that has won the support of many people of goodwill around the world."

Zionism Is Not Racism

Benjamin Netanyahu

Benjamin Netanyahu, a former Israeli commando, is Israel's former deputy foreign minister and was elected leader of the conservative Likud party in 1993. In the following viewpoint, Netanyahu argues that the charge by Arabs and others that Zionism equals racism unjustly libels the Jewish people. Netanyahu maintains that Zionism is a color-blind movement that, for example, has welcomed the immigration of tens of thousands of black Ethiopian Jews to Israel. Netanyahu asserts that the libel against Zionism is the same type of libel as was spread by the Nazis. He is the author of *A Place Among the Nations: Israel and the World*, from which this viewpoint is excerpted.

As you read, consider the following questions:

1. Why does Netanyahu believe that Israel's greatest strength is its moral stature?
2. How have anti-Semites exploited the term "Zionist," according to the author?
3. In Netanyahu's opinion, why do many people continue to believe that Zionism equals racism?

In November 1975, a mere eight years after their great defeat in the Six Day War, the Arabs achieved their greatest victory on the field of propaganda: The General Assembly of the United Nations, by a vote of 72 to 35, with 32 abstentions, resolved that Zionism, the national movement of the Jewish people, constituted "racism."

Such an achievement had eluded even the great anti-Semitic propagandists of our millennium like Tomás de Torquemada and Joseph Goebbels. For what they and their disciples had failed to do in the Inquisition and in the Holocaust had at long last been achieved by the General Assembly of the United Nations. Never before had anti-Semitism acquired a tool of such *universal* dissemination as the UN. Never before had a slander of the Jewish people, of which there had been so many, been promulgated and applauded by an organization that purported to represent humankind.

Israel's Moral Strength

The Arabs knew that Israel's strength was not rooted in its numbers, its size, or its resources. In all these areas the Arabs were far stronger. Israel's greatest shield, they understood, was its moral stature. They therefore sought to tarnish that shield, to crack it, and ultimately to crush it. Their weapon was an extraordinary vilification of a movement that had inspired millions. For Zionism is a unique moral phenomenon that has won the support of many people of goodwill around the world. The Jewish people had suffered degradation, humiliation, oppression, and mutilation like no other. The Jewish legacy is one of the principal founts of Western civilization, contributing above all to advancing the concepts of freedom and justice. The Zionist movement had come into being to seek for its own people freedom and justice; after two millennia of bondage, the Jewish people was entitled to its own liberation as an independent nation.

This is the true and only meaning of Zionism. At the close of World War I, and again after World War II, it had been so understood not only by the Jewish people but by virtually the entire world. Many nations and peoples had admired the tenacity, courage, and moral strength of the Zionist movement. They had marveled at Israel's achievement in rebuilding a modern state on the ruins of an ancient homeland. They had applauded the ingathering of the exiles from a hundred lands and the seemingly miraculous revival of an ancient tongue. And they had thrilled at Israel's ability to maintain its democratic and human ethic in the face of one of the most remorseless campaigns of hatred in history. All this had been appreciated by people not only in Europe and America but in Africa and elsewhere in the developing world, where Israel and Zionism had served as a shining example of the independence and progress that so many other nations, coming out from under the heel of empire, hoped to achieve.

These realities were not lost on the Arab regimes or on the Soviets [who sponsored the resolution together]. Indeed, their attack on Israel was not driven by political interest alone. Deep down, they experienced an unforgiving resentment. For nothing so effectively unmasks dictators and despots who hide behind the rhetoric of "liberation" and "self-determination" as a genuine movement of national liberation. Israel and Zionism, by their very existence, exposed the claims of the tyrants and totalitarians for the sham that they are.

Concern Toward Blacks

But the sham was particularly preposterous in labeling so completely color-blind a movement racist. Theodor Herzl, the founder of modern Zionism, had himself declared the plight of blacks to be a cause of fundamental concern to him, like that of the Jews:

> There is still one problem of racial misfortune unresolved. The depths of that problem, in all their horror, only a Jew can fathom. . . . I mean the Negro problem. Think of the hair-raising horrors of the slave trade. Human beings, because their skins are black, are stolen, carried off, and sold. . . . Now that I have lived to see the restoration of the Jews, I should like to pave the way for the restoration of the Negroes.

Almost a century later, Israel's rescue of Ethiopia's Jews showed Zionism to be the only movement in history to transport blacks out of Africa not to enslave them but to liberate them.

In 1985, on the tenth anniversary of the adoption of the resolution defaming Zionism, I organized a symposium on the United Nations premises to attack this infamy. The Arab states and the PLO [Palestine Liberation Organization] were especially irked by this affront (how dared we convene a conference on "their" ground?), and they tried unsuccessfully to block it. But what irritated them even more was that one of the speakers, Rahamim Elazar, was an Ethiopian Jew. He described in moving terms his own personal salvation in coming to Israel. Since then, tens of thousands of members of his community have followed in their great exodus from Ethiopia. An accusation of racism against the Zionists by the Arab world—whose contemporary customs include the keeping of indentured black servants in the Gulf states and a prolific history of trading along the slave coast of Africa, as well as the repeated massacres of blacks by the Sudanese Arabs—should have been received like a witless joke.

It wasn't. The combined power of the Arab and Soviet blocs gave them complete control of the UN, its microphones, and its printing presses. To be sure, even without the campaign against Israel, one would have been hard pressed to consider the UN General Assembly a pure arbiter of moral truth. Indeed, what can be said of an institution that failed to curb in even the slightest way the Soviet aggression in Afghanistan, a war that claimed a million lives and turned five million people into refugees; that for seven years did not lift a finger to stop the sickening carnage of the Iran-Iraq War, in which another million perished; that did not even address, much less remedy, such outrages as the genocide in Cambodia, the horrific slaughter of the Ibo in Biafra, and the massacre of hundreds of thousands of civilians in Uganda under Idi Amin, all in flagrant violation of the UN's own Universal Declaration of Human Rights?

Feelings of Inferiority Breed Discrimination

The means used by all the governments of Israel to discriminate against Arabs might be unacceptable, and even very disturbing, but they do not constitute racism. Racism is bound up with feelings of superiority. There are phenomena in Israel which on the surface appear to be racist, but they are really the opposite of racism, and in fact derive from feelings of inferiority.

Aryeh Naor, *New Outlook*, March/April 1992.

Yet despite all these and other enormous affronts to conscience, nothing injected such calumny into the arteries of international opinion as the Zionism-racism resolution did against Israel. It may be tempting to dismiss this resolution as a meaningless absurdity, especially after its belated renunciation in December 1991. But that would be a mistake. We must remember that the Arabs had a full sixteen years to drive home their racism message, and that even after its formal renunciation, this defamation lives on in the minds of many nations and their leaders. I stress again that, for the first time in history, a world body had given its stamp of approval to the libeling of an entire people. In the very century of the Holocaust, one must not forget the insidious power of uninhibited libel. Without the torrents of slander poured on the Jews by the Nazis, the Holocaust would never have been possible. Had the Nazis not succeeded in brainwashing Germans and non-Germans alike into believing that the Jews were reprehensible, subhuman, and in fact a different species, they would not have secured the collaboration of thousands upon thousands of ordinary people in moving the machinery of genocide.

We know that in the two or three European countries where such collaboration did not take place, the majority of Jews were saved. Well known is the example of Denmark, in which the king himself declared that if any of his subjects wore the yellow

badge, then he too would wear it; Denmark's Jews were successfully smuggled to safety in Sweden. Less well known but
equally dramatic is the case of Bulgaria, where the entire educated elite of the country opposed the implementation of official
anti-Semitism. Thus, the Union of Bulgarian Lawyers and the
Union of Writers respectively denounced the German-imposed
anti-Jewish legislation as "socially damaging" and "very harm-
ful." The head of the Bulgarian Orthodox Church described the
directives as "thunder from a clear sky." A German report at-
tributed Bulgarian disobedience of these laws to the "inactivity
of the police and the complete indifference of the majority of
the Bulgarian people." Particularly telling is the explanation that
the German ambassador in Sofia offered to his superiors in
Berlin: He told them that the "Bulgarian public lacks the understanding of the Jewish question in historical terms." This failure
of understanding was in fact directly due to the stubborn refusal
of the country's leadership—writers, clergy, teachers, politicians—to spread the Nazi slander, as a consequence of which
Bulgarian Jewry was saved.

In other words, libel is the prelude to murder. It is a license to
kill. The libeling of an entire people separates that people from
the rest of humanity, making the lives of its members dispens-
able, its oppressors and murderers immune to blame.

Disguised Anti-Semitism

Appearances notwithstanding, the libel of "Zionism equals
racism" is the very same libel that was spread by the Nazis. It is
the same anti-Semitism dressed up in trendy terminology. For
the bitter truth is that the horrors of the Holocaust did not make
anti-Semitism unfashionable; they only made some of the old
terminology embarrassing. *Zionism* and *Zionist* now serve as eu-
phemisms for *Judaism* and *Jew*. And since there is no worse epi-
thet in today's lexicon than *racist*, it is the term that is used to
replace the whole range of old-fashioned invective. It is the contemporary equivalent of *Christ-killer, traitor, usurer, international
conspirator*. All this has stolen into vogue under the sham dis-
claimer of "I'm not anti-Semitic, I'm just anti-Zionist"—the
equivalent of "I'm not anti-American, I just think the United
States shouldn't exist."

Building on the Zionism-racism resolution, the Arab propaganda machine has now been at work for a quarter of a century,
ever since the Six Day War, spinning a web of falsehoods that
have permeated every issue and colored every opinion on the
subject of Israel. Even now, with the resolution overturned, the
spires of untruth that it erected and buttressed remain standing,
having taken on a terrible life of their own. So successful has
been the demonization of the Jewish state that many people are

willing to overlook the most heinous crimes, to pardon virtually any excess on the part of the Arabs, since, after all, one has to take into account their "plight" and "all they have suffered." Just as they had planned, the Arabs have succeeded in foisting their historical fabrications into the media and from there onto the world public and its representatives everywhere. With this, the Arabs have achieved an astonishing transformation, making themselves over into the aggrieved party demanding justice, and Israel into an "entity"—unnatural, alien, immoral—capable of virtually no right because its very existence is itself an irredeemable wrong.

Guilty for Being a Nation

Thus it is that Zionism, once considered a noble and legitimate national movement worthy of broad international support during the establishment of the new world order at the opening of the twentieth century, finds itself the odd man out at the initiation of the new world order at the close of the century. Israel is the only nation on the face of the globe that important sections of opinion consider to be *guilty* for being a nation—wrong for claiming its homeland as its own, culpable for building its homes, schools, and factories on this land, and unjust for trying to defend itself against enemies who wish its destruction.

Periodical Bibliography

The following articles have been selected to supplement the diverse views presented in this chapter.

The Christian Century   "UN Repeals Resolution," January 15, 1992.

Arie Dayan   "The Debate over Zionism and Racism: An Israeli View," *Journal of Palestine Studies*, Spring 1993.

Lawrence S. Eagleburger   "UN Repeals Zionism-Is-Racism Resolution," *U.S. Department of State Dispatch*, December 23, 1991.

Douglas J. Feith   "A Mandate for Israel," *The National Interest*, Spring 1993. Available form PO Box 3000, Dept. NI, Denville, NJ 07834.

Arthur Hertzberg   "Waiting for the Messiah," *Commonweal*, May 8, 1992.

Allen Lesser   "Waiting for the End of the World," *The Humanist*, September/October 1992.

Bernard Lewis   "Muslims, Christians, and Jews: The Dream of Coexistence," *The New York Review of Books*, March 26, 1992.

Robert A. Licht   "Israel Among the Nationalisms," *First Things*, April 1991. Available from PO Box 3000, Dept. FT, Denville, NJ 07834.

A.L. Motzkin   "Ancestors," *The New Republic*, April 13, 1992.

News from Within   Special issue on Zionism, March/April 1992. Available from the Alternative Information Center, PO Box 31417, Jerusalem, Israel.

Daniel Pipes   "Israel, America, and Arab Delusions," *Commentary*, March 1991.

Sheldon L. Richman   "Anti-Semitism: What It Is and What It Isn't," *Issues of the American Council for Judaism*, Winter/Spring 1992. Available from PO Box 9009, Alexandria, VA 22304.

Michael Strassfeld   "Toward a Torah of Zion," *Tikkun*, July/August 1993.

What Are the Prospects for Arab-Israeli Peace?

Chapter Preface

With a handshake outside the White House on September 13, 1993, Israeli prime minister Yitzhak Rabin and PLO chairman Yasir Arafat sealed the breakthrough Israeli-PLO accord, which grants limited Palestinian autonomy in Israel's occupied territories. After the signing, Palestinian delegation spokeswoman Hanan Ashrawi proclaimed, "We have become partners in peace and no longer adversaries in conflict."

While most supporters expressed more cautious optimism for the accord's success, many Jews and Palestinians denounced the agreement outright, arguing that Arafat and Rabin had betrayed their people. On one side, Jewish opposition protested Israel's consent to allow PLO authority in the territories. On the other, Palestinians argued that the accord merely glossed over as issues for future negotiation important grievances such as Israeli control of Arab East Jerusalem and the banishment of refugees to Jordan and other Arab states.

Whether in favor of or opposed to the accord, many Jews and Palestinians predicted that the plan was a formula for increased violence, particularly by extremist Jewish settlers and Palestinian militants who felt cheated by the agreement. For example, a Guttman Institute poll taken in Israel prior to the signing found that 75 percent of Israelis expected Palestinian violence to increase as a result of the accord. Indeed, both Arab and Jewish extremists had promised to step up violence, not only against each other, but against those backing the accord within their own national group as well.

The success of the peace accord, many experts believe, rests on the ability of both Jews and Palestinians to forsake or prevent violence. Whether both sides are committed to peace is debated by the authors of the following viewpoints.

"This government is determined to expend all the energy, to take any path, to do everything necessary . . . to achieve peace."

Israel Is Committed to Peace

Yitzhak Rabin

Yitzhak Rabin is a former Israeli general who helped plan the defeat of Arab forces in the 1967 Six Day War. In 1992, Rabin was elected to his second term as Israel's prime minister. In the following viewpoint, excerpted from a speech to the Knesset (Israel's parliament), Rabin argues that Israel must join the international movement toward peace. He asserts that the key to peace is self-government for Palestinians, whom he urges to take control of their destiny and end hostilities with Jews by accepting autonomy. Rabin warns, however, that the security of Jewish settlers in the occupied territories is Israel's utmost concern and will take priority over peace if the offer of autonomy is met with continued violence.

As you read, consider the following questions:

1. Why does Rabin believe that Palestinians can gain nothing through violence?
2. How will Israel respond if Palestinians reject autonomy, according to Rabin?
3. In Rabin's opinion, how serious is the threat of nuclear weapons in the Middle East?

From "Peace: The Future of Israel" by Yitzhak Rabin, a speech delivered before Knesset, Jerusalem, Israel, July 13, 1992.

The citizens of Israel and people in countries throughout the world look forward today to our embarking upon a new path, to fresh momentum, to turning a new page in the annals of the state of Israel. Attended by their best wishes and concern, we are today setting out on the long and difficult journey.

This government is determined to expend all the energy, to take any path, to do everything necessary, possible, and more, for the sake of national and personal security, to achieve peace and prevent war, to do away with unemployment, for the sake of immigration and absorption, for economic growth, to strengthen the foundations of democracy and the rule of law, to ensure equality for all citizens, and to protect human rights. We are going to change the national order of priorities. We know very well that obstacles will stand in our path. Crises will erupt; there will be disappointments, tears, and pain. But after it all, once we have traveled this road, we shall have a strong state, a good state, a state in which we will be proud to be citizens and partners in the great effort. . . .

Peace and Security

We must join the international movement toward peace, reconciliation, and cooperation that is spreading over the entire globe these days—lest we be the last to remain, all alone, in the station.

The new government has accordingly made it a prime goal to promote the making of peace and take vigorous steps that will lead to the conclusion of the Arab-Israeli conflict. We shall do so based on the recognition by the Arab countries, and the Palestinians, that Israel is a sovereign state with a right to live in peace and security. We believe wholeheartedly that peace is possible, that it is imperative, and that it will ensue.

"I shall believe in the future," wrote the poet Shaul Tcherniknovsky. "Even if it is far off, the day will come when peace and blessings are borne from nation to nation"—and I want to believe that that day is not far off.

The government will propose to the Arab states and the Palestinians the continuation of the peace talks based upon the framework forged at the Madrid Conference. As a first step toward a permanent solution we shall discuss the institution of autonomy in Judea, Samaria [together the West Bank], and the Gaza District. We do not intend to lose precious time. . . .

To you, the Palestinians in the territories, I wish to say from this rostrum—we have been fated to live together on the same patch of land, in the same country. We lead our lives with you, beside you and against you. You have failed in the war against us. One hundred years of your bloodshed and terror against us have brought you only suffering, humiliation, bereavement, and pain. You have lost thousands of your sons and daughters, and you are losing ground all the time. For 44 years now, you have been living under a delusion. Your leaders have led you through lies and deceit. They have missed every opportunity, rejected all the proposals for a settlement, and have taken you from one tragedy to another.

Paul Conrad, © 1993, Los Angeles Times Syndicate. Reprinted with permission.

And you, Palestinians in the territories, who live in the wretched poverty of Gaza and Khan Yunis, in the refugee camps of Hebron and Shechem; you who have never known a single day of freedom and joy in your lives—listen to us, if only this once. We offer you the fairest and most viable proposal from our standpoint today—autonomy—self-government—with all its advantages and limitations. You will not get everything you want. Perhaps neither will we. So once and for all, take your destiny in your hands. Don't lose this opportunity that may never return. Take our proposal seriously—to avoid further suffering, and grief; to end the shedding of tears and of blood.

The new government urges the Palestinians in the territories to give peace a chance—and to cease all violent and terrorist activity for the duration of the negotiations on the subject of autonomy. We are well aware that the Palestinians are not all of a single mold, that there are exceptions and differences among them. But we urge the population, which has been suffering for years, and the perpetrators of the riots in the territories, to forswear stones and knives and await the results of the talks that may well bring peace to the Middle East. If you reject this proposal, we shall go on talking but treat the territories as though there were no dialogue going on between us. Instead of extending a friendly hand, we will employ every possible means to prevent terror and violence. The choice, in this case, is yours. . . .

The plan to apply self-government to the Palestinians in Judea, Samaria, and Gaza—the autonomy of the Camp David Accords [Israel's 1979 treaty returning the Sinai Peninsula to Egypt]—is an interim settlement for a period of five years. No later than three years after its institution, discussions will begin on the permanent solution. It is only natural that the holding of talks on the subject creates concern among those among us who have chosen to settle in Judea, Samaria, and the Gaza District. I hereby inform you that the government, by means of the IDF [Israeli Defense Force] and the other security services, will be responsible for the security and welfare of the residents of Judea, Samaria, and the Gaza District. However, at the same time, the government will refrain from any steps and activities that would disrupt the proper conduct of the peace negotiations.

We see the need to stress that the government will continue to enhance and strengthen Jewish settlement along the lines of confrontation, due to their importance for security, and in greater Jerusalem. . . .

A Volatile Middle East

The winds of peace have been blowing from Moscow to Washington, from Berlin to Beijing. The voluntary liquidation of weapons of mass destruction and the abrogation of military pacts have lessened the risk of war in the Middle East, as well. And yet this region, with Syria and Jordan, Iraq and Lebanon, is still fraught with danger. Thus when it comes to security, we will concede not a thing. From our standpoint, security takes preference even over peace. A number of countries in our region have recently stepped up their efforts to develop and produce nuclear weapons. According to published information, Iraq was very close to attaining nuclear arms. Fortunately, its nuclear capability was discovered in time and, according to various testimonies, was damaged during and following the Gulf War. The possibility that nuclear weapons will be introduced into the Middle East in the coming years is a very grave and negative development from Israel's standpoint. The government, from its very outset—and possibly in collaboration with other countries—will address itself to thwarting any possibility that one of Israel's enemies will possess nuclear weapons. Israel has long been prepared to face the threat of nuclear arms. At the same time, this situation requires us to give further thought to the urgent need to end the Arab-Israeli conflict and live in peace with our Arab partners.

From this moment forward the concept of "peace process" is no longer relevant. From now on we shall not speak of a "process" but of making peace. In that peace-making we wish to call upon the aid of Egypt, whose late leader, President Anwar Sadat, exhibited such courage and was able to bequeath to his people—and to us—the first peace agreement. The government will seek further ways of improving neighborly relations and strengthening ties with Egypt and its President, Hosni Mobarak.

I call upon the leaders of the Arab countries to follow the lead of Egypt and its president and take the step that will bring us—and them—peace. I invite the King of Jordan and the presidents of Syria and Lebanon to this rostrum in Israel's Knesset, here in Jerusalem, for the purpose of talking peace. In the service of peace, I am prepared to travel to Amman, Damascus, and Beirut today, tomorrow. For there is no greater victory than the victory of peace. Wars have their victors and their vanquished, but everyone is a victor in peace.

"Israel isn't interested in peace, but in conquest."

Israel Is Not Committed to Peace

Yeshayahu Leibowitz, interviewed by Chaim Shur

Yeshayahu Leibowitz is a well-known liberal intellectual and philosopher in Israel who has long opposed what he views as his nation's oppression of the Palestinians. In the following viewpoint, Leibowitz argues that since the end of the 1967 Six Day War, Israel has been intent on violently dominating the Palestinian people rather than seeking peace with Arabs. Leibowitz contends that continuing the occupation will lead to the murder of more Palestinians and a "war to the finish with the entire Arab world." Chaim Shur is editor-in-chief of *New Outlook*, a bimonthly Israeli magazine that promotes peace and cooperation among all the peoples of the Middle East.

As you read, consider the following questions:

1. In Leibowitz's opinion, why should a state's powers be limited?
2. Why does Leibowitz believe that Israel may become a fascist state?
3. According to the author, why should both Jews and Palestinians renounce claims to statehood based on historic borders?

From "The March to Bestiality" by Yeshayahu Leibowitz, interviewed by Chaim Shur, *New Outlook*, July/August 1992. Reprinted with permission.

Shur: *In your book,* Am, Eretz, Medinah (People, Land, State) *you differentiate between the concept of statehood as an instrument and the concept of etatism, which you say eventually leads to fascism. Can you elaborate on this?*

Leibowitz: Every state—in the past, the present, and the foreseeable future—is an apparatus of coercion, but if I am not an ideological anarchist I acknowledge its necessity. Men cannot live together except within the framework of some overriding law. Statehood, while necessary, is thus contrary to human freedom. This means that the power of the state ought to be limited to the minimum required for people to coexist. To regard a state as a human value is the essence of fascism.

Are these differing attitudes toward statehood reflected in Israeli society today?

Israel certainly was conceived as a democracy. The State of Israel was meant to be the framework for the political-national events of the Jewish people. But for the last 25 years, since the Six-Day War, the State of Israel has become an apparatus of violent domination over another people. This is the corruption of the State.

No Peaceful Intentions

Those who see the state as an instrument for the oppression of another people see the state as an end in itself. Is this what you call fascism, namely the state not as a means, but as an end in itself?

That's the essence of the fascist idea. Think of the 19th century, of 1848, the year of the spring of the nations, the national renaissance of the Hungarians, the Italians under [military hero] Giuseppe Garibaldi. These movements were considered to be expressions of progress, of liberty. Yet [Austrian dramatist] Franz Grillparzer already warned then: there is a way leading from humanity through nationality to bestiality.

That's the way the German people went, to the end. And we started on this path after the Six-Day War. Some months after the war I wrote an article in [the newspaper] *Ha'aretz* saying that the seventh day—the day after the Six-Day War—would prove to be a decisive date in our history, because that was the day we had to decide what to make of this brilliant military victory. We decided not to strive for peace with the Arab world but to maintain a violent domination over the Palestinians. That was a fateful decision. And it was taken not by a [conservative] Likud government, but by a [more liberal] Labor government.

Are you saying that if there is no turning back, we are heading toward a fascist state?

This march to bestiality can be stopped. The German people didn't stop it. They went to the end. To Auschwitz.

To return to your book for a moment, I think it was in your discus-

*sion with Boas Evron that you claimed that nationality was indepen-
dent of statehood. Can you explain this?*

This is a statement of fact, not an idea. Certainly the Jewish
people are an instance of this. In fact, our Declaration of Independence begins with a lie: "The Land of Israel was the birthplace of
the Jewish people." The Jewish people conquered the land. . . .

Al Hayat (Beirut), 1992.

*You mentioned that after the Six-Day War it was the Labor Party
that made the decision not to strive for peace with the Arab world
and to maintain a violent domination over the Palestinians. Nevertheless, there is a significant difference between the Labor Party and
the Likud, and while [Labor Prime Minister] Yitzhak Rabin may not
be a declared dove, he is far from being the kind of hardliner that
[former Likud Prime Minister] Yitzhak Shamir is.*

When he was still a Labor Party leader [former general] Moshe
Dayan said: "I prefer Sharm el-Sheik [a strategic promontory on
the Sinai Peninsula] without peace to peace without Sharm el-
Sheik"—which means that the State of Israel isn't interested in
peace, but in conquest.

A Deadly Occupation

*But Dayan then wrongly believed that it was possible to have a lib-
eral occupation.*

A liberal occupation—that's a quadrilateral triangle. If you
maintain a policy of occupation, you will have to murder Arab
children. That's an indelible fact. In three years we've killed
160 Arab children up to the age of 14. That's on the domestic
front. Externally, continuing the occupation means that we will

have a war to the finish with the entire Arab world, and that the sympathy of the international community will be on their side.

Let me put it this way. Already in 1967 Yeshayahu Leibowitz said that the occupation would lead to bestiality. The great majority of people did not believe it at that time. Today more and more people realize that you were right. There has been a change. So you can't say that Yitzhak Rabin of 1967 is the same Yitzhak Rabin of 1992.

Concerning Rabin, I don't know whether the Rabin of yesterday is the Rabin of today, or whether the Rabin of today is the Rabin of tomorrow. Some years ago he said it would not be a disaster if we had to visit Gush Etzion [a large urban settlement near Jerusalem] with a visa. He was right then. . . .

If the State of Israel will not agree to a partition of the Land of Israel, which is the one and only possibility for a peaceful solution, it will become a fascist state, with concentration camps not only for Arabs, but also for Jews like myself. Externally, as I have said, we will face a war to the finish with the entire Arab world.

Claims to Historic Land

Do you see any hope?

Certainly, there is no necessity in history. Policies can be changed. Nobody foresaw the dissolution of the Soviet Union. No historian, no sociologist.

We have had peace with Egypt for 15 years now. Egypt was one of the signatories of the Arab Khartoum statement after the 1967 war never to recognize the State of Israel and never to maintain relations with the State of Israel. But the moment we agreed to the evacuation of the occupied Egyptian territories, Egypt recognized Israel and made peace with her. This means that peace is possible on condition that we renounce the claim to maintain the State of Israel within the borders of the historic Land of Israel, and that the Palestinians renounce the claim to a State of Palestine within the borders of the entire historic Palestine. This is certainly a very difficult psychological process, because it is deeply rooted in the consciousness of Jews that the entire country is the Land of Israel, and the same goes for the Palestinians—for them the entire country is Palestine. Both peoples will have to accept that they cannot have their statehood within the full borders of the historic Land of Israel/Palestine. This is impossible.

"The Israeli-PLO agreement . . . will be seen as the prelude to peace in the Middle East."

The Israel-PLO Accord Is a Prelude to Peace

Khalil E. Jahshan

In the following viewpoint, Khalil E. Jahshan argues that the Israel-PLO accord is a significant step toward ending Arab-Israeli hostilities. But Jahshan maintains that revitalization of the occupied territories' infrastructure and a framework of genuine democracy there are needed for the accord to succeed. He concludes that Israel and the United States must accept the inevitability of an independent Palestinian state and warns that their failure to do so may derail the peace process. Jahshan is a Palestinian activist and the executive director of the National Association of Arab Americans in Washington, D.C.

As you read, consider the following questions:

1. In Jahshan's opinion, what role should the United States play in ongoing peace negotiations?
2. Why should Israel and the PLO include neighboring countries in the peace process, according to Jahshan?
3. In the author's opinion, what must the PLO accomplish in the occupied territories?

"The Road Ahead" by Khalil E. Jahshan, *In These Times*, October 4, 1993. Reprinted with permission of the author.

The extraordinary ceremony marking the peace accord between Israel and the Palestine Liberation Organization brought hope to Arabs and Jews entangled by decades of confrontation, mistrust and violence. But as the dust produced by this emotional and surprising event settles, it becomes necessary to put things in perspective.

First of all, the Israeli-PLO agreement on interim self-government in the West Bank and Gaza and the letters of mutual recognition exchanged by the former antagonists are simply the first steps in a long and arduous journey toward a comprehensive, just and lasting peace throughout the region. They provide a basis to establish the mutual trust necessary to negotiate the details for implementing Palestinian self-government.

Second, the road toward this objective is riddled with dangers, political pitfalls and potential diplomatic setbacks. Therefore, the overwhelming task of fleshing out and implementing this agreement requires new thinking and solid commitment on the part of all parties concerned to meeting the long-term objectives of the ongoing peace process.

The U.S. Role

What needs to be done to avoid or overcome these potential roadblocks?

In contrast to the negotiating phase of the Israeli-PLO accord, the role of the sponsors—particularly that of the United States—is vital and indispensable during the implementation stage. President Clinton and Secretary of State Warren Christopher have emphasized the U.S. commitment to the process and its success. Now, they face the awesome task of translating their words into deeds. The price required for "not allowing this agreement to fail" may prove to be a heavy one in both financial and political terms. The administration must be willing to shoulder this responsibility in its capacity as a "full partner" in the Madrid peace negotiations that have been taking place since 1991.

The Israeli-Palestinian accord was negotiated in secret, outside the Madrid framework and without direct U.S. participation. The Clinton administration acted wisely by quickly giving enthusiastic support for the finished agreement, providing a venue for its signing, and committing its active involvement in future negotiations. The United States must move swiftly to combine the two diplomatic processes. This means bringing the new accord into the Madrid framework, making the necessary adjustments to reconcile the two approaches, removing the restrictive conditions and terms of reference that paralyzed the Madrid negotiations and taking advantage of the momentum generated by the agreement to rejuvenate those negotiations.

Although the importance of the agreement must not be underestimated, it left many important issues unresolved. The substantive and historically most difficult issues separating the parties were postponed to a phase of negotiations—scheduled to start no later than September 1996—that will determine the final status of the West Bank and Gaza. This postponement of negotiations on such vital issues as Jerusalem, refugees, settlements and borders requires an awesome leap of faith on the part of a majority among the Palestinians, especially those in the diaspora, who remain largely skeptical about the accord. Thus it is incumbent upon the signatories and the witnesses to this agreement to ensure that these items remain on the agenda and are adequately addressed at the appointed time.

Ushering in Peace

My people are hoping that this agreement, which we are signing today, marks the beginning of the end of a chapter of pain and suffering which has lasted throughout this century. My people are hoping that this agreement which we are signing today will usher in an age of peace, coexistence and equal rights. We are relying on your role, Mr. [Clinton], and on the role of all the countries which believe that without peace in the Middle East, peace in the world will not be complete.

Yasir Arafat, *The New York Times*, September 14, 1993.

One of the weaknesses of the Madrid formula that contributed to the stalemate of the past was the absence of a clear and enforceable timetable. The agreement overcomes this problem by committing the parties to specific deadlines—the first one of which came on October 13, 1993, when the Declaration of Principles entered into force. The sponsors must see to it that these deadlines are strictly adhered to by the parties, regardless of changes on the Israeli or the Palestinian sides.

The nature of the agreement between Israel and the PLO and the secret manner in which it was concluded have directly or indirectly contributed to the isolation of Jordan, Lebanon and Syria, the other three partners in the peace process. It is of utmost importance to the welfare of the Israeli-PLO accord to get all the parties quickly on board. Those excluded from the deal are left with only two choices: to become full partners in the process of reconciliation by promptly reaching similar accords in their own respective tracks or to oppose the agreement and seek to undo it. The U.S.-brokered 1983 agreement between Israel and Lebanon, which failed because it excluded other nations in the region, is a case in point.

Once successful, peacemaking is exciting and politically rewarding. However, like war, peace has a price tag. The agreement between Israel and the PLO will never be fulfilled unless those who support it mobilize their financial resources to translate the document into reality. The United States must take a leading role in convincing the international community—particularly the European allies, Japan and members of the Arab Gulf Cooperation Council—to overcome donor fatigue and contribute the funds needed to restructure Palestinian society. Palestinian needs are massive indeed. Experts estimate that a minimum of $1 billion per year will be needed over the next five years to rebuild the infrastructure of the West Bank and Gaza. At this price, peace might look very expensive—but it is nowhere near as expensive as war or the status quo.

In his meetings with U.S. officials in Washington, PLO Chairman Yasser Arafat said that the agreement rests on two pillars: security and economic prosperity. The Palestinians must ensure stability in order to allow economic development to take place. The first challenge that lies ahead for the Palestinian leadership is to fashion strong and democratic political institutions that will be able to govern a Palestinian state and, at the same time, ensure free, democratic expression. They must determine how to achieve a stable environment without being oppressive or intolerant toward legitimate and democratic opposition.

Genuine Democracy

Palestinian chaotic democracy or "the democracy of the guns," as Arafat prefers to call the current situation, must be transformed into genuine democracy, in which basic and universal civil, human and political rights are respected and protected. After 25 years of oppressive Israeli occupation, the Palestinians in the territories have extremely high expectations in this regard.

The second challenge lies in the Palestinian leadership's ability and willingness to rebuild an independent and strong Palestinian economy and effect rapid and steady economic growth through free enterprise, private initiative and entrepreneurship. The adoption of the classic Third World pattern of a centrally directed and strictly controlled economy will not appeal to Palestinian and international investors, whose capital is vital in the attempt to transform the West Bank and Gaza into a Middle Eastern Singapore.

Article III of the Israeli-Palestinian agreement on interim self-government provides for direct, free and general political elections for a Palestinian Council in the West Bank and Gaza. The elections will be held under international supervision no later than June 1994. The world community, friend and foe alike, will look at these elections as a test of PLO willingness to live and let live. In order to secure and maintain support for his cause, Arafat must ensure that these elections are free, democratic and all-inclusive. They should signal that a Palestinian multi-party system is emerging in the territories. The opposition must have a fair and unimpeded chance to present its case.

The Goal Is Independence

Arafat must also focus his attention on the concerns of many Palestinians in the diaspora who, under the leadership of the PLO, have come to espouse a two-state solution to the crisis and who perceive the Israeli-PLO agreement as offering only a truncated entity in the Gaza Strip and the Jericho area. The PLO must reassure them that self-determination, including the option of independent statehood, remains its primary long-term objective. Furthermore, both Israel and the United States must come to terms with the fact that an independent Palestinian state is inevitable and that their continued opposition to it, which stems from various domestic considerations, is liable to derail the whole process as the parties get closer to the permanent status phase.

It is obvious that the list of challenges and potential obstacles is long and overwhelming. The Palestinians cannot overcome these difficulties alone. If the breakthrough achieved in the Israeli-PLO agreement is to be capitalized upon, it is essential that both Palestinians and Israelis see concrete, tangible improvements on the ground. The world community must be willing to commit the financial, technological and humanitarian assistance necessary to improve the standard of living of Palestinians in the West Bank and Gaza. The Palestinian interim self-governing authority must be successful in providing the stability necessary to ease the security concerns of Israelis.

The Israeli government must exhibit the flexibility necessary to negotiate the remaining details for Palestinian self-government and the critical issues that must be resolved in the future. Finally, the Clinton administration must provide the leadership to nudge the process forward whenever negotiations stagnate.

If all parties are willing to make the necessary commitments and compromises, the signing of the Israeli-PLO agreement in Washington on September 13, 1993, will be seen as the prelude to peace in the Middle East. The prospects for a successful implementation of the Israeli-PLO agreement are limited, however, unless such determination and goodwill are forthcoming.

"Arabs will slaughter each other on Sundays, Tuesdays and Thursdays, while on Mondays, Wednesdays and Saturdays they will murder Jews."

The Israel-PLO Accord Is a Prelude to Violence

Ze'ev Benjamin Begin

Ze'ev Benjamin Begin is a Likud (conservative) member of the Knesset, Israel's parliament, and son of the late Prime Minister Menachem Begin. In the following two-part viewpoint, Begin argues that the Israel-PLO accord endangers Israel's security because the PLO remains intent on destroying Israel. Begin criticizes the agreement for mistakenly granting Palestinians legislative powers over autonomous territories instead of administrative powers over Arabs only. He predicts that the outcome of the agreement will be the creation of a terrorist Palestinian state and an increase in violence against both Arabs and Jews. Part I is a syndicated piece that was published in American newspapers. Part II is an open letter addressed to Israeli prime minister Yitzhak Rabin, criticizing him for orchestrating the accord. It appeared in the *Jerusalem Post International Edition.*

As you read, consider the following questions:

1. Why does the author believe that Israel cannot trust Yasir (Yasser) Arafat?
2. In Begin's opinion, how has Rabin weakened Israel's sovereignty over Jerusalem?
3. What specific limits on combating terrorism has Rabin approved, according to Begin?

From "Assessing Israel's Risk" by Ze'ev Benjamin Begin, *The Washington Times*, September 8, 1993, and "Rabin's Self-Entrapment," *The Jerusalem Post International Edition*, September 18, 1993. Reprinted with permission.

I

In order to understand the implications of the agreement between the government of Israel and the terrorist organization of the Palestine Liberation Organization, one must scrutinize Israel's position in this region.

It is a tiny speck on the map, somewhere between Marrakech and Bangladesh. It is the Jewish democracy, faced with 1 billion Muslims, all of whom see Jerusalem as their holy city, all of whom view Eretz Yisrael, the Land of Israel, as the sacred Muslim Arab Land of Phalasteen.

We know better: Eretz Yisrael belongs to the Jewish people, period.

This is the source of a longstanding dispute, and the political structure of modern Arab society is the source of the violence. Among the 20 independent Arab states, none has produced a democracy. Rather, they are all armed autocracies, with varying degrees of violence applied to assume and retain power.

I concur with Israeli Prime Minister Yitzhak Rabin's observation that Islamic fundamentalism is on the rise in the Arab world, and that it threatens not only Israel. However, the assumption of some—that if the PLO assumes control in the Gaza district and the Jericho area it will suppress the fundamentalist terrorist movement of Hamas—is sheer fantasy. Israel is now combating Hamas because it has the will and because it keeps a foot on the ground: effective intelligence supported by trained army units. It is important to note that the Israeli military sees tremendous difficulties in securing Israel and its citizens. Once the area is relinquished to the PLO, and Israel evacuates, hell will break loose, and Hamas will take over.

Same PLO Goals

I also concur with Mr. Rabin's longstanding observation that the acronym of the terrorist mafia called the PLO stands for an "organization for the liberation of Palestine" from the Jewish presence. This gang is not changing its nature or goals; it changes only tactics.

Let us remember that, back in 1988, PLO commander Yasser Arafat publicly and emphatically renounced terrorism; let us not forget that, since then, hundreds of Arabs and dozens of Israelis have been killed by direct order of this moderate "chairman," and the U.S. government refused to accept Mr. Arafat's political bid for legitimacy.

After attempting to delude people that he "recognized" Israel, when we were viciously attacked by Iraqi Scud missiles in 1991, Flying Henchman Arafat warmly embraced Saddam Hussein, who promised to scorch half of Israel. "A horse that can count to 10," observed Samuel Johnson, "is a remarkable horse, not a remarkable mathematician." A disguised terrorist, seeking the annihilation of Israel, who signs an agreement with it, is not a remarkable peace champion. He is a remarkable impostor. Are we going to be remarkable fools?

It is worth noting that for many years some pundits advocated that only a strong PLO would be able to come to terms with Israel. Now many of them insist it is the current weakness of the PLO that makes an agreement possible. For many years, Western politicians were parroting that the "PLO is the sole legitimate representative of the Palestinian people." Suddenly they realize that a financial crisis within that corrupt gang threatened the PLO's stature in the Arab street. There goes the money— and the legitimacy goes with it.

A Launching Pad for War

This is the first step toward the establishment of a Palestinian state, which I think will happen sooner rather than later. And far from being a cause of peace and stability, I think it will be the cause of another war. As I see it, the Palestinians have finally decided to adopt the so-called phase strategy, which calls for getting a foothold to begin with, with a state in phase 2, and then using the state as a launching pad for a final assault.

Norman Podhoretz, *The New York Times*, September 3, 1993.

This gang will never be able to withstand the tide of the fundamentalist Hamas puritan murderers. For a butchered Jew or Arab, a knife is a knife, whether wielded in religious or secular terror.

A wise aspect of the Camp David Accords [Israel's 1979 treaty returning the Sinai Peninsula to Egypt] lies in the fact that it affords Israel a five-year period of temporary arrangements that can be used to test Arab readiness and ability to peacefully live with Jews. The countdown of this period was designed to begin once the Arab Administrative Council is freely elected and established.

Under the proposed agreement, the countdown will start before there is even an agreement on the modalities for elections. This means that the prospect of a proper, full-scale test of Arab-Israeli coexistence is being practically removed from the scenario.

A Terrorist State

There are grave difficulties in the conclusion of the agreement, and grave dangers in its implementation. In the Camp David Accords, the perceived political organ for running Arab autonomy is an Administrative Council, with administrative powers. But since it has been agreed now that the Arabs will rule through an Arab Council with legislative powers, the creation of an embryonic PLO terrorist state is at our doorstep.

The consequences of the agreement are not easy to predict, but they must be viewed through the greedy eyes of the victorious terrorists. For them, "Gaza and Jericho First" is exactly that: a foothold, a bridgehead, to be extended later through the joint efforts of further violence and diplomacy. Their goal has never changed, and they have repeatedly stated it clearly: a two-phase strategy to completely do away with the Jewish state.

The words of Faisal Husseini, a "moderate" Arab resident of Jerusalem, must be taken seriously. In Amman in 1992 he emphasized (in Arabic, of course) that "our goal is to bring about the dissolution of the Zionist entity, gradually."

This incompatibility of long-range goals—destruction vs. coexistence—is the crux of the issue. Yielding to terrorism is morally wrong and is practically of no avail. Under the slogan of "peace at any price," Israel paid a dear price while peace remains elusive.

The PLO and Hamas want Israel to "rest in peace." We shall insist on our right to live in peace.

II

Dear Mr. Prime Minister,

In your continuous attempt to deceive the public, you refuse to allow it to debate the document approved by your government of fools and by the PLO gang. . . .

Over the past few years, you have repeatedly warned against capitulation to PLO demands. You stated that granting Arab residents of Jerusalem the right to be elected to the Arab Autonomy Administrative Council would severely damage Israel's sovereignty over the city.

Now you have given in. The agreement, written as per PLO demands, states that Jerusalem's Arab population will have "the right to participate in the elections, in accordance with the agreement between the two sides."

This is rather vague, but your health minister made sure to clear the haze, congratulating you on granting Jerusalem Arabs the right to elect representatives to the Autonomy Council.

Jerusalem Arabs will thus become an integral part of the Legislative Arab Council. This is the prologue to your shameful agreement to include Jerusalem (in its entirety, according to the formulation) as a specific item in the negotiations toward a final settlement.

Impaired Security

You have also impaired the security of Israel and of Israelis. On this issue, you approved five relevant points. The PLO will have authority over the territory; Israel will withdraw from the Gaza district and the Jericho area; responsibility for "internal security" (including combating terror, now the job of the General Security Service, border police and the army) will be transferred to the PLO forces; international forces will be deployed in these areas; Israeli forces will be allowed to patrol the roads only, without entering the adjacent areas.

The compounded summation of these details is what alarmed the IDF [Israeli Defense Force] chief of staff and his deputy. For the sake of fairness, you should provide the public with the chief of staff's viewpoint, as expressed in the government meeting which approved the agreement. Under the conditions you created, we will have no ability whatsoever to combat terrorist activity—no intelligence, no preventive detention, no chasing of murderers into sanctuary towns.

However, this fact holds no importance for you, as I have learned from Foreign Minister Shimon Peres's announcement explaining the facts of life to the IDF chief of staff: "Must we be the defenders of Islam? Let the Palestinians kill each other. This is what the chief of staff is not taking into account."

These remarks account for the foreign minister's calling the future areas of Gaza and Jericho "experimental farms."

In order to explain clearly the ramifications of the experiment, you added your own view, with typical vulgarity: "I hope that a partner can be found who will be responsible for the internal problems in Gaza. He will deal with them without the Supreme Court, without B'tselem [an Israeli human rights group], without some diehard liberals, and without all sorts of mothers and fathers."

The Coming Bloodbath

Who will win this "bloodbath" (to quote an expert, Health Minister Haim Ramon)? This is your Catch 22: You hope that the PLO will control Hamas after it has notified the refugees from Jaffa [who fled the city during the 1948 Arab-Israeli war] that the PLO has relinquished, on their behalf, their right of return there. You want to sign an agreement only with such a tamed PLO, but a PLO like that will be decimated by the religious Hamas priests.

And don't try to fool the public: On the foreign minister's advice, the Arabs will slaughter each other on Sundays, Tuesdays and Thursdays, while on Mondays, Wednesdays and Saturdays they will murder Jews, "without B'tselem." On Friday, they will all go to refuel in the local mosque.

You have damaged Jerusalem, and you have hurt our security.

On the issue of an independent Arab state west of the Jordan, too, the Arab terrorists have broken your political backbone. . . .

115

In your eagerness for an agreement now, you have approved a mechanism for its self-destruction. You agreed that disputes regarding the implementation of the principles would be subject to external arbitration. If the PLO does not capitulate to all your demands, or if you do not acquiesce in all theirs, crucial issues will be submitted to international arbitration. This will essentially remove the source of authority on every issue from Israel's hands and hand it over to outsiders.

An Agreement All Will Pay For

Since you find abstract thought difficult, here's an example: A committee will be established to decide "by agreement" upon the possible return of persons displaced in the 1967 war. Until now, through the agreed mechanism, Israel retained its right of veto.

However, in the agreement you affirmed that such a dispute will be handled by arbitration. The PLO has demanded the return of 600,000 people, and you will agree to only 6,000. The international arbitrator will establish a compromise, by which only 160,000 will return. You see?

The agreement you affirmed is not an "Improved Camp David Accord." It isn't even a poorer version. In spirit, in principle and in detail, it is the opposite of the Camp David Accord. It is even a breaching of that fine document.

You have entrapped yourself in the stupidity of a commitment "to reach an agreement within six to nine months." In negotiations with the PLO gang and through the agreement you approved, you preferred to retain your public "credibility." In doing so, you sold out on your political credo.

You wanted an agreement at any price. What you got is one we shall all pay for.

"Attacks on Israeli targets by [the armed wing of Hamas] have increased . . . and will intensify."

Hamas Terrorists Are a Growing Threat to Peace

Lamia Lahoud

Hamas ("zeal" in Arabic and an acronym for the Islamic Resistance Movement) is a fundamentalist group whose goal is to destroy Israel and create an Islamic state. In the following viewpoint, Lamia Lahoud argues that both the popularity of Hamas and their number of armed attacks are increasing in the occupied territories. Lahoud contends that the militancy of Hamas appeals to many young Palestinians who desire more violent opposition to Israel. Lahoud maintains that despite the Israeli-Palestinian autonomy agreement, the safety of Israelis in the occupied territories remains jeopardized. Lahoud writes for the *Jerusalem Post* daily newspaper.

As you read, consider the following questions:

1. How do Hamas and the Moslem Brotherhood differ, according to Lahoud?
2. According to Lahoud, what effects did Israel's mass deportation of Palestinian activists have?
3. Why is Hamas more popular than other armed Palestinian groups, according to the author?

"A Youthquake Shakes Up Hamas" by Lamia Lahoud, *The Jerusalem Post International Edition*, September 4, 1993. Reprinted with permission.

Hamas has a new look: youthful and more feminine.

The Islamic Resistance Movement has become more open to women and to young leaders, including those who are not extremely religious.

"Hamas is replacing its old leadership, which is made up of members of the Moslem Brotherhood [the leading international fundamentalist organization], and is raising a new and younger leadership which has taken part in the *intifada* [Palestinian uprising]," says a 26-year-old storekeeper from Hebron. He says he is "associated with" Hamas.

The storekeeper and other Hamas members and supporters would not agree to be quoted by name for fear of arrest on charges of belonging to an illegal organization.

The Hamas youthquake was strengthened by the deportation of 415 Hamas and Islamic Jihad activists in December 1992, according to Hamas members and Israeli experts.

One aftershock has been an increase in the level of violence.

"The young leaders are more political and less conservative, and they are ready for military action," the storekeeper says.

"Their political and Islamic outlook attracts a greater number of Palestinians who want to fight the Israeli occupation, but who don't agree with the Moslem Brotherhood in all respects. For example, contrary to the old leadership, the young leaders encourage the participation of women in Hamas."

Some of the wives of the deportees have become politically active, he says, naming the wife of Sheikh Bassam Jarrar of Ramallah.

Far More Radical

Yigal Carmon, who left his job as adviser to the prime minister on terrorism, says Hamas, which was founded in 1988, is far more radical than its parent organization, the Moslem Brotherhood.

He describes the young leaders as more militant, more pragmatic and less religious than the older leaders in the Moslem Brotherhood.

"The Brotherhood was not involved in terrorist actions. They were less political and tried to exert their influence through education and social institutions. The maximum of their political activism was to infiltrate unions and other organizations through elections.

"Their religious and spiritual influence was for them the most important aspect of their movement," says Carmon, who is currently doing research on the subject of Islamic terrorism.

"The young guard is more practical and involved with the everyday realities. They . . . are more open to less religious supporters. Also, their main goal is to fight and resist Israel. They use terrorism to achieve their goal, which is to get rid of Israel and establish an Islamic state in Israel and the territories."

Rafi Israeli, an expert on Islamic fundamentalism and a professor of Islamic studies at the Hebrew University, agrees that Hamas is opening up to less religiously extreme supporters.

"Any Palestinian Moslem who . . . wants to fight Israel can join Hamas, even if that person is not a pious, practicing Moslem."

A Vow to Kill

We have vowed to continue shooting the skulls of the Jews with the bullets of [Hamas], and we are also sworn to respond to the conspiracy that [Prime Minister Yitzhak] Rabin is planning in order to humiliate our people. . . .

Rabin, your soldiers and settlers will be our targets everywhere, and we will not let you sleep or move in our land safely. Death will chase you everywhere.

Hamas statements, quoted in *Los Angeles Times*, October 25, 1993.

Kader Sawendaq, the head of the Islamic Shariah College at An-Najar University in Nablus, says that by deporting 400 Islamic leaders, Israel radicalized Hamas by depriving the movement of its spiritual leaders.

He says the younger Hamas supporters are far more radical than their elders. Sawendaq describes himself as a member of the Moslem Brotherhood.

Hamas Appeals to the Young

According to a Hamas student council representative at Bir Zeit University, "Hamas attracts a lot of young people because it represents today the only real armed Palestinian resistance to Israel." He says that Hamas members believe armed struggle is the only way to achieve its aim of establishing an Islamic state in all of mandatory Palestine [Israel, the West Bank, and the Gaza Strip].

That student's opinion reverberates beyond the campus of Bir Zeit, Carmon says. Student lists at the universities represent the political parties outside the academic institutions.

"Those who run for the student council elections are members of the political parties and represent them. They are elected on the basis of political ideas and motives. Many Palestinians who have been arrested for terror activities here were students," Carmon says.

Sawendaq says Hamas is gaining influence because it offers an easy ideology for the traditional Palestinians from the villages.

"Most Palestinians are Moslems and relatively traditional. They can identify with Islamic values but do not understand slogans of secularism and democracy," Sawendaq says.

Hamas has become too powerful to be ignored in a future settlement, he says.

Attacks on Israelis Increase

Ibrahim, a member of An-Najar's student council, says the number of attacks on Israelis by Izzadin al-Kassam, the armed wing of Hamas, has increased since the mass deportation.

"The attacks have continued despite the deportations. On the contrary, the number of attacks on Israeli targets by Izzadin al-Kassam have increased in the last months and will intensify," says Ibrahim, who claims he was imprisoned for two years on charges of belonging to Hamas. . . .

Both Carmon and Israeli agree that there has been an increase in armed terrorist attacks in the territories by the Izzadin al-Kassam.

"The deportations don't serve any purpose," Israeli says.

"Ahmed Rantisi and other leaders of Hamas who were deported to south Lebanon are great demagogues, but they don't carry out terror attacks against Israeli targets. It's the rank and file of Hamas who are active, and they will continue to operate despite the deportation," Israeli says.

Israeli says Hamas has managed to overcome the difficulties created by the deportations. Initially, there was an increase in attacks on Israeli targets inside the Green Line [Israel's pre-1967 border], he says. Later, primarily because of the closure of the territories, those attacks dropped drastically.

"Armed attacks on Israeli soldiers inside the territories have increased since the deportations. Such attacks have not been affected by the closure of the territories," Israeli says.

Growing Support

According to Ibrahim, the results of the student council election at An-Najar University represent the political balance of power in the northern West Bank.

Hamas in 1993 picked up at least 5 percent more of the total votes at An-Najar University, Ibrahim says.

"At An-Najar University, we got 45 percent of the votes while Fatah only won with a slight majority of 47 percent. The results show that Fatah has lost votes and Hamas has gained support. This is also true for the political balance outside the university," Ibrahim says.

Carmon says student elections are indicative of the general public's mood because the student lists run as political parties with political slogans. At An-Najar, Hamas ran under two slogans, the return of the deportees and opposition to the peace process.

The Hamas student from Bir Zeit University says Hamas has gained influence in the Ramallah area, too, although Ramallah is less traditional than Nablus and has a strong Christian community. He says Izzadin al-Kassam has increased the popularity of Hamas in the territories.

"Izzadin al-Kassam was founded in 1991 in Gaza by members of Hamas because we felt the need for military action other than violent demonstrations and some individual attacks. The group is popular among most Palestinians because it carries out daring attacks against Israeli military targets. Although they also kill collaborators, they have concentrated on attacking Israelis," he says.

According to the student, that focus makes them more popular than Fatah's Black Panthers or the Red Eagles of the Popular Front for the Liberation of Palestine, two armed PLO [Palestine Liberation Organization] groups who concentrate on killing Palestinians accused of collaboration rather than attacking Israeli targets.

He says the group started operating in Gaza but has extended its reach to Hebron and also to Nablus, Jenin, Tulkarm, Ramallah and Jerusalem.

No Safety for Israelis

Ibrahim says the attacks by Izzadin al-Kassam always have a political purpose and message. He mentions the murders of three soldiers [in the West Bank in August 1993] as an example.

"These killings were a message to the Palestinian negotiators and to the Israelis. Hamas wanted to show them that even under an autonomy agreement with a Palestinian police force, the Palestinian delegates cannot guarantee the safety of Israelis in the area," Ibrahim says.

According to Israeli, Hamas's message to the Palestinian peace-talks delegates goes further than that.

"Hamas is not only trying to show the delegates that they are unable to guarantee the safety of Israelis under an autonomy deal, but is directly threatening them too. They are saying that they will continue their fight, not only against Israel but also against those Palestinians whom they consider to be traitors."

"Both Palestinian and Israeli commentators know that [settlers' threats of violence] are not idle."

Violence from Jewish Settlers Is a Growing Threat to Peace

Marguerite Michaels and Graham Usher

In the West Bank and Gaza Strip, many Jewish settlers vehemently oppose the Israel-PLO accord as a threat to their safety and their settlements. In Part I of the following viewpoint, Marguerite Michaels describes how settlers who fear Palestinian attacks and the relinquishment of Jewish settlements are prepared to use violence against Palestinians, as well as Israeli soldiers, to try to foil the accord. Michaels asserts that thousands of settlers are well-armed and considered dangerous by Israel. In Part II, Graham Usher chronicles Jewish reprisals for the killing of settlers and contends that settlement leaders are determined to fight violence with violence. Michaels is an associate editor for *Time* magazine. Usher is a correspondent in the West Bank and Gaza Strip for *Middle East International*, a pro-Palestinian bimonthly magazine published in London.

As you read, consider the following questions:

1. According to Michaels, what nonviolent tactics are settlers using to protest the Israel-PLO accord?
2. In Usher's opinion, why should settlers' threats of violence be taken seriously?
3. Why did Palestinian negotiators protest Israeli proposals to withdraw from the Gaza Strip, according to Usher?

I

Jews fighting Jews. Jews killing Jews. The idea is anathema in Israel—yet becoming thinkable to some of the 115,000 settlers who have laid claim to the West Bank land they call Judea and Samaria, an integral part of Eretz Yisrael, the land God gave to the Jews. Although none have yet been asked to relinquish their settlements, many fear the worst is soon to come, and they are determined to resist.

White-bearded, grandfatherly Rabbi Eliezer Waldman looks more like a prophet than a revolutionary. When he helped found Kiryat Arba, now home to 7,000 Jews near the Palestinian city of Hebron, in 1968, he says, "we felt that God had opened the gates and brought us back to the heart of Eretz Yisrael." As spiritual leader of the Jewish settlement movement, Waldman and a handful of other settlers must decide how they are going to force the Israeli government to renege on the peace agreement. The rabbi is convinced that with demonstrations, the blocking of some roads, interference in the routine workday of government officials in Jerusalem, the settlers will prevail. "If it's your homeland, you must say, 'It's mine,'" explains Waldman. "If you begin speaking about the rights of others, people will think it's not yours."

But some settlers are prepared to go much further: in the past, West Bankers have embraced violence, even against Israeli soldiers, as part of their protests. "We are reacting with violence," said Aaron Domb, spokesman for the Council of Settlements in Judea, Samaria and Gaza, "because the government has acted with violence by forcing this agreement on the nation." Former Chief Rabbi Shlomo Goren asserted, "[Yasir] Arafat is responsible for thousands of murders. Therefore, everyone in Israel who meets him in the streets has the right to kill him."

Threats of violence and civil war horrify most Israelis and divide the settlers. Last week the most respected pollster in Israel asked Jewish settlers what they would do if the Gaza-Jericho first plan [granting limited autonomy there] is adopted. Only 2% said they would take part in armed resistance against the Israeli authorities; 11% promised to take up arms but only against the future Palestinian police. Nearly half said they would actively resist the accord without the use of arms.

Settlement leaders are caught between the few who embrace violence to continue doing what they believe is God's work and those who have, after years of the Palestinian uprising, lost their taste for the hatred and death that violence breeds. Ahiram Nagar is 18 years old, and has lived in Kiryat Arba for the past three years. He is about to enter the Israeli army, and he is not averse to taking part in violence because "it can help." Far more typical is Michal Petel, 31, a Jerusalem-born mother of five who has lived in Kiryat Arba since 1981. "The peace proposal hurts, but if a few less people get killed, that would be O.K."

Israeli security services are taking the threats of mayhem seriously. According to their assessment, there are at least 30,000 settlers who are armed legally with rifles and handguns, and have access to illicit stockpiles of grenades, mines and other explosives. Many of the men are well-trained reserve officers in the Israeli Defense Force [IDF]. Half the 30,000 are considered hardcore troublemakers, and they live mainly in the West Bank. An informal vigilante police force of settlers already operates in the West Bank.

Rampage in Hebron

Jewish settlers went on a shooting spree in the occupied West Bank for the second straight day and wounded three Palestinians, one of them critically, police and Arab sources said.

Residents said about 80 settlers armed with at least 10 submachine guns shot at Arab cars in the Hebron area. . . .

On the first day, settlers went on the rampage in Hebron and wounded at least three Arabs after Palestinians stoned a leading settler's car. Soldiers stood by without intervening.

Hebron is the only town in the occupied West Bank and Gaza Strip where Jews have settled in the middle of a Palestinian population.

Reuters News and Associated Press, *The San Diego Union-Tribune*, December 5, 1993.

Shlomo Gazit, Israel's first coordinator of the occupation and now a senior research fellow at the Jaffee Center at Tel Aviv University, believes the militants will be heard from but will fail to stop the peace process. "[Yitzhak] Rabin's message is clear: they have lost the war for Greater Israel. They will try to mobilize public opinion, but public opinion will be happy with this agreement. If in the next five years there will be no *intifadeh* [Palestinian uprising], and no terror, then who the hell cares about Greater Israel?"

II

Events in the occupied territories have concentrated Palestinian minds on what PLO [Palestine Liberation Organization] delegation head Nabil Sha'th has called "the main problem of the current PLO-Israeli negotiations" on Palestinian self-rule, and what many others regard as potentially the most contentious issue of the entire Oslo [peace] package—that of Israeli settlements and settlers in the West Bank and Gaza Strip, and Israel's apparently irrevocable commitment to preserve and defend them.

On 7 November 1993, Palestinian assailants ambushed an Israeli car near the West Bank village of Beit Kahil, killing the driver and wounding the passenger. The driver was Ephraim Ayyub, an Israeli from the Kfar Darom settlement in the Gaza Strip, while the passenger was Rabbi Haim Druckman, former Knesset [Israeli parliament] Member of the National Religious party and staunch advocate of the settlers' cause. While the attack was initially claimed by the armed wing of the DFLP [Democratic Front for the Liberation of Palestine], a communique circulated by Hamas [Islamic Resistance Movement] subsequently declared that it had mounted the operation as a warning to the Israelis "to withdraw their cowardly army from our holy land".

Settlers' Revenge

Coming less than a week after Hamas' killing of another settler near Ramallah, the attempted assassination of so prestigious a figure as Druckman sent the settlers—in Rabin's parlance—"spinning" into a paroxysm of fury. On news of the ambush, West Bank settlers went on the rampage in Hebron, torching Palestinian cars, vandalising shops and homes and—for three and a half hours the next morning—blockading a total of 49 roads throughout the occupied territories.

In three consecutive days of rioting in the Gaza Strip, settlers from the Gush Qatif settlement block shot and wounded at least 4 Palestinians, injured a further 30, burnt to the ground ten greenhouses, destroyed one house and closed the main Gaza-Khan Yunis road with burning tyres. In a grotesque reversal of roles, IDF units had to declare "closed military areas" to let Palestinian schoolchildren pass safely between Kfar Darom and their homes in Gaza's Deir al-Balah refugee camp. "It's a Jewish *intifada* [uprising]", said one Israeli conscript at the scene of the havoc.

The ferocity of the settlers' reprisals sent tremors not just through the ranks of Palestinians—who feared that Rabin would exploit the settlers' rage to backtrack still further on such "confidence-building measures" as releasing Palestinian prisoners—but through mainstream Israeli opinion generally. Writing in the Israeli daily *Ha'aretz*, Ron Kislev argued that the "scope of the settlers' retribution for both killings showed that it had clearly been prepared in advance" and amounted to "a violent threat against the Israeli government's sovereignty and against the majority which gave it the power to conduct a peace policy".

Settler leaders seemed only too eager to confirm this prognosis. "We warned that we are capable of foiling these [peace] agreements on the ground and we will now prove this", said a spokesman for the Yeshiva Settler Council in the wake of the

October 1993 Haim Mizrahi [a settler] assassination while head of the Kiryat Arba Settler Movement, Zvi Katzover, presaged apocalyptically that the days of "Jewish terrorist action were close". Both Palestinian and Israeli commentators know that these are not idle threats. In the Israeli *Yediot Aharonot* newspaper, N. Barnea reports a meeting between Katzover and a "senior figure in the IDF" in which the settlers' leader forewarns a time "when a settler would take a gun, enter an Arab village and slaughter 30 to 40 Arabs". The "settler" Katzover was referring to, says Barnea, was "himself".

Whatever the settlers' game-plan vis a vis the PLO-Israeli agreement, Palestinians fear that the stakes are likely to be their lives and their property. Speaking after the settlers' actions on 9 November, [Palestinian negotiator] Faisal Husseini aired the anxieties of the Palestinian street by calling for "international protection to separate Palestinians in the territories from the IDF and settlers until the complete withdrawal of the army from all occupied Palestinian lands. If the Israelis want to implement the Israeli-Palestinian agreement", he added, "they should prove they can control the settlers".

Questions of Withdrawal

It was just the question of the IDF's "control" of the settlers that caused the first crisis of the round of PLO-Israeli negotiations at Taba [Egypt] on 2 November 1993. The Palestinian delegation walked out of the talks in protest at the army's plan for "withdrawal" from the Gaza Strip. According to Palestinian and Israeli sources, the Israelis had proposed that the IDF withdraw "in stages" to one kilometre buffer zones around Gaza's Gush Qatif settlement chain and along the Green Line [pre-1967] border, retaining, however, 20 look-out posts to ensure "freedom of movement" for soldiers and settlers on all the Strip's main roads and arteries leading to the chain. Nabil Sha'th dismissed the plan out of hand as "the continued Israeli occupation of Gaza". While there are only 3,000 settlers in the Strip—compared to 130,000 in the West Bank—the land area they command, coupled with army-controlled "state lands", comprises something like 40 per cent of all the territory.

For many Palestinian analysts the deadlock at Taba was simply a crisis waiting to happen since such a vista is written into the Oslo Accords. One clause of the Declaration of Principles speaks of Israel's "withdrawal from the Gaza Strip and Jericho", while another talks only of the IDF's "redeployment away from Palestinian population centres". Yet, as Israeli journalist Yoel Marcus drily points out—"it is impossible to both withdraw from Gaza and remain there at the same time".

"The problem between Syria and Israel was one of who would speak out first for peace. We have beaten them to it."

Syria Is Committed to Peace

Hafez al-Assad, interviewed by Patrick Seale

Hafez al-Assad was elected president of Syria in 1971 after leading a coup a year earlier. In the following viewpoint, an interview with British journalist and Syria expert Patrick Seale, Assad (Asad) argues that Syria wants peace with Israel and has proposed full peace in exchange for Israel's full withdrawal from the Golan Heights. Assad maintains that there is a strong peace movement among Syria's political parties and people that the West should realize exists. Seale is the author of the extensive biography *Assad of Syria: The Struggle for the Middle East*.

As you read, consider the following questions:

1. What kind of peace does Syria want, according to Assad?
2. Why does Assad believe that Western journalists fail to acknowledge Syria's peace movement?
3. According to Assad, what is the current Arab view toward coexistence with Israel?

From "Interview with Syrian President Hafiz al-Asad" by Patrick Seale, *Journal of Palestine Studies*, Summer 1993. This interview originally appeared in and is reprinted with permission from the May 10, 1993, daily newsletter *Mideast Mirror*, London.

Asad: We now assert that our aim is peace, and that peace must be comprehensive. In the past, we used to insist that peace should be arrived at through an international conference. We did not want the conference to be divided into bilateral committees, if that precluded overall coordination between the Arab parties. In all the speeches we made during visits paid to us by foreign leaders, and in our own visits abroad, we invariably stressed the need for such a peace conference. But even as we spoke, we were utterly convinced that Israel did not want peace.

Seale: Is that still your view today?

If you had waited, I was about to answer that. We now say that we want peace and, in point of fact, we do not say anything which we do not truly mean. We do mean it. Such behavior may sound strange in today's world, where you might speak with a top official and, a mere hour later, hear him declare the very opposite of what he had told you.

The suspicions we had about Israel—that it does not want peace—these suspicions still stand. As evidence, one might point to the fact that the Israeli delegations at the first eight rounds of peace negotiations [following the 1991 Madrid conference] did not take a single step forward.

Peace Trends

However, there is a phenomenon emerging in Israel which we may consider new, and which we have noticed particularly since 1991. This is that the trend of opinion in Israel in favor of peace is growing. This phenomenon is bound to have an impact on Israel's rulers. We did not notice this trend in the past because, if the trend existed at all, it was very limited. But today, it seems to be gaining strength.

Of course the fanatics are still there, in the religious parties, for example, and even among the members of the Labor party—although, of course, not all of them.

At any rate, there is not the slightest doubt that we want peace. We would not otherwise have talked about peace for the past twenty years. Nevertheless, we will work to secure our rights and our goals. The peace we want must be just, it must be comprehensive, and it must be based on UN resolutions.

You have said that your policy is "full peace for full withdrawal." Does this remain your position?

Yes!

Can you spell out some of the steps towards this objective? For example, if Israel were to recognize Syrian sovereignty over the whole of the Golan [Heights], what would Syria give in return? Would you agree to end the state of war?

When Syria put forward the notion of "total peace for total withdrawal" it was a great leap forward. It was intended to throw the ball into the Israeli court. We are waiting for an answer from the Israelis. The ball is now in their court, but they have not yet answered. So, until they do, any talk of later steps is meaningless. At any rate, this is not one of the current tasks of the political leadership. Such matters will have to be discussed at other levels. I advise you to discuss the question with the Israelis. Put the question to them!

Syria's Defensive Mode

The arsenals of the [Persian] Gulf countries will be expanded. But given their isolationist trend, their total absorption in their own priorities, and their newly ingratiating proclivities towards Israel, the likelihood that they would turn these weapons against it is nil. Such a likelihood is rendered even more improbable because of the central role these countries assign the United States in the new Gulf security system.

Nor is Syria in a position to pose a serious military threat to Israel. Syria now finds itself alone facing Israel. If it had illusions about strategic parity in the past, these had already been knocked out by Glasnost Moscow before the Gulf War. To be sure, Syria is using the funds recently received from the Gulf countries to build up its armed forces with Russian, Chinese and North Korean hardware. But it is doing so in strictly defensive mode. . . .

Hafez al-Assad will not subscribe to a peace process that precludes the return of the Occupied Territories and Israeli withdrawal to the 1967 frontiers. He will continue to refurbish his second strike capacity to deter an Israeli first strike.

Walid Khalidi, *Palestine Reborn*, 1992.

You mean that I should ask them if, were you to agree to end the state of war, they would give up the whole of the Golan?
No! We proposed "full withdrawal in exchange for full peace." They have not agreed to this. That is why it makes no sense to ask hypothetical questions or raise possibilities when the other party has not agreed to the basic principle. If you and I were the belligerents, we could easily move on to subsequent questions!

Peace Initiators

You mentioned that there were new forces emerging in Israel.
People used to say that the problem between Syria and Israel was one of who would speak out first for peace. We have beaten them to it. We have gone ahead of them. We have spoken first. We presented the idea. It was not an idea current in the street, but we put it forward. We said this is an equation with two

parts—"full peace for full withdrawal." We are in favor of this equation. But is Israel for it? That is the question. . . .

Would you agree that Syria and Israel are doomed to remain rivals, even if a peaceful settlement is reached?

Why?

Because of their geopolitical situation. They are like two kings on a chess board. Between them are three pawns: Lebanon, the Palestinians, and Jordan. Each king wants to control all the pawns. Would you agree that this struggle underlies the peace negotiations?

As I have said, in Israel itself there is a growing current in favor of peace, which demands peace. People who express such views—and they are growing in number—want peace between Israel and the Arab nation. Whatever anyone might say, the whole world knows that the Arab nation lives in this region. No one, in the East or West, can ignore the Arab nation, even though the Arabs may differ among themselves and may even, on occasion, fight each other. In the end, they will stand together. . . .

Attitudes of Peace

Just as you say there is a movement for peace in Israel, is there a movement for peace in Syria? Is public opinion here ready?

Everything we do in Syria is well-known to our people. Our policy concerning peace was not decided by a single man or a single institution. It was discussed year by year by children at school and by our parties and state institutions. If you want to be sure of this, talk to anyone.

Our complaint against the West is that it never seems to seek the views of our ordinary people. It seeks out just one man to talk to him about what it wants to hear. Representatives of the Western media come here simply to find confirmation of their preconceived ideas. This is my experience both with Western politicians and with journalists. They come with images of Syria in their heads and, as I've said, they look for some individual to confirm their prejudices.

So far as I know, we have never prevented anyone coming to Syria. Of course some have a grudge against us. They come here to serve our enemies. We are not talking about them. We are talking of people who really want to know the truth. But this is the way they go about their work. They don't address themselves to the masses of the people and their leaderships. They don't even seek to consult our political parties. The West talks a lot about parties, but when it wants to know what is happening in Syria, it does not go to our parties.

If you consult our parties in Syria—and there are seven of them—you will find that they are long-established movements. There are differences between them, but if you were to consult them about their attitude to the peace process you would find them expressing the same ideas, which they would defend with the same spirit. The same would be true of our trade unions and popular organizations.

What helps in this respect is that, what we say in our contacts about the peace process, we also say to our own people. The views we have expressed from the start of the process after the 1991 Gulf war were first discussed inside the National Progressive Front and in the popular organizations. What we are now doing is the outcome of these deliberations.

This is not to say that 100 percent of all Syrians share the same uniform opinions. There are people in our country who say the Israelis do not want peace and that we should not, therefore, waste so much effort over it.

They maintain that the negotiations themselves represent a gain for Israel and a loss for the Arabs. Thousands of people hold such views, tens or perhaps even hundreds of thousands. But this has not led to serious splits or feuds inside our country. Because, in spite of differences of approach, no one person believes that another wants to forfeit our national rights. No such accusations are made.

Isn't it difficult for a Ba'thist [member of Syria's ruling party] or an Arab nationalist to accept Israel's presence in this region?

Ever since the establishment of the PLO [Palestine Liberation Organization], the PLO asserted and the Arabs eventually accepted that the PLO was the representative of the Palestinian Arab people. Many Arabs differed with the PLO—and this was reciprocated—but most of these differences remained within the bounds of brotherly sympathy. On this subject, there were certain basic things to which we were committed. So, when the PLO said that it wanted to reach a settlement on the basis of international resolutions, this view was shared by other Arab countries. This implied the adoption of a new position which was that Palestine contained both Arabs and Israelis.

So there was an acceptance of Israel's place in the region?

I am speaking about how the Palestinians see things. And, of course, Egypt also. Accepting the UN resolutions means that the Arabs have agreed, de facto, that both the Israelis and the Arabs have their place in Palestine. . . .

We want to live as a nation in the midst of this modern world. We want to cooperate with others, to serve mutual interests— our own and those of others. Each should respect the will and the opinions of others, and the dignity of everyone should be protected in the interests of everyone, and we should always seek to resolve our differences on the basis of international law and conventions. Thus we strive to achieve a lasting peace everywhere in the world, our region included.

131

"There still exist serious doubts as to [Syria's]
very commitment to peace with Israel."

Syria Is Not Committed to Peace

Zalman Shoval

Zalman Shoval is a former Israeli ambassador to the United
States. In the following viewpoint, Shoval argues that the policies of Syria and its president, Hafez al-Assad, do not reflect a
strong commitment to peace. Of serious concern, he insists, is
Syria's support of Arab terrorists and its advanced weapons
buildup. Shoval states that Assad does not believe Syria is
bound by Arab acceptance of Israel, and he believes that Syria
would not hesitate to disrupt a peace agreement. Shoval asserts
that Syria considers Israel, its territories, Jordan, and Lebanon
as part of a future "Greater Syria."

As you read, consider the following questions:

1. Why does Shoval believe that Syria could easily nullify a
   peace agreement with Israel?
2. According to Shoval, how has Israel offered to settle the
   Golan Heights dispute?
3. What would be the main benefit of peace with Syria,
   according to the author?

From "On Syria, the Jury Still Deliberates" by Zalman Shoval, *The Washington Times*, June 15,
1993. Copyright 1993 by The Washington Times Corporation. Reprinted with permission.

There still exist serious doubts as to [Syria's] very commitment to peace with Israel.

Contrary to some commentaries in the press about Syrian President Hafez Assad's supposed greater flexibility and willingness to embark on "Public Diplomacy"—all this based on a single press interview [by Patrick Seale]—closer examination of the interview, which appeared in a London-based Arab-language newspaper (i.e., a publication that is *not* readily accessible to readers in tightly censored Syria itself [the interview was also published in English in *Mideast Mirror* and *Journal of Palestine Studies*])—proves only that Syria's wily president is still a master of Orwellian double talk. One Israeli official even went so far as to write, rather over-optimistically, that the interview was proof the Syrians now understood they must address themselves to the three subjects essential to Israel: the real nature of peace, security arrangements between the two countries, and the adoption of open and public diplomacy that would make the change in Syria's approach to the Jewish state clear to both Syrians and Israelis. But a more realistic analysis of Mr. Assad's statements provides a far from clear answer to the question, how the Syrian attitude has really changed to warrant its description as a "most impressive public move—signaling the chance of a breakthrough in the coming months."

An Irreversible Concession

A senior U.S. diplomat involved in the peace process once privately admitted to me that "what you are being asked to give up is irretrievable—while what the Arabs will give you is easily reversible." This is particularly apt with regard to Syria—since what Israel is being asked to do—and the Syrian leader reiterates his demands in no uncertain fashion—is quite clear: To give up *in their entirety* the Golan Heights from which, till Israel seized them in 1967 after reversing Syria's aggression, the Israeli Kibbutzim [communes] and towns in the valley down below had been exposed to almost daily acts of shelling and terror—and to dismantle and abandon military installations, towns, and economic investments—the lot! The Syrians? Well, they would, it is hoped, sign a peace treaty that, though an important achievement in itself, could be nullified at any given moment, either as a result of changing Syrian policy perspectives or of an upheaval in the regime—both not entirely inconceivable, considering Syria's history.

President Assad's so-called new "public diplomacy" must be viewed also in light of his other actions, some equally "public," some less so: The continued hampering of the exit of Syrian Jews; the ongoing terrorist attacks on Israel by organizations abetted by Syria; the fact that Damascus is still the headquarters of numerous anti-Israel and anti-Western terrorist organizations. Add to that the enormous arms buildup, including improved "Scud-C" missiles and launchers from North Korea, advanced combat aircraft and tanks from Eastern Europe, the development—perhaps jointly with Iran—of chemical and biological warfare implements—and one cannot help asking against whom Syria intends to employ this arsenal of death—if it is really intent on peace?

Stronger than Israel

Syria directs the operation of Radio Al Quds, beamed to [Israel's] administered territories, which incites Palestinians against the "traitors" in their midst who negotiate with Israel. Unlike their Israeli apologists, the Syrians are quite frank about supporting the "armed struggle" as long as Israel occupies "Arab land." And they have flatly rejected Israeli demands to disarm Hezbollah [militias] and the Palestinians in southern Lebanon. In the peace talks the Syrians have rejected all Israeli suggestions to discuss a truce in Lebanon.

Nor has Hafez al-Assad slowed down the feverish pace of Syrian arming. Having replenished and modernized all branches of its armed forces, Syria surpasses Israel in virtually all major classes of military equipment, let alone in the number of troops. In April 1993, Syria began to manufacture Scud-C missiles in factories near Hama and Aleppo.

David Bar-Illan, *Commentary*, September 1993.

The fact is that, since the start of the present peace-process, Syria has not budged an inch, nor has it responded in kind to the Yitzhak Rabin government's agreeing to apply to the Golan U.N. Security Resolution 242 [mandating peace in the region], including Israeli withdrawals from [occupied] territories. As a matter of fact, the question whether Syria would agree to fully normalize relations even *after* a peace treaty is still moot.

The news is not all bleak. Mr. Assad hints in the interview that if the Palestinians do not reach an agreement with Israel, Syria (and other Arab states) might go it alone. But almost in the same breath he deflates the positive aspects of the above, by practically claiming Syrian hegemony over other Arab parties—especially the Palestinians. What's more, any Arab party giving up "Arab Rights" would face Syria's wrath!

And when asked by the interviewer if the fact of Israel's very existence is now acceptable to Mr. Assad's Ba'athist [ruling party] and Pan-Arab credo—he becomes even more evasive: After all, he says, it is up to the Palestine Liberation Organization, which *others* have recognized as the Palestinians' representatives. If they as well as the Egyptians deem that there is room for both Palestinians and Israelis—that is their business. Syria, however, would not necessarily be bound by their position. Furthermore, as—"according to Assad"—the subject of "Palestine" isn't the Palestinians' exclusive domain, but one that concerns the Arab people as a whole (which in the Syrian-Ba'athist interpretation means that all of the lands to the south and west of Syria—including Israel, the "territories," Jordan and Lebanon—are really part of a future "Greater Syria"), it isn't up to the Palestinians alone to decide their fate. An illuminating sidelight in the interview is the way the Syrian dictator refers to his relationship with Lebanon. Indicating that Damascus has no intention of ever letting go of its unfortunate neighbor, he states that should Beirut ever try to reach a separate peace with Israel, Syria won't hesitate to once again make war against it.

There are some passages in the interview that must have brought wry smiles to the lips of the many victims of Mr. Assad's political persecutions (those who are still alive, that is). London's *Economist* [magazine] recently described Syria as "an old-fashioned dictatorship," but Mr. Assad declares, without blinking, that policies in his country are not the preserve of one man alone—and that they are adopted only after deliberation by all political parties (?) and institutions.

The benefits for Israel and the entire Middle East region of peace with Syria are obvious—the most important perhaps being that the Syrians would stop threatening other Arab parties that want to reach an understanding with Israel. Most Israelis probably realize peace will not be achieved without heavy sacrifices on Israel's part—or refuse to consider such sacrifices for the sake of a *real* peace, to use one of the late David Ben-Gurion's [Israel's first prime minister] expressions. But at the same time, opinions in Israel and elsewhere are divided with regard to the question if Syria has in fact undergone a genuine "strategic change" in its long-term aims—or whether its present policies merely reflect a tactical shift, dictated by the disappearance of its previous Soviet patron, and by the need to get into Washington's good graces and appear solicitous for the latter's policy goals—as well as for the wishes of its Saudi financial benefactors.

One swallow does not make a summer, and one newspaper interview—even if it includes a few positive elements, and none too many at that—cannot replace real diplomatic flexibility. And to judge by Syria's intransigent stance during the Madrid [peace] Conference, the jury is still out with regard to the verdict about her commitment to peace and co-existence with Israel.

Periodical Bibliography

The following articles have been selected to supplement the diverse views presented in this chapter.

Noam Chomsky	"The Israel-Arafat Agreement," *Z Magazine*, October 1993.
George J. Church	"All Together Now," *Time*, September 20, 1993.
E.J. Dionne Jr.	"Blessed Are the Realists," *The Washington Post National Weekly Edition*, September 20-26, 1993.
Steven Emerson	"Farewell to the Old PLO," *The Wall Street Journal*, September 10, 1993.
William F. Jasper	"The Mideast Peace Charade," *The New American*, October 18, 1993. Available from The Review of the News Incorporated, 770 Westhill Blvd., Appleton, WI 54915.
Henry Kissinger	"Turning a Fairy Tale into Reality," *Newsweek*, September 27, 1993.
Benjamin Netanyahu	"Peace in Our Time?" *The New York Times*, September 5, 1993.
Edward W. Said	"Arafat's Deal," *The Nation*, September 20, 1993.
Brent Scowcroft	"The Kick-Start That Gave Peace a Chance," *Newsweek*, September 13, 1993.
Ariel Sharon	"'Arafat Should Be Tried as War Criminal,'" *The Jerusalem Post International Edition*, September 11, 1993. Available from 211 E. 43d St., Suite 601, New York, NY 10017.
Joseph Sobran	"Old Enemies," *The Wanderer*, September 23, 1993. Available from 201 Ohio St., St. Paul, MN 55107.
U.S. Department of State Dispatch	Special issue on the Israel-PLO accord, September 1993.
The Wall Street Journal	"The Perils of Peace," September 10, 1993.
Washington Report on Middle East Affairs	Special issue on the Israel-PLO accord, November/December 1993. Available from American Educational Trust, PO Box 53062, Washington, DC 20009.
Mortimer B. Zuckerman	"Risks for the Pain of Peace," *U.S. News & World Report*, September 27, 1993.

Should Israel Give Up Land for Peace?

Chapter Preface

In 1967, border clashes between Israel and Syria and Egypt's troop buildup in the Sinai Peninsula led to the Six Day War, in which Israel soundly defeated Egypt, Jordan, and Syria. As a result, Israel gained much territory from each nation: the Sinai and the Gaza Strip from Egypt, the West Bank of the Jordan River and the Old City of Jerusalem from Jordan, and the Golan Heights from Syria. Months after the war, the UN Security Council passed Resolution 242, which called for the "withdrawal of Israeli armed forces from territories occupied in the recent conflict" and the "acknowledgment of the sovereignty, territorial integrity and political independence of every State in the area and their right to live in peace."

Although Egypt and Israel reached a "land for peace" agreement in 1979 to return the Sinai based on these conditions, Israel has steadfastly refused to give up the West Bank or the Golan Heights, citing the strategic military edge the territories' elevation provides (they overlook much Arab and Israeli land), and citing the fact that more than a quarter-million Israeli settlers inhabit these territories.

But many Palestinians and Syrians contend that no lasting peace can be achieved unless Israel withdraws to its pre-1967 borders. Many experts agree that Israel must make some concessions of land for peace. Israel thus faces this dilemma: risking its security by ceding land versus the continuation of hostilities with Arab neighbors. The authors of the following viewpoints debate whether Israel should give up land for peace.

"Self-determination . . . is a sacred and inviolable right which we shall relentlessly pursue and exercise with dedication and self-confidence and pride."

Palestinians Should Have Their Own Nation

Haydar 'Abd al-Shafi

Haydar 'Abd al-Shafi led the Palestinian delegation at the 1991 Middle East peace conference in Madrid, Spain. In the following viewpoint, excerpted from a speech delivered at the conference, 'Abd al-Shafi argues that Israel must end its hostile occupation of the West Bank and Gaza Strip and recognize Palestinians' independence. 'Abd al-Shafi asserts that Israel's occupation suppresses the Palestinian people and denies their United Nations–sanctioned right to self-determination. The author contends that Palestinians are willing to live peacefully with Israel, but insists that Israel must end its hostility in order to achieve peace. 'Abd al-Shafi is the head of the Gaza Strip's Red Crescent Society, the Muslim counterpart of the Red Cross.

As you read, consider the following questions:

1. What injustices has Israel committed in the occupied territories, according to 'Abd al-Shafi?
2. In 'Abd al-Shafi's opinion, why must Palestinians become independent as soon as possible?
3. According to the author, why is Jerusalem important to Palestinians?

From "A Cry for Freedom" by Haydar 'Abd al-Shafi, *Al-Fajr*, November 4, 1991. Reprinted with permission.

For too long the Palestinian people have gone unheeded, silenced and denied—our identity negated by political expediency, our rightful struggle against injustice maligned, and our present existence subsumed by the past tragedy of another people.

For the greater part of this century, we have been victimized by the myth of "a land without a people," and described with impunity as "the invisible Palestinians." Before such willful blindness, we refused to disappear or to accept a distorted identity. Our Intifada [Palestinian uprising] is a testimony to our perseverance and resilience, waged in a just struggle to regain our rights.

It is time for us to narrate our own story, to stand witness as advocates of a truth which has long lain buried in the consciousness and conscience of the world. We do not stand before you as supplicants, but rather as the torchbearers who know that in our world of today, ignorance can never be an excuse. We seek neither an admission of guilt after the fact, nor vengeance for past inequities, but rather an act of will that would make a just peace a reality. We speak out from the full conviction of the rightness of our cause, the verity of our history, and the depth of our commitment. Therein lies the strength of the Palestinian people today, for we have scaled the walls of fear and reticence and we wish to speak out with the courage and integrity that our narrative and history deserve. . . .

Life Under Occupation

Regardless of the nature and conditions of our oppression, whether the dispossession and dispersion of exile or the brutality and repression of the occupation, the Palestinian people cannot be torn asunder. They remain united, a nation wherever they are, or are forced to be.

And Jerusalem, that city which is not only the soul of Palestine but the cradle of three world religions, is tangible even in its claimed absence from our midst at this stage [Arab Jerusalemites were barred from the Madrid conference]. . . . Palestinian Jerusalem, the capital of our homeland and future state, defines Palestinian existence—past, present and future—but itself has been denied a voice and an identity. Jerusalem defies exclusive possessiveness or bondage. Israel's annexation of Jerusalem remains both clearly illegal in the eyes of the world community and an affront to the peace that this city deserves.

We come from a tortured land and a proud, though captive, people, having been asked to negotiate with our occupiers, but leaving behind the children of the Intifada, and a people under occupation and under curfew, who enjoined us not to surrender or forget. As we speak, thousands of our brothers and sisters are languishing in Israeli prisons and detention camps, most detained without evidence, charge or trial, many cruelly mis-

treated and tortured in interrogation, guilty only of seeking freedom or daring to defy the occupation. We speak in their name
and we say: set them free.

The State of Palestine

The State of Palestine is an Arab state, an integral and indivisible
part of the Arab nation, at one with that nation in heritage and
civilization, with it also in its aspiration for liberation, progress,
democracy and unity. The State of Palestine affirms its obligation
to abide by the Charter of the League of Arab States, whereby the
coordination of the Arab states with each other shall be strengthened. It calls upon the Arab compatriots to consolidate and enhance the emergence in reality of our state, to mobilize potential
and to intensify efforts whose goal is to end Israeli occupation.

Palestine National Council, Palestinian Declaration of Independence, November 15,
1988.

As we speak, the tens of thousands who have been wounded
or permanently disabled are in pain: let peace heal their wounds.
As we speak, the eyes of thousands of Palestinian refugees, deportees and displaced persons since 1967 are haunting us, for exile is a cruel fate: bring them home. They have the right to return. As we speak, the silence of demolished homes echoes
through the halls and in our minds: we must rebuild our homes
in our free state.

Willing to Share

And what do we tell the loved ones of those killed by army
bullets? How do we answer the questions and the fear in our
children's eyes? For one out of three Palestinian children under
occupation has been killed, injured or detained. How can we explain to our children that they are denied education, our schools
so often closed by army fiat? . . . What requiem can be sung for
trees uprooted by army bulldozers? And, most of all, who can
explain to those whose lands are confiscated and clear waters
stolen, the message of peace? Remove the barbed wire, restore
the land and its life-giving water.

The [Jewish] settlements must stop now. Peace cannot be
waged while Palestinian land is confiscated in myriad ways and
the status of the Occupied Territories is being decided each day
by Israeli bulldozers and barbed wire. This is not simply a position; it is an irrefutable reality. Territory for peace is a travesty
when territory for illegal settlement is official Israeli policy and
practice. The settlements must stop now.

In the name of the Palestinian people, we wish to directly address the Israeli people with whom we have had a prolonged exchange of pain: let us share hope instead. We are willing to live side by side on the land and the promise of the future. Sharing, however, requires two partners willing to share as equals. Mutuality and reciprocity must replace domination and hostility for genuine reconciliation and coexistence under international legality. Your security and ours are mutually dependent, as entwined as the fears and nightmares of our children.

We have seen some of you at your best and at your worst, for the occupier can hide no secrets from the occupied, and we are witness to the toll that occupation has exacted from you and yours. We have seen you anguish over the transformation of your sons and daughters into instruments of a blind and violent occupation—and we are sure that at no time did you envisage such a role for the children whom you thought would forge your future. We have seen you look back in deepest sorrow at the tragedy of your past and look on in horror at the disfigurement of the victim turned oppressor. Not for this have you nurtured your hopes, dreams and your offspring. . . .

Quest for Peace and Freedom

We pledge our commitment to the principle of justice, peace and reconciliation based on international legitimacy and uniform standards. We shall persist, in our quest for peace, to place before you the substance and determination of our people, often victimized but never defeated. We shall pursue our people's right to self-determination, to the exhilaration of freedom, and to the warmth of the sun as a nation among equals.

This is the moment of truth; you must have the courage to recognize it and the will to implement it for our truth can no longer be hidden away in the dark recesses of inadvertency or neglect. The people of Palestine look at you with a straightforward, direct gaze, seeking to touch your heart, for you have dared to stir up hopes that cannot be abandoned. You cannot afford to let us down, for we have lived up to the values you espouse, and we have remained true to our cause.

We, the Palestinian people, made the imaginative leap in the Palestine National Council of November 1988, during which the Palestinian Liberation Organization (PLO) launched its peace initiative based on U.N. Security Council resolutions 242 and 338 [calling for withdrawal of Israeli forces from occupied territories], and declared Palestinian independence based on Resolution 181 of the United Nations, which gave birth to two states in 1948: Israel and Palestine. In December 1988, a historic speech before the United Nations in Geneva led directly to the launching of the Palestinian-American dialogue. Ever since then, our people have responded positively to every serious peace initiative and have done their utmost to ensure the success of this process. Israel, on the other hand, has placed many obstacles and barriers in the path of peace to negate the very validity of the process. . . .

Statehood Now

These historic decisions of the Palestine National Council wrenched the course of history from inevitable confrontation and conflict toward peace and mutual recognition. With our own hands, and in an act of sheer will, we have molded the shape of the future of our people. Our parliament has articulated the message of a people with the courage to say "yes" to the challenge of history, just as it provided the reference, in its resolutions in Algiers and in the Central Council meeting in Tunis, to go forward to this historic conference. We cannot be made to bear the brunt of other people's "no." We must have reciprocity. We must have peace.

A Step Toward Independence

Our [Israel-PLO] agreement is only a step toward an independent Palestinian state which will confederate with Jordan, according to the free choice of the two peoples. We are committed to that.

Yasir Arafat, *Time*, September 27, 1993.

In the Middle East there is no superfluous people outside time and place, but rather a state sorely missed by time and place— the state of Palestine. It must be born on the land of Palestine to redeem the injustice of the destruction of its historical reality and to free the people of Palestine from the shackles of their victimization. Our homeland has never ceased to exist in our minds and hearts, but it has to exist as a state on all the territories occupied by Israel in the war of 1967, with Jerusalem as its capital, in the context of that city's special status and its non-exclusive character.

This state, in a condition of emergence, has already been a subject of anticipation for too long. It should take place today, rather than tomorrow. However, we are willing to accept the proposal for a transitional stage, provided interim arrangements are not transformed into permanent status. The time frame must be condensed to respond to the dispossessed Palestinians' urgent need for sanctuary and to the occupied Palestinians' right to gain relief from oppression and to win recognition of their authentic will. During this phase, international protection for our people is most urgently needed, and the *de jure* [by law] application of the Fourth Geneva Convention is a necessary condition. The phases must not prejudice the outcome; rather they require an internal momentum and motivation to lead sequentially to sovereignty. Bilateral negotiations on the withdrawal of Israeli forces, the dissolution of Israeli administration and the transfer of authority to the Palestinian people cannot proceed under coercion or threat in the current asymmetry of power. Israel must demonstrate its willingness to negotiate in good faith by immediately halting all settlement activity and land confiscation while implementing meaningful confidence-building measures. Without genuine progress, tangible constructive changes and just agreements during the bilateral talks, multilateral negotiations will be meaningless. Regional stability, security and development are the logical outcome of an equitable and just solution to the Palestinian question, which remains the key to the resolution of wider conflicts and concerns.

The Cry for Freedom

In its confrontation of wills between the legitimacy of the people and the illegality of the occupation, the Intifada's message has been consistent: to embody the Palestinian state and to build its institutions and infrastructure. We seek recognition for this creative impulse which nurtures within it the potential nascent state. We have paid a heavy price for daring to substantiate our authenticity and to practice popular democracy in spite of the cruelty of occupation. It was a sheer act of will that brought us here, the same will which asserted itself in the essence of the Intifada, as the cry for freedom, an act of civil resistance, and people's participation and empowerment. The Intifada is our drive toward nation-building and social transformation. We are here today with the support of our people, who have given itself the right to hope and to make a stand for peace. We must recognize, as well, that some of our people harbor serious doubts and skepticism about this process. Within our democratic, social and political structures, we have evolved a respect for pluralism and diversity, and we shall guard the opposition's right to differ within the parameters of mutual respect and national unity.

The process launched here must lead us to the light at the end of the tunnel, and this light is the promise of a new Palestine— free, democratic and respectful of human rights and the integrity of nature.

Self-determination can neither be granted nor withheld at the whim of the political self-interest of others, for it is enshrined in all international charters and humanitarian law. We claim this right; we firmly assert it here before you and in the eyes of the rest of the world, for it is a sacred and inviolable right which we shall relentlessly pursue and exercise with dedication and self-confidence and pride.

Let us end the Palestinian-Israeli fatal proximity in this unnatural condition of occupation, which has already claimed too many lives. No dream of expansion or glory can justify the taking of a single life. Set us free to re-engage as neighbors and as equals on our holy land.

A Just Cause

To our people in exile and under occupation, who have sent us to this appointment laden with their trust, love and aspirations, we say that the load is heavy and the task is great, but we shall be true. In the words of our great national poet, Mahmoud Darwish: "My homeland is not a suitcase, and I am no traveler." To the exiled and the occupied, we say: You shall return and you shall remain and we will prevail for our cause is just. We will put on our embroidered robes and *kuffiyehs* and, in the sight of the world, celebrate together on the day of liberation.

Refugee camps are no fit home for people who had been reared on the land of Palestine, in the warmth of the sun and freedom. The hail of Israeli bombs, almost daily pouring [on the] defenseless civilian population in the refugee camps of Lebanon is no substitute for the healing rain of the homeland. Yet, the international will had ensured [Palestinian refugees'] return in United Nations Resolution 194—a fact willfully ignored and unenacted.

Similarly, all other resolutions pertinent to the Palestinian question, beginning with Resolution 181 through resolutions 242 and 338, and ending with Security Council Resolution 681 [condemning Israel's deportation of Palestinians], have until now been relegated to the domain of public debate, rather than real implementation. They form the larger body of legality, including all relevant provisions of international law, within which any peaceful settlement must proceed. If international legitimacy and the rule of law are to prevail and govern relations among nations, they must be respected and, impartially and uniformly, implemented. We, as Palestinians, require nothing less than justice.

The Olive Branch of Peace

To Palestinians everywhere: today we bear in our hands the precious gift of your love and your pain, and we shall set it down gently here before the eyes of the world and say— there is a right here which must be acknowledged, the right to self-determination and statehood; there is strength and there is the scent of sacred incense in the air. Jerusalem, the heart of our homeland and the cradle of the soul, is shimmering through the barriers of occupation and deceit. The deliberate violation of its sanctity is also an act of violence against the collective human, cultural and spiritual memory and an aggression against its enduring symbols of tolerance, magnanimity and respect for cultural and religious authenticity. The cobbled streets of the Old City must not echo with the discordant beat of Israeli military boots; we must restore to them the chant of the *muezzin*, the chimes of the church bells, and the prayers of all the faithful calling for peace in the City of Peace.

From Madrid, let us light the candle of peace and let the olive branch blossom. Let us celebrate the rituals of justice and rejoice in the hymns of truth, for the awe of the moment is a promise to the future, which we all must redeem. The Palestinians will be free, and will stand tall among the community of nations in the fullness of the pride and dignity which by right belongs to all people. In the words of Chairman Yasir Arafat in 1974 before the U.N. General Assembly: "Let not the olive branch of peace fall from my hands." Let not the olive branch of peace fall from the hands of the Palestinian people.

"Palestinian Arabs . . . are in the minority in the forty miles west of the Jordan River, and . . . they will receive no additional independent states there. "

Palestinians Should Not Have Their Own Nation

Benjamin Netanyahu

Benjamin Netanyahu is the leader of Israel's conservative Likud party and a staunch opponent of ceding land controlled by Israel. In the following viewpoint, Netanyahu argues that there is no reason to create a new Arab state for Palestinian Arabs in the West Bank (Judea-Samaria) because Jordan—a nation created from the division of the land of Palestine—is their legitimate homeland, as Israel is for Jews. Netanyahu contends that Palestinian claims for self-determination are misleading because until Israel's occupation of the West Bank in 1967, Arabs there had never claimed to be a people distinct from Arabs in Jordan. Netanyahu is the author of *A Place Among the Nations: Israel and the World*, from which this viewpoint is excerpted.

As you read, consider the following questions:

1. In Netanyahu's opinion, how did Arab propagandists define the Middle East conflict as a Palestinian problem?
2. Why does Netanyahu believe that there is no distinction between Palestinians in Israel and those in Jordan?
3. How has Jordan accommodated Palestinians wishing to live there, according to the author?

On a visit to the United States in May 1990, I was besieged by some of Israel's staunchest Jewish-American allies who were concerned about an altercation that had occurred near St. John's Hospice in East Jerusalem. A yeshiva had rented, with Israeli government aid, a building adjacent to a Christian monastery and turned it into a dormitory for its students. The furor that arose when the church objected to this arrangement gave much comfort to Israel's enemies and much discomfort to its friends. Some of these friends, members of the Presidents of Major American Jewish Organizations, were now pressing me on how Israel's government, which was then led by the Likud party, could allow such a "fiasco" to take place.

"You're right. It's a big problem for us now," I said. "But it will blow over in a week. There's a much bigger problem that won't go away."

"What's that?" they asked.

"Saddam," I answered. "Saddam Hussein is the Middle East's, and Israel's, number one problem."

The response to that was as dismissive as it was scornful: "Come on," I was told in exasperation. "That's just a Likud diversion."

Few incidents illustrate the distortion of Middle Eastern reality . . . as well as this exchange, three months before Saddam's invasion of Kuwait. Israel's friends and foes alike falsely believed the "Palestinian Problem" to be synonymous with the "Middle East Problem." This perversion of truth is a monument to the success of the Arab propaganda machine, and it certainly has done great damage to Israel. . . .

The Reversal of Causality

If the Arabs said that all the problems in the Middle East were telescoped into the Palestinian Problem, they now proceeded to explain exactly what that problem was: not a by-product of wars in which the Arab states attacked Israel, but in fact the *cause* of those attacks in the first place.

With each year's harvest of propaganda, the reality of the Arab world's war against Israel began to recede in the popular mind, leaving only the image of Israel against the Palestinian Arabs. (Saddam's missile attacks on Israel during the Gulf War were a rude but brief reminder of this larger context.) The Arab Goliath was turned into the Palestinian David, and the Israeli David was turned into the Zionist Goliath. Not only were size and power reversed, so was the sequence of events. In the Reversal of Causality, it is not the Arabs who attacked Israel, but Israel that attacked the Arabs—or more specifically, since the Arab states deliberately substituted "Palestinians" for "Arabs," it was Israel that attacked the Palestinians. In a nutshell, the new chain of reasoning went like this: All the problems in the

Middle East are rooted in the Palestinian Problem; that problem itself is rooted in Israel's occupation of Palestinian lands. Ergo, end that occupation and you end the problem. . . .

Brandishing the ever-popular slogan of "self-determination," [Arab propagandists] asserted that the "Palestinian people" have been denied their "legitimate rights," and one of the rights that has been denied, they claimed, is the right to a "homeland." Significantly, the slogans of "Palestinian self-determination" and "legitimate rights" were introduced into common currency only after the failure of the Arab attempt to destroy Israel in [the Six Day War in] 1967.

For it is an uncontested fact that during the nineteen years of Jordanian rule over Judea-Samaria [1949-67], the Arab leaders, the Arab media, and Arab propaganda said virtually nothing about a "homeland" or "legitimate rights" for the Palestinian Arabs living in Judea-Samaria. When "Palestinian rights" *were* spoken of, it was always in reference to Israel behind its 1967 lines, to Haifa, Jaffa, and Acre, and the message was crystal clear: Israel was to be destroyed in order for the Arabs to obtain those rights.

No Distinct Nationhood

It is noteworthy that under the 1922-1947 British Mandate [giving Britain administrative powers in Palestine], it was the Jews of the country who called themselves Palestinians. The *Palestine Post* and the Palestine Philharmonic were Jewish. Likewise the Jewish soldiers who made up the Jewish Brigade of the British Army were called by the British "Palestinians," a term that at the time referred mainly to Jews. There were thus Palestinian Jews and Palestinian Arabs, although in those days the Arabs did not stress a distinct Palestinian nationhood but always emphasized that they were part of the larger Arab nation.

This deep-rooted identification with the Arab nation did not diminish over the years. Yasser Arafat, head of the PLO [Palestine Liberation Organization], has said, "The question of borders does not interest us. Palestine is only a small drop in the great Arab ocean. Our nation is the great Arab nation extending from the Atlantic to the Red Sea and beyond." And Zuhair Mohsin, a member of the PLO executive, put it this way: "There are no differences between Jordanians, Palestinians, Syrians and Lebanese. We are one people." Yet soon after 1967, the Arab world began speaking with one voice about the newly occupied "Palestinian people," as though a distinct Palestinian nation had somehow come into being out of thin air.

The process of forming a separate nation is a complex one. The development of a unique "peoplehood" is always a long historical process, and its culmination is expressed by the emergence of several shared attributes, most often a distinct language, culture, religion, and history. But let us grant that through a miraculous telescoping of history, what took other peoples centuries was achieved by the Palestinian Arabs almost overnight, by dint of declaration, and that they are entitled to a national home. But who are the Palestinian Arabs, and where is their homeland? Let us hear what the Arab leaders themselves say.

PLO Designs

The PLO, supposedly committed to "Palestinian self-determination," asserted from its inception in 1964 that its design encompasses the entirety of Palestine, both its western and eastern parts, *both* Israel and Jordan. This was underscored time and again, as in the Palestine National Council's Eighth Conference, in February-March 1971:

> In raising the slogan of the liberation of Palestine . . . it was not the intention of the Palestine revolution to separate the east of the river from the west, nor did it believe that the struggle of the Palestinian people can be separate from the struggle of the masses in Jordan.

Given the current embrace between the PLO and Jordan, PLO leaders are naturally reluctant to publicize this long-standing claim. But their candid statements in the past are revealing. For example, Chafiq el Hout, a PLO official, said in 1967, "Jordan is an integral part of Palestine, just like Israel." And Arafat made this same point in his speech before the United Nations in 1974: "Jordan is ours, Palestine is ours, and we shall build our national entity on the whole of this land."

No Independent Palestine

The Palestinians should have the right—as specified in the Camp David Accords—to participate in the determination of their future. But they do not have the right to determine Israel's future. For that reason, we oppose the creation of an independent Palestinian state.

Bill Clinton and Al Gore, *Putting People First*, 1992.

Some would expect the Jordanians to contest this claim. But until very recently they did not. In 1970, Crown Prince Hassan, addressing the Jordanian National Assembly, said, "Palestine is Jordan, and Jordan is Palestine. There is one people and one land, with one history and one destiny." King Hussein (also—significantly—before an Arab audience) said on Egyptian television in 1977, "The two peoples are actually one. This is a fact." In an interview with an Arab newspaper in Paris in 1981, Hussein said, "The truth is that Jordan is Palestine and Palestine is Jordan." And in 1984, he told the Kuwaiti paper *Al-Anba* that "Jordan is Palestine. . . . Jordanians and Palestinians must . . . realize that their fate is the same," and that "Jordan in itself is Palestine." In 1988 the PLO leader Abu Iyad reemphasized precisely the same point: "We also insist on confederation with Jordan because we are one and the same people."

In recent years, to ward off the inevitable conflict between them over who will control eastern Palestine (Jordan), Hussein and the PLO have somewhat amended such pronouncements. But whether whispered or spoken out loud, these declarations of the Arabs themselves confirm what both history and logic tell us: The area of Palestine is indeed the territory of Mandatory Palestine, as decreed in 1922 by the League of Nations, and comprises the present-day states of Israel and Jordan. It is absurd to pretend that an Arab in eastern Palestine who shares the language, culture, and religion with another Arab some ten miles away in western Palestine, an Arab who is often his close relative if not literally his own brother, is a member of a different people. Indeed, the PLO's officials and Jordan's rulers have been the first to admit this.

Two States Only

Those who accept the notion of a "Palestinian people" must therefore wonder: How *many* Palestinian Arab peoples are there? Is there a "West Palestinian Arab people" on the West Bank, and just across the border an "East Palestinian Arab people" in Jordan? How many Arab states in Palestine does Palestinian Arab self-determination require?

Clearly, in eastern and western Palestine, there are only two peoples, the Arabs and the Jews. Just as clearly, there are only two states in that area, Jordan and Israel. The Arab state of Jordan, containing some three million Arabs, does not allow a single Jew to live there—it expelled those Jews who came under its control in 1948. Jordan also contains four-fifths of the territory originally allocated by the League of Nations for the Jewish National Home. The other state, Israel, has a population of five million, of which one-sixth is Arab. It contains less than one-fifth of the territory originally allocated to the Jews under the Mandate. In the territory disputed between these two states (Judea, Samaria, and East Jerusalem) live another 1,150,000 Arabs and 250,000 Jews (another 650,000 Arabs live in Gaza).

The claim of "self-determination," then, is misleading. For the inhabitants of Jordan—which Hussein's grandfather Abdullah originally wanted to call the Hashemite Kingdom of Palestine— are all Palestinian Arabs (Arabs from Palestine), and within that population western Palestinian Arabs—those whose families came from the part of Palestine west of the Jordan River—are the decided majority. It cannot be said, therefore, that the Arabs of Palestine are lacking a state of their own, the ultimate expression of self-determination. The demand for a second Palestinian Arab state in western Palestine, and a twenty-second Arab state in the world, is merely the latest attempt to push Israel back to the hopelessly vulnerable armistice lines of 1949. . . .

Jordan Is Palestine

Much as the Arab ideologues and irredentists living in Israeli territory may not like it, it is in the Arab-controlled portion of Mandatory Palestine, in the state of Jordan, that they may exercise Palestinian Arab self-determination.

That Jordanian leaders are uncomfortable with this is understandable. King Hussein's Hashemite royal family—Bedouins whom the British imported from Mecca to rule over the Palestinian majority in Jordan—fears for its survival and prefers to herd the PLO onto the Israeli side of the Jordan River rather than share power with it. Hussein himself has survived several assassination attempts and has had the experience of losing his grandfather and his prime minister to Palestinian terrorists. The PLO, for its part, seems always willing to set up shop on any piece of territory available. But neither of these motives alters the fact, as both Hussein and Arafat have said on numerous occasions, that Jordan is Palestine—or to be precise, the lion's share of Mandatory Palestine. That Palestinian Jordan is ruled by a monarch of Bedouin extraction no more justifies the creation of an additional Palestinian state than the election of a Hispanic-American president in the United States would justify the creation of a separate country for Americans of, say, Anglo-Saxon extraction. The fact remains that Jordan is a state that encompasses the overwhelming majority of Palestine's territory and that has a majority of Palestinian Arabs.

The question of who rules this Palestinian state is of great interest to the contending parties, and to Israel as well. For strategic reasons, many people in Israel prefer the continuation of a Jordan under the less aggressive Hashemites. But this in no way alters the fact that a national home, indeed a sovereign state, exists for Palestinian Arabs. Even now, many of the principal functionaries of the Jordanian regime have been Palestinian Arabs who originated on the West Bank, including Prime Minister Zaid al-Rifai and Foreign Minister Taher Masri, both from Nablus. If the inhabitants of this Palestinian state wish to replace the head of government with a Palestinian as well, that should be up to them, although I do not see in Jordan or anywhere else in the Arab world a movement to facilitate such democratic choice. In any case, the question of who rules the

Palestinian state is quite separate from the fact that such a state exists and endows the Palestinian Arabs with a national home.

No Right to Independence

Accordingly, Jordan has granted its citizenship to Palestinians who wish to live there, and it has absorbed three hundred thousand Palestinian Arabs who were expelled by Kuwait for their role in the Gulf War. Thus Jordan has served as a home for Palestinian Arabs, much as Israel has served as a home for Jews. Of course, the existence of a Palestinian national home does not mean that all Palestinians have to live there. A West Bank Palestinian Arab may choose to remain in Israel, just as a Jew may choose to remain in America rather than come to live in the Jewish state. But a Samarian Arab or a Judean Arab who freely makes this choice also chooses to be part of a minority in the Jewish state, just as have the Arabs of Galilee and Jaffa. He or she has no more right to demand a second Palestinian Arab state in Samaria than do Palestinian Arabs to demand a third Palestinian Arab state in Galilee and a fourth in Jaffa. If there is to be peace, it will have to mean, at long last, the recognition by the Palestinian Arabs that they are in the minority in the forty miles west of the Jordan River, and that they will receive no additional independent states there.

"Israel cannot defend itself against an Arab offensive . . . unless its present borders are retained."

An Independent Palestine Would Threaten Israel's Security

Yohanan Ramati and Shlomo Baum

Since 1967, Israel has asserted that giving up the West Bank region to Arab rule would make Israel vulnerable to an attack or invasion from the east. In the following viewpoint, Yohanan Ramati and Shlomo Baum agree and argue that the topography of the West Bank region makes it ideal defensive territory for Israeli artillery and radar. Ramati and Baum contend that an Arab-controlled West Bank would place Israel at a strategic disadvantage, leaving much of its industry, military, and population exposed to terrorists or well-armed Arab forces. Only by retaining its present borders, the authors conclude, can Israel possibly defend itself. Ramati is the director and Baum is the head of the Jerusalem Institute for Western Defence.

As you read, consider the following questions:

1. How have Arab militaries grown stronger, according to the authors?
2. Why do Ramati and Baum believe that the Jordan River valley is an ideal border?
3. In the authors' opinion, why is unconventional warfare unlikely to break out between Arab nations and Israel?

From "Can Israel Survive the Loss of Judea and Samaria?" by Yohanan Ramati and Shlomo Baum, *Midstream*, August/September 1992. Reprinted by permission of the Theodor Herzl Foundation, New York.

Many claim that Israel can be defended within its pre-1967 borders with minor modifications. When pressed, nobody can explain *how*. The truth is that within such borders Israel is indefensible and therefore certain to be attacked.

Since the late 1960s, when weapons and munitions began to be propelled through the air and guided from afar, some politicians and so-called military experts began to claim that territory and topography are losing their value in war. They are wrong— both in theory and in practice. The land area required to wage war or deter war increases with advances in military technology which improve the lethality, accuracy and range of weapons, as well as the mobility and speed of weapons platforms (land and air). In his classic book, *Numbers, Predictions and War*, Col. T.N. Dupuy shows that waging war in 1973 required nearly 200 times more land area than during the Napoleonic War, 16 times more than in World War I and 29 percent more than in World War II. Otherwise, casualties become prohibitive. Principles valid for centuries have not suddenly ceased to apply in the 1990s.

Topography

The topographical shape of territory has also become more important. Throughout history, topography often determined the outcome of battles, being of special importance to the defending side. But high ground and dominating strongholds are more essential for defense today than in the past. This follows inevitably from the physical laws governing the transmission of electromagnetic radiation, because modern control systems and all sophisticated weapons and munitions using sensors and antennas must be deployed from line-of-sight locations. A tank can be hit by a guided missile from three to five miles, but only if there is a line-of-sight from the missile's launching point to its target. Thus, mountain strongholds with extended visibility greatly increase the spotting distance and targetability of enemy armored forces, artillery and combat aircraft.

It is a military axiom that radar stations must be situated on the highest topographically suitable mountain sites available. This is true especially in front-line defense zones. AWACS [Airborne Warning and Control System] aircraft cannot substitute for radar stations on the ground, as their low speed and vulnerability to air-to-air and ground-to-air missiles compel their stationing in remote stand-off positions.

All these are universal military truths that any good nonpolitical American general will confirm. For Israel, they are especially meaningful because the asymmetry between the warring parties in the Arab-Israeli conflict is unprecedented in military history. The 20 Arab states that surround Israel cover an area exceeding 5.1 million square miles, which is larger than Europe up to Russia's Ural mountains. The size of "Greater Israel" is less than 11,000 square miles—roughly the size of Maryland.

The population of the Arab states is about 215 million. The Jewish population of Israel is about 4.1 million.

Israel has few natural resources. The natural resources of the Arab states account, inter alia, for about 60 percent of the world's total oil reserves, enabling them to acquire modern weapons systems on a scale making any normal military balance between them and Israel impossible.

The universal conclusion is that the importance of territory relative to the two other basic components of the battlefield—manpower and weapons systems—increased as a result of advances in military technology. How does this apply to Judea and Samaria [West Bank]?

Israel's "green line" borders were indefensible already in 1967. Therefore, Israel's national security doctrine advised preemptive strikes into Arab territory whenever an Arab attack was imminent. This doctrine was implemented in the Six-Day War.

In the Yom Kippur War of 1973, the territory acquired in 1967 proved critical. Some Syrian tanks reached the Jordan River near the Sea of Galilee after 48 hours. An advance of another six miles would have given Syria control of the power station that pumps water for three-quarters of Israel.

Does ceding Judea and Samaria to Arab rule reduce or increase the likelihood of war? The aspects that must be considered before answering this question are deterrence, defense, counterattack, terrorism and irregular forces. They will all be examined.

Arab Weapons

Since 1973, a vast change has occurred in the technological level and quantities of the weapons systems owned by the Arab states:

a) Egypt, Syria, Jordan and Iraq have purchased thousands of modern tanks and self-propelled artillery, as well as hundreds of modern combat aircraft and combat helicopters. They have also purchased and deployed sophisticated modern antiaircraft systems, including missiles.

b) Large numbers of ground-to-ground missiles with ranges covering the whole area of Israel have been acquired and/or developed with foreign aid by Egypt, Syria, Iraq and Saudi Arabia.

The Arab-Israel conflict is not about borders, though some Arab states now find it convenient to present it as a border dispute for tactical reasons. The existence of Israel—not the size of Israel—is the cause of the conflict; therefore, territorial concessions by Israel cannot end the conflict. The key question is not: "Will the Arabs want to attack Israel?" but "Under what conditions are they less likely to attack?" The Arabs evaluate prospects of success versus risks of failure like anyone else.

In the case of Israel, topography is a key factor in both defense and deterrence. It largely determines the amount of risk the Arab side takes when launching an attack.

Judea and Samaria is a mountainous area of 2,270 square miles, reaching at some points 3,300 feet above sea level. It can be divided from north to south into three operational zones.

©1992 International Copyright by CARTOONEWS inc., N.Y.C., USA

"Have a cigar."

Lurie/Cartoonews, Inc., © 1992. Reprinted with permission.

The eastern zone borders the Jordan River (which itself forms a natural border). It includes the western part of the Jordan rift valley and the mountains dominating it. Even tanks can climb these mountains only along five routes, which can be easily blocked by the defenders. Observation posts and firing positions in the eastern mountainous area dominate the Jordan Valley and these five routes alike. Firefinding radar, radar jammers and forward observation posts for artillery have excellent placements here. Thus the topographical structure of the eastern zone makes the Jordan Valley a natural tank trap and killing ground. Israel can stop an Arab offensive across the Jordan River by numerically superior forces—inflicting heavy losses. It should be stressed that the topography on the Jordanian side of the Jordan Valley is roughly similar, providing excellent defensive positions against an attack from the west.

The central zone encompasses the mountainous spine and all the major ridges and peaks of Judea and Samaria. This zone is approximately 80 miles from north to south and is 5 to 10 miles wide. Due to major developments in radar technology since 1967, these mountains house Israel's early warning radar system and have become the country's front air defense line. This is not all. As already stressed, the high ground and dominating strongholds are more essential for defense than in 1973, as all sensors, antennas and control systems must be deployed from line-of-sight locations.

Due to Israel's small area and the fast speeds of modern aircraft, the time needed for air defense procedures is very limited. Identification, decision, scramble and intercept must be executed accurately without hesitation. The same applies to orders from radar stations on the ground given to combat aircraft on intercept missions. As already stated, airborne radars like the AWACS cannot substitute for these ground-based radar stations.

In time of war, radar stations in the central zone provide warning depth both for the coastal strip and for the eastern front. They also provide essential tactical depth for the defense of Israel's densely populated coastal plain against enemy bombers attacking from the east, as these can be attacked by AA [antiaircraft] cannon and missile fire even before they reach the Jordan Valley. The central zone is also an ideal location for passive electronic warfare and for jammers of enemy radars.

Israel's Vulnerable Plain

The western zone extends inland from the foothills of Israel's pre-1967 border (the so-called "green line") to the 2,000 feet contour. The western slopes of the central zone and the hills of the western zone completely dominate most of the coastal plain by surveillance and fire. Some of Israel's military bases and most of its major population centers, airfields, harbors, traffic arteries, fuel depots and power stations are in line-of-sight from there. Half of Israel's population, 75 percent of its energy and 80 percent of its industry are concentrated in the area dominated by Judea and Samaria. A withdrawal to the "green line," or anywhere near it, will put Israel's airfields in this area under constant enemy surveillance. In time of war, the enemy will be able to confuse Israel's warning radar system. The airfields will be under artillery fire. Every combat aircraft on takeoff will be exposed to missile attack. Under such conditions, not only is air supremacy unattainable, but it will be impossible to utilize the Israeli air force.

Air supremacy in Israel's skies is a necessary precondition for the mobilization of Israel's reserves, which constitute most of its military strength. Without air supremacy, the reserves' safe arrival at their military depots upon call-up, their equipment there and their transfer to the fronts cannot be accomplished. Under such conditions, the coastal plain from Benyamina (south of Haifa) through Tel Aviv to Ashdod is indefensible.

Why Demilitarization Is Useless

Even those who want Israel to retreat to its pre-1967 borders agree that the evacuated areas must be demilitarized. But in case of a war initiated by the Arabs, demilitarization is useless. Local irregular forces, coordinated with the attackers, will seize all dominating positions at night. (Already in the Camp David agreements, Egypt demanded and obtained "a strong local police force" for Judea, Samaria and the Gaza Strip, which will be ideal for this purpose. It will probably consist of thousands of trained soldiers in police uniforms.) Simultaneously, commando units of Arab armies to the east of the Jordan River or the Golan Heights can be transferred by helicopter to these positions within minutes and dig in. Arab armored forces will reach these dominating positions the same night, only three to five hours later. It should be stressed that Israel needs, at the very least, 24 hours to mobilize its reserves.

In other words, demilitarization leaves Israel no effective deterrence and only increases the incentive to attack.

Owing to lack of space, we mention only one point [about terrorism]: even from a supposedly demilitarized Judea and Samaria, Katyusha rockets can be launched into the Tel Aviv area and other densely populated areas of Israel's coastal plain. There are some 15 Palestinian Arab terrorist organizations, and no Palestinian authority will be strong enough to control all of them, even if it wants to. No Israeli government can accept such a situation, and this factor alone will cause war, as it did in Lebanon.

Territory and Unconventional Warfare

From Pakistan and Iran to Iraq, Syria, Libya and Algeria, there is a race to acquire ground-to-ground missiles and develop nuclear or other unconventional weapons. The U.S. cannot prevent this. However, for as long as the existing borders and the technological gap between the Arab states and Israel are maintained, the Arab-Israel balance of deterrence is in principle much as it was between the U.S. and the USSR during the Cold War. So unconventional wars are unlikely to break out.

In unconventional war, second strike capability is the key deterrence factor. Unlike the U.S., Israel cannot maintain a fleet of nuclear submarines for this purpose. But it can maintain dozens of mobile missile launchers safe in underground tunnels hewn into rock just as Iraq did during the Gulf War.

Despite all the technology available to the U.S. during the Gulf War and three satellites on the job, the Allies failed to locate the mobile missile launchers in the Iraqi tunnels. Though the launching area was relatively small and the range of the Iraqi missiles nearly constant (about 400 miles), the U.S. failed to destroy even one of these launchers or to prevent the launching of missiles from these Iraqi sites. It could not have prevented such launchings even had it found the sites, as the [launchers] move out of the tunnels for firing and retreat back into them afterwards.

Judea and Samaria provide many ideal locations for underground tunnel missile sites, thus assuring Israel's unconventional second strike capability, whatever the nature of the unconventional Arab attack. Sites in the Galilee and the Negev [regions] are insufficient to provide an assured second strike capability. Thus, those arguing that in an age of missiles territory and topography lose their military value could not be more wrong.

After the limitations imposed by the secession of Sinai, the existing borders provide Israel with the maximum of attainable deterrence against both conventional and unconventional Arab attacks. They raise the cost of war to the Arabs to an almost prohibitive level.

Conversely, the pre-1967 borders nearly nullify Israel's deterrence, leaving it only an offensive, preemptive option. They maximize the cost of war to Israel, while sharply reducing it to the Arabs. This greatly increases the Arab incentive to attack.

Keep Present Borders

Israel cannot defend itself against an Arab offensive, regardless of whether missiles are or are not used, unless its present borders are retained. Moreover; these borders provide Israel with its only chance of executing an effective counterstrike against vital enemy objectives if attacked by missiles with conventional warheads and of executing a "second strike" after an enemy "first strike" by enemy missiles with unconventional warheads.

The observation posts, firing positions, missile sites and radar in Judea, Samaria and the Golan Heights serve, first and foremost, purposes of deterrence. But they are also essential for defense, counterattack and decision of the battle if deterrence collapses. Without them, war is much more likely. So is defeat.

The end of the Cold War intensified the arms race in the Middle East. The former Soviet republics need foreign currency badly and are selling huge quantities of modern weapons systems to the Arabs at ridiculous prices. The United States is doing the same—at higher prices. This has upset the military balance between the Arab states and Israel. . . .

The arguments produced by the Israeli Left for ceding territory are not serious and serve mainly internal political purposes. No responsible Israel government should make Israel's survival dependent on nonexistent Arab goodwill. Articles in Egypt's semiofficial *Al Ahram* openly admit that "the problem of the Arabs *today* is that they cannot fight Israel, so peace is the only way of gaining *some* of their stolen rights" (10 February 1992), and that the Arab goal in the negotiations is to give Israel frontiers that make the use of its land forces impossible (22 November 1991). . . . The Arab strategic goal [is to] push Israel back to indefensible borders. For Israel this is a matter of survival.

"A Palestinian state can be devised which is totally compatible with Israel's security."

An Independent Palestine Would Not Threaten Israel's Security

Walid Khalidi

Walid Khalidi is a Palestinian scholar and a graduate of Harvard University in Cambridge, Massachusetts. In the following viewpoint, Khalidi argues that an independent Palestine could be established that would not threaten Israel. Khalidi maintains that this new state would be demilitarized, have no military alliances, and be monitored by multinational forces to deter attacks on Israel. Khalidi contends that an independent Palestine that acquired armed forces would be no match against Israel's army and would have no incentive to attack. Khalidi is the author of *Palestine Reborn*, from which this viewpoint is excerpted.

As you read, consider the following questions:

1. According to Khalidi, how does Israel hold a logistical advantage over the West Bank and Gaza Strip?
2. Why does Khalidi believe that a Palestine controlled by radicals would be no threat to Israel?
3. Why is the author confident that Israel could defeat an Iraqi tank invasion?

I believe a Palestinian state can be devised which is totally compatible with Israel's security. The rock on which this state will be built is its weakness, not its strength. Its defence will not be in its hands, since no defence establishment it can build could possibly match Israel's crushing military preponderance. The defence of this Palestinian state will therefore be based solely on international guarantees. In a word, it would be a voluntarily demilitarized state in its own self-interest and contractually so, except for the requirements of internal security.

The demilitarized regime could be monitored by international observers, and by regular and unannounced on-site inspections. The state could commit itself à la Austria not to enter into any military alliance or arrangement with any Arab or non-Arab country. It will have no defence installations on its borders with Israel. A multinational force could be stationed in it for ten-year renewable periods: to act as trip-wire along the Jordan to deter any hostile move from the East, to police the border with Israel against infiltration into Israel, to act as a strategic reserve to help the Palestinian state against radical Palestinian elements, and to move against any Palestinian radical takeover of the state.

The treaty between the Palestinian state and Israel could be endorsed by the Arab League and guaranteed by the super powers. Violation of the treaty could be subject to sanctions and international military collective action if necessary.

The demilitarized regime could be politically reinforced by some federal/confederal arrangement with the moderate monarchical regime in Amman, whose maintenance is an essential component of the plan. The demilitarized regime could be economically reinforced by economic treaties and arrangements with Israel which could empirically be developed towards a full economic union between Israel and the Palestinian/Jordanian federation/confederation. . . .

Contexts of a Settlement

Any Palestinian regime would be subject to several constraints. . . .

There would be *the regional context of the settlement*. An overall settlement would have to remove the causes of a specifically Egyptian and Syrian irredentism. It would have to involve full withdrawal to the 1967 frontiers on the Golan and in Sinai. This need not entail the stationing of Egyptian or Syrian troops on the frontiers. With pan-Arab irredentism defused by a PLO [Palestine Liberation Organization] endorsement of the Palestinian state, and Egyptian and Syrian irredentism defused by return to the 1967 frontiers, the stage will have been set for the generation of an Arab consensus in favour of an overall settlement. Within such a framework, a collective Arab guarantee of the settlement could be made and the modalities elaborated for economic assistance to the Palestinian state. Given its non-aligned status, it is difficult to see what expectation would prompt a Palestinian regime to withdraw from such an arrangement.

Geographical Points

Let us look at *the military balance between Israel and a Palestinian state. . . .* Even if for argument's sake a Palestinian state acquired armed forces one-half or one-third those of Jordan, the balance of power between it and Israel would be crushingly in favour of the latter. The deterrence Israel would command would be eminently credible. It would be all the more enhanced by a sober assessment of the military implications of the new state's geography. Note specifically the following:

Discontinuity. The Gaza Strip and the West Bank are separated from one another by Israeli territory from twenty to thirty-five miles wide. Even with East Jerusalem restored to the Palestinian state, West Jerusalem dominates the main road linking Nablus to the north and Hebron to the south.

Encirclement. Both the Gaza Strip and the West Bank are almost completely surrounded by Israel, the former on the north and east, the latter on the north, west, south and southeast.

Accessibility of Palestinian territory. If Tel Aviv is fifteen miles from the West Bank, the West Bank is the same distance from Tel Aviv. Accessibility is not only a function of distance. It is a function of terrain, vegetation, communication routes and transport capacities, but above all it is a function of the balance of power. Visual accessibility with the naked eye is a bonus.

The Gaza Strip is five to ten miles wide, thirty miles long. Every square yard is penetrable from the Israeli side by foot within an hour, by vehicle within minutes. It has no warning time against aircraft. It is totally accessible to the naked eye from land and sea.

The West Bank is some eighty-five miles long. Its greatest width is under forty miles, its narrowest at Jerusalem is under twenty miles. No point on the West Bank falls outside a twenty-five-mile radius from the nearest point along the Israeli frontier, and most of it falls within a twenty-mile radius of the frontier. No impenetrable vegetation or inaccessible terrain prevents arrival from the Israeli frontier anywhere on the West Bank, by foot within six hours, by vehicle within one. Warning time against aircraft is to all intents and purposes nil. No dense forests cover any part of it.

Links to the outside world. The Gaza Strip has no direct land link to the outside world. If the Israelis dismantled their settlements in the Arish area on the southern frontier of the Gaza Strip, they could be replaced by a UN buffer zone. The single airport in the Strip is a stone's throw from Israel. The only harbour is small and makeshift. The figures for the Palestinian forces that might be deployed in the Strip under the formulae discussed above and their relation to the Israeli forces speak for themselves. The Israeli Navy is also available to monitor the Gaza coastline.

A Preposterous Idea

[An] argument regularly used to discredit the idea of Palestinian self-determination is that it will result in a hostile "rump state" from which Palestinians can directly continue their war against Israel. U.S. President George Bush endorsed this view. Yet Abba Eban, Israel's foreign minister during the 1967 war, has complained that Israel is often depicted in such scenarios as some kind of "demilitarized land like Iceland . . . or Costa Rica" while the PLO is likened to "Ghengis Khan . . . able to exterminate Israel," and he dismisses the idea of a Palestinian threat to Israel's existence as "preposterous."

Robert Vitalis, *The Struggle for Peace: Israelis and Palestinians*, 1992.

The West Bank has no direct access to the sea. It has one airport north of Jerusalem with limited capacity. It is within medium mortar range from the Israeli frontier. It is accessible to the naked eye to aircraft flying within Israeli airspace. The West Bank's land link to the Arab world is through Jordan. Vehicular travel to and from Jordan is along two main routes with two crossing points on the Jordan River. The routes leading to the crossing points from the Jordanian side pass through gorges and open country. As they come out of the open country on the Palestinian side, they start their climb up the mountains of Nablus and Jerusalem. Given Israeli air superiority, the terrain on both sides of the Jordan River is an ideal burial ground for armour.

As a party to the settlement, Jordan would be anxious to monitor the armed forces of the Palestinian state. Its position astride the land routes of access to the state as well as the state's only contact with the sea through Arab territory (Jordanian Aqaba) enables it to exercise effective control on vehicular traffic to the state. This could be reinforced by UN inspection and verification personnel at the two crossing points on the Jordan River, as indeed at the Jerusalem airport. The orifices of the state would thus be sealed.

The West Bank has the configuration of a bulge abutting on Israel, with its base on the Jordan River. The length of this base from north to south is forty-five miles. A road runs along the base parallel to the river from the Israeli frontier near Lake Tiberias. An army crossing the Syrian desert in the direction of the Jordanian routes of access to the Palestinian state would have to cover hundreds of miles before reaching the eastern frontiers of Jordan, themselves hundreds of miles from the Jordan River. An armoured Israeli column travelling southward from the direction of Lake Tiberias could in less than two hours sever all contact between the Palestinian state and the Arab hinterland. Israel could also draw on its five paratroop brigades and 186 helicopters (not to mention its 574 combat aircraft) to take possession in time of the two crossing points on the Jordan River.

Therefore, any PLO leadership would take the helm in a Palestinian state with few illusions about the efficacy of revolutionary armed struggle in any direct confrontation with Israel. They would be acutely aware of its costs. They would have little incentive on national or corporate grounds to incur it.

To one observer, the real security question posed by the Palestinian state is: For how long would the Israeli brigadier generals be able to keep their hands off such a delectable sitting duck? . . .

Radicals' Supposed Threat

The assumption that a Palestinian state will be radical in its policies is highly questionable. Its government is bound to be a coalition of the intifada and Diaspora leaderships. This will be a seasoned veteran leadership with no illusions about what is and what is not possible. They would be only too aware of the cost and sacrifices suffered to achieve statehood. They would have a vested interest in not embarking on or encouraging suicidal policies that would provoke renewed Israeli occupation.

But even if a radical group did seize power, the worst it could do would be very limited and containable and it would be more than likely that such a group would be ousted by Palestinian public opinion sooner rather than later.

But what is the worst a radical group could do? . . .

The radical group could decide to launch an all-out attack against Israel with the forces available to it. Given the miniscule forces the Palestinian state would have in comparison to Israel's, even if such an attack could get under way before its very early detection, it would be crushed within hours, bringing about the downfall of the group.

The radical group could initiate continuous small-scale attacks against Israel. These would activate the sanctions mechanisms of the agreement, justify Israeli retaliation and sooner rather than later arouse Palestinian public opinion against the group, forcing it to resign or desist.

The argument that the retention of the West Bank and the

Gaza Strip is needed as a security measure in the event of an Arab invasion is also highly questionable.

We are talking about a comprehensive settlement involving the PLO, with collective Arab endorsement and the neutralization of Arab irredentism. One would assume that the chances of an Arab war against Israel would be enhanced by the continued occupation and colonization by Israel of Arab land and not by the termination of this occupation.

But even in the unlikely event of a post-settlement future Egyptian or Syrian government reneging on the settlement, the presence in such a scenario of a Palestinian state along the lines we described cannot hamper Israel's ability to deal with the Syrian or Egyptian threat. Should the Palestinian government be reckless enough to have colluded with the Syrian or Egyptian governments or both, then Israel would have a clear *casus belli* [act justifying war] and the ability to gobble up the Palestinian territories in no time.

The worst-case scenario is of Iraq's serried tank divisions suddenly lumbering up the Eastern slopes of the Judaean hills. But how will they get there?

The shortest distance between Baghdad and the Israeli frontier via Rutba, Mafrak and Irbid is 580 miles—some five times the distance between the Suez Canal and Israel. The other routes via Mafrak and then Jerash or Amman are both about 680 miles each, six times the distance between the Suez Canal and Israel, or about the distance between Paris and Berlin. The terrain throughout is open, vulnerable, vegetationless desert—ideal burial ground for tanks to the side which enjoys mastery of the skies, as Israel does. This terrain can be and is kept under constant surveillance by Israel through a combination of devices: on-site intelligence at source and in transit, friendly intelligence and satellites, incessant Israeli overflights in Saudi and Jordanian airspace, the Israeli Hawkeye AWAC [Airborne Warning and Control] system, long-range drones, radar, and the Israeli satellite *Offek*.

The mass movement of tanks in such an environment cannot escape early detection, giving ample time for Israeli mobilization and aerial interception with conventional and less conventional weapons. A Palestinian state in the West Bank and the Gaza Strip would in no way hinder or diminish Israel's ability to detect, intercept or mobilize for a hypothetical Iraqi invasion. Jewish settlements in the Golan and the Palestinian Occupied Territories cannot defend Haifa and Tel Aviv in the missile, chemical and nuclear warfare of the future. A Palestinian state will not prevent Israel from reaching the high ground of the West Bank next door long before the Iraqi tanks hundreds of miles away could get there.

*"The Palestinian flag would be raised in Al Quds
and the Israeli flag would fly over Yerushalaim."*

Israel Should Share
Control of Jerusalem

Adnan Abu Odeh

Adnan Abu Odeh is the Kingdom of Jordan's ambassador to the
United Nations. In the following viewpoint, Odeh argues that
the debate over control of Jerusalem can be settled if Israel ad-
heres to UN Security Council Resolution 242 and relinquishes
the eastern Arab portion of Jerusalem that it acquired during
the 1967 Six Day War. Odeh asserts that the western and eastern portions of Jerusalem, except for the holy walled part of the
city, should be controlled by Israelis and Palestinians respectively. Since the ancient walled section is the site of shrines sacred to Christians, Jews, and Muslims, Odeh maintains that it
should remain open to all followers of these faiths, and be governed only by a multireligious council.

As you read, consider the following questions:

1. Why do Arabs and Jews defer settling the Jerusalem dispute,
   according to Odeh?
2. Why does the author believe that parts of Jerusalem outside
   the walled city cannot be considered holy?
3. According to Odeh, how do Arabs and Jews lose nothing
   under his proposal?

From "Two Capitals in an Undivided Jerusalem," by Adnan Abu Odeh. Reprinted by
permission of *Foreign Affairs*, Spring 1992. Copyright 1992 by the Council on Foreign
Relations, Inc., New York.

Between 1948, the year of Israel's establishment, and the war of 1967, when the Israeli army occupied all of mandate Palestine and other Arab territories belonging to Egypt and Syria, the Arab-Israeli conflict was viewed as being composed of three major issues: mutual recognition of the parties involved; the status of Jerusalem; and the right of repatriation or compensation for Palestinian refugees. Bipolarization was at its peak, and unfortunately there were no serious international efforts at solving the conflict. It was hoped that after the legitimate rights of the Palestinian people, including the refugees, were addressed, the Arabs would recognize the Jewish state, and peace treaties would ultimately be signed. After the 1967 war the U.N. Security Council passed resolution 242 as the basis for solving the conflict: Israel would return land it occupied in 1967 in return for peace and recognition. However, with its own interpretation of resolution 242, which I regard as self-serving, Israel's occupation was prolonged, its attitudes hardened and it introduced other factors that further complicated the conflict. Chief among these was the incessant practice of building Jewish settlements in the occupied territories, thus disrupting the cardinal formula of "land for peace" and intensifying the Palestinian national identity, which made the Palestinian people look for a solution beyond resolution 242.

What is now required is a genuine effort to avoid entanglement in details and discussion of peripheral issues. I propose that we proceed to the heart of the matter.

Address the Issue Now

The future status of Jerusalem has long been regarded as the most intractable of issues in the Arab-Israeli conflict: it is controversial, emotional and intricate. The parties to the conflict have long agreed, at least tacitly, to defer settlement of Jerusalem to a later phase in the peace process. The Arabs hold that they have a right to reclaim their lands seized in the 1967 war, East Jerusalem as well as the surrounding West Bank. The government of Israel asserts its right to Greater Jerusalem undivided, including those new areas built out beyond the city center into the West Bank after the 1967 war. The world community never acquiesced in the division of the city in 1948 or its annexation by one side in 1967.

I would like to propose for consideration that the problem of Jerusalem be addressed now, and not deferred until later. I argue, contrary to the prevailing attitudes, that with the ongoing peace negotiations this is the most propitious time to introduce constructive concepts. The approach described here builds upon a concept of Jerusalem that flows from analysis and diagnosis of the competing claims over a city that all consider holy and that addresses all the parties' declared positions.

We start from the simple fact that Jerusalem has both Arab and Jewish inhabitants. Arabs (Muslims and Christians) and Jews are equally bound to Jerusalem with the same intensity for the same reasons: religious attachment, historical attachment and political attachment.

In 1967, within weeks of the conquest of the West Bank, Israel expressed its devotion to Jerusalem by annexing the Arab part of the city that forms an integral part of the West Bank. Ever since, Israel has proclaimed that Jerusalem will remain the undivided capital of Israel and that it will never compromise on the eastern, Arab, part of the city. For their part, the Arabs and virtually all of the outside world affirm that resolution 242 applies to East Jerusalem no less than it does to the West Bank and the rest of the occupied territories. The position of the United States is that the final status of East Jerusalem, though the Security Council resolution applies, should be decided through negotiations and that Jerusalem should remain undivided.

What precisely is this Jerusalem that Israelis, Arabs and the world community are talking about? Is it the Jerusalem of 1850, of 1910, 1948, 1967 or of 1992? Like other important cities Jerusalem is a living entity that has grown over time, both through natural progress and prosperity and as a result of an increase in its population. What Israelis consider Greater Jerusalem now comprises an area about one-fifth of the occupied West Bank.

My first point, therefore, is to draw a distinction between the ancient walled city and the areas outside the walls. Is every hectare now called Jerusalem to be considered holy? Does every hectare annexed to the city, due to natural growth, thus become holy?

The Holiness of Jerusalem

In its essence the holiness of Jerusalem is an attribute of the holy places themselves. As a conceptual matter it is reassuring to note that the main holy places of three religions are clearly marked, distinct and known: the Church of the Holy Sepulcher for Christians, the Wailing Wall for Jews, and the Dome of the Rock and Al Aqsa Mosque for Muslims. All three shrines are located within the ancient walled city. Around these shrines have grown up over the years quarters inhabited by the followers of each religion, all believers in one God. Thus within the walled city we have the Christian (and Armenian) Quarter, the Jewish Quarter and the Muslim Quarter. Each quarter contains buildings inhabited and used by the followers of each religion, and each quarter has cultural characteristics separate and distinct from the others.

Over time a shade and degree of holiness has been extended to these quarters of the walled city surrounding the shrines themselves. Beyond that, however, it is stretching the point to call "holy" every building, every neighborhood and every street corner that has been built up around the walled city, extending out many kilometers in some directions. When Jerusalem is called a holy city, this can only mean the walled city where the holy places are located and their immediate surroundings inhabited for centuries by believers.

Source: Foundation for Middle East Peace.

It can be argued that the holiness of the walled city is God-given, for the existence of the houses of God associated with the three monotheistic religions. We must distinguish between the God-given holy areas and those added to the city in response to population growth and the decisions of successive government acts.

For example, in 1933 the British High Commissioner expanded the city limits; this did not expand the areas of God-given holiness. The same holds true for other extensions of the city limits by the municipality of Arab Jerusalem in 1955 and by Israel in 1980. It is hard to find either religious or historical justification for a refusal to compromise on the areas of Arab Jerusalem that lie outside the walled old city but still within present municipal boundaries.

Direct negotiations between Israel and the Arab side began on the basis of U.N. Security Council resolution 242, which declares inadmissible the acquisition of territory by war. I propose to maintain a distinction between the areas that were made holy by God and those incorporated into Jerusalem by man. The essential dispute about Jerusalem concerns not the modern secular city—restaurants, nightclubs and apartment blocks, the King David and Intercontinental hotels—but rather the ancient walled city.

Three Components

It is fortunate for the solution of the problem of Jerusalem, at least conceptually, that the city has three names: Al Quds in Arabic, Yerushalaim in Hebrew, and Jerusalem as it is known to the rest of the world. Here is the first component of my conceptual framework.

The walled city, the true and holy Jerusalem, would belong to no single nation or religion. Rather, it would belong to the whole world and to the three religions: Muslim, Christian and Jewish. Thus no state would have political sovereignty over it, so that Jerusalem would remain a spiritual basin, as it was originally founded and universally conceived.

My second component concerns the urban areas that stretch beyond the ancient walls to the east, northeast and southeast, the Arab part of the city. These would be called Al Quds, the name used by Arabs and Muslims.

The third component concerns the urban areas that stretch beyond the walls to the west, northwest and southwest. These would be called Yerushalaim, the name used by Jews.

The Palestinian flag would be raised in Al Quds and the Israeli flag would fly over Yerushalaim. Over the walled city of Jerusalem, however, no flags would fly, for the sacred shrines would be the symbol of the city's God-given holiness and spiritual significance to all believers in one God, belonging not to this state or that.

The holy walled city of Jerusalem would be open to all; Muslims, Christians and Jews must not be separated from their holy shrines, from which they all derive their cultural and religious identities. It would be governed by a council representing the highest Muslim, Christian and Jewish religious authorities. Each authority would be responsible for running and maintaining the holy sites of its faith and participating on equal footing in the administration of "Jerusalem."

As far as political identity is concerned, the Arabs would be Palestinian nationals and vote for their national institutions. The Jews would be Israelis and vote, as now, in their national elections. Administrative details of the spiritual city of Jerusalem would be left to creative minds in negotiations. As for the Jewish settlements in Al Quds, they would be subject to the same solution reached for the other settlements in the occupied territories.

Arabs and Jews Lose Nothing

In the Arab mind (Muslims and Christians alike), Al Quds would extend as far as their own holy sites in the walled city. Yerushalaim, to the Jews, would stretch as far as their holy sites inside the old city. In other words the Dome of the Rock, Al Aqsa Mosque and the Holy Sepulcher, both the Muslim and Christian surrounding quarters within the walled city and the Arab community at large outside the walls would form one uninterrupted entity, linked geographically and demographically. On the other hand the Wailing Wall, the Jewish Quarter surrounding it and the Israeli community at large outside the walls, linked geographically and demographically, would likewise form one uninterrupted entity. Thus Jews and Arabs (Muslims and Christians) alike would not lose the city so holy to them; the Arabs would not lose Al Quds, the Jews would keep Yerushalaim as the undivided capital of Israel and the world would be assured that Jerusalem was not being assimilated into either.

I offer this proposal to refute the view that the problem of Jerusalem is too complex to be addressed. In this framework the issue of Jerusalem would be resolved not only as a symbol of peace but also as an embodiment of its essence—assuming, of course, that the parties negotiate in good faith in a quest for a balanced, just and desirable peace based on U.N. Security Council resolution 242.

"Jerusalem will remain a city with a clear Jewish majority and under Israeli sovereignty forever."

Israel Should Control All of Jerusalem

Ehud Olmert and Bernard I. Lindner

Ehud Olmert, a member of Israel's conservative Likud party, was elected mayor of Jerusalem in November 1993. In Part I of the following viewpoint, Olmert argues that control of Jerusalem is not a negotiable issue between Arabs and Jews; Jews will never relinquish any part of it. Olmert contends that in contrast to Muslims, Jews have guaranteed the rights of all worshipers in Jerusalem. In Part II, Bernard I. Lindner describes the Jews' founding and settlement of Jerusalem and its historical significance to them, and argues that the city is the exclusive center of Judaism. Lindner contends that in the past, Muslims violently disrupted Jewish worship in Jerusalem and that only Jews are capable of keeping the sacred sites open to all. Lindner is a technology law and contract law attorney in Los Angeles.

As you read, consider the following questions:

1. How did Muslims desecrate Jewish shrines in Jerusalem, according to Olmert?
2. According to Lindner, how has control of Jerusalem shifted between Arabs and Jews?
3. Why does Lindner believe that Muslims have no claim to Jerusalem as a holy city?

"Jerusalem Is Not Negotiable—It Will Be Israel's Forever" by Ehud Olmert, *Los Angeles Times*, October 4, 1993. "Jerusalem: The Eternal Jewish City" by Bernard I. Lindner was written expressly for inclusion in the present volume.

I

Twenty-five minutes. That's all it takes to go from Jerusalem to Jericho.

When Israeli Foreign Minister Shimon Peres sat down with Secretary of State Warren Christopher in 1993, it was to explain a new policy dubbed "Gaza-Jericho first," in which Israel is to grant some Palestinian autonomy in those two areas.

For Americans accustomed to vast distances, it should come as a frightening realization that Yasser Arafat, a man who has long wielded terrorism against Israel and the United States, is considering moving into a house in Jericho—25 minutes away from our Parliament.

The incorrect premise we're hearing these days is that if Gaza and Jericho are dealt with first, everything else will fall or be pushed into place until the sticky issue of Jerusalem is reached—last. The flaw is the misperception that the fate of Jerusalem is somehow negotiable. Ask any schoolchild in Israel, and the answer will be firm, clear and simple: Jerusalem will be the united capital of the state of Israel forever, for as long as the Star of David flutters over our hard-won sovereign state—and that should be a pretty good spell.

Christopher has perhaps judiciously advised the parties to the peace talks to save Jerusalem for last. That is also the position of the Yitzhak Rabin government. The State Department and other friends and outsiders might believe that this tactic makes sense as a negotiating stratagem.

I speak for most Israelis—well over 90%, according to polls—when I say that it ultimately does not matter. We can either start with Jerusalem or conclude with it. The result will be the same or there will be no result: Jerusalem will be ours.

Horrible Arab Rule

For 19 horrid years, Jordanians and Palestinians controlled part of our capital city, the so-called Old City and environs of East Jerusalem. From the outset in 1948, every Jew who survived the onslaught was summarily expelled. Their property was seized. The many historic synagogues of the walled enclave were gutted, trashed, some turned into makeshift barns. The most famous Jewish cemetery in the world, on the Mount of Olives, was randomly plowed under and built over. The ghastly photos of gravestones turned into latrines for occupying Jordanian troops are still seared irrevocably in our consciousness. East Jerusalem became our *Judenrein* [German for "Jewish excluded"].

Other non-Muslims fared little better. Christian children were compelled to spend long hours every day learning about the Islamic religion, and the Christian populace of the Jordanian-controlled sector was decimated by emigration.

Jordanian snipers wantonly fired from the walls into civilian West Jerusalem. Bullet holes still adorn buildings in what was then no-man's-land, scant yards away from City Hall, silent testimony to the Arab concept of rule in the holy city.

In stark contrast to places bearing the ignominious names of Belfast, Beirut and Sarajevo, Jerusalem for 26 years [since the 1967 Six Day War] has been a paradigm of freedom and guaranteed rights for all. Tourists roam everywhere, greenery abounds, new roads are helping to ease the traffic congestion and Jews and Arabs coexist, albeit separately. It's the best that can be hoped for. Much needs to be done still, but the foundation is firmly in place.

Jerusalem: First in Jewish History

Jerusalem will remain the capital of Israel, undivided. . . . Jerusalem should be open to all believers. There is no contradiction between having Jerusalem united politically as the capital of Israel and open religiously to every person that has God in his heart. Jerusalem is first in our heart, first in our history, first in our land. It was never an Arab capital and the Jewish people have never had any capital but Jerusalem. And when the Muslims are praying, they are bowing to Mecca, and when the Jews are praying, they are bowing to Jerusalem.

Shimon Peres, *The MacNeil/Lehrer News Hour*, October 8, 1993.

During this time, the facts on the ground have been changed, largely through the smart planning and hard work of the Likud-led government that guided Israel from 1977 until 1992. Today, Jerusalem is a city with an unshakable Jewish majority. The new neighborhoods of Gilo, Ramot and others now claim no less than 160,000 Jewish residents among a total of nearly 400,000 Jews in the capital. Palestinian Arabs in these areas account for about 155,000. Yet another 40,000 Jews live in surrounding suburbs, all within 15 minutes or so by car. Most of these people have sunk their roots in the past 15 years.

The negotiators in Washington may discuss Jerusalem now or discuss it later. But they dare not suggest that we return to the living hell that preceded 1967. There remains perhaps but one overwhelming consensus in Israeli politics today, and that is an unequivocal truth that cannot be chipped away at or watered down by semantics: Jerusalem will remain a city with a clear Jewish majority and under Israeli sovereignty forever.

Anyone who will not or cannot understand this bedrock reality is doomed to fail in facilitating peace in the Middle East.

II

Almost exactly three thousand years ago, David, king of Israel, moved his capital from the city of Hebron in Judea to Jerusalem, which is on the border between the Land of Judea and the Land of Benjamin. Juda and Benjamin were two of the thirteen tribes of Israel. The total lands included the east and west side of the Jordan River, including the lands of Syria up to the river Euphrates and the Red Sea in the south.

Jerusalem's holiness originates from being chosen by David through divine inspiration to be the resting place of the Golden Holy Arc with the stone tablets containing the Ten Divine verbal Statements made by G-d [spelling reflects author's religious beliefs] to the Jewish people (also known as the ten commandments) at Mount Sinai. The grounds were further sanctified by the son of David, King Solomon, when he built the First Temple of Jerusalem. The ceremonies involved millions of Jews from all the tribes and is amply described in Kings I of the Hebrew Bible available in English translation. Jerusalem and the surrounding lands were ruled by continuous filial descendants of King David for over four hundred years until, in the year 587 B.C.E. [Before Common Era, or B.C.], the city and Temple were destroyed in a fiercely aggressive war by the armies of the empire of Babylonia. The inhabitants of Jerusalem were then exiled to Babylon.

Return to Jerusalem

When Koresh [Cyrus], emperor of Persia, conquered Babylonia he gave permission to the Jews to return to Jerusalem and rebuild the Temple.

The Second Temple of Jerusalem lasted through the lifetimes of the Persian and Greek Empires. However, a Jewish alliance with the Roman Empire, which started about the year 150 B.C.E., eventually brought about the destruction of Jerusalem in the year C.E. [A.D.] 70. It turned out to be a misunderstanding. While Israel wanted an alliance among friends, Rome insisted on domination.

Even after the year 70, and the Bar Kochba rebellion of C.E. 135 [that liberated Jerusalem for three years], the population in the country remained essentially Jewish until after the year 600 when the Moslems conquered the country. In spite of restrictions the country of Judea and Jerusalem were never without Jews. Jerusalem never ceased to be for Jews the unique and exclusive center of their personal and religious aspirations.

Jews have constituted a major part of the city's population since the 15th century, and from the middle of the 1850s onward Jerusalem has had a substantial Jewish majority.

The very identity of Jews stems from their coming from Judea, and even the Koran mentions several passages referring to G-d's commanding the Sons of Israel to enter the land and keep it. Ironically, if the Jews were to oblige the Arabs and leave the land at the Arabs' request, the Arabs could then fault the Jews for disobeying G-d's words. The Koran does not mention Jerusalem by name and makes Mecca and Medina the religious centers of Islam. None but the Jews cried (and continue still) over Jerusalem's destruction, and prayed and continue to pray every day for its rebuilding.

The Jews' Exclusive Capital

The Arabs controlled the land of Israel from the year 600 until the Crusades of the 11th century. After the Crusaders were removed from the land, the Mamelukes took over until the land was eventually taken over by the Turkish Empire, which owned it until the British conquered Palestine in 1917. It is to be kept in mind that during the past three thousand years none but the Jews made Judea their only and exclusive homeland and Jerusalem their exclusive capital.

Arabs, Mamelukes, Turks, Christians and others conquered and kept the land as part of some empire or foreign interest. Jerusalem was kept small and was usually governed from afar. Far from being a capital to Arabs, Jerusalem was kept as a neglected town, one of many governed from Damascus, Baghdad or Amman.

The only possibly legitimate interest that Moslems and Christians have for Jerusalem is access to their designated holy places. Israel is most qualified to provide access to all peoples because of its history of allowing access. In dedicating the First Temple, King Solomon stated to the whole public and to G-d (Kings I 8:41) "To the stranger who is not of your people Israel who comes from a far land for the sake of your name . . . and he will come to pray in this House, You should listen to him from your Heavenly abode, and you should do as the stranger calls upon you." The Jewish people have kept this faith as law during the two temples and to this very day. The Arabs and Islam are the most unqualified to guarantee access to holy places. For hundreds of years Jews have been either completely prohibited or severely restricted in visiting their holy places. Visits to the Western Wall remnant of the Temple Mount were often accompanied by riots, killings and stone throwing. Look at a picture of the Western Wall (some call it the Wailing Wall) and you will see that on top of it are many rows of small bricks to prevent stone-throwing, placed there by British Count Moses Montefiore by special permission of the Turkish Empire during the middle of the 19th century, before political Zionism was ever even thought of. The Arab riots and killings during the British occupation to prevent Jewish religious services at the Western Wall; the complete prohibition of Jewish visits to the Wall during the 1948-67 Jordanian occupation (in spite of an agreement to the contrary); the desecration of all synagogues in the Old City; and the use of tombstones to build military latrines make any further discussion on this matter superfluous. Arabs walk safely in Jewish cities. Jews do not dare to visit Arab cities for fear of being killed. Saudi Arabia and Jordan are *Judenrein*, and the PLO [Palestine Liberation Organization] is attempting to make East Jerusalem and all of Judea the same. Is racial discrimination so virtuous that we should help them achieve such goals?

Under Jewish Control

The world will be better off if the Jews control Jerusalem, since the Jews are ruled traditionally by a combination of democracy tempered and improved upon by the time-verified scholarly tradition of live and let live. The Arabs have Mecca and Medina (which was a Jewish city before Mohammed executed the Jews and appropriated their property; see the Koran), and twenty other capitals. The Christians have Rome as their holy city. Should the Arabs also take Jerusalem from the Jews? Or perhaps should the Arabs move their holy places to Baghdad? The story (Samuel II 12:1-4) told by the Prophet Natan to King David explains it a little more: "There were two people in one town; one was rich, the other very poor. The poor man had a little sheep which he bought and raised together with his children. It would eat from his bread, drink from his cup, sleep on his side, and be like his daughter. There arrived a Guest to the Rich man who had pity to give his Guest from his sheep and cattle, so he took the little sheep from the Poor man, and prepared it for the man who came to him." King David thought the Rich man deserved capital punishment. If Israel, the Poor man in this instance, gives Jerusalem to the Arabs, it too would suffer capital punishment.

> *"Under international law, Israel is required to restore the Golan Heights . . . to their original sovereignty. "*

Israel Must Return the Golan Heights to Syria

Laura Drake

In 1981, Israel formally annexed the Golan Heights region, won from Syria during the Six Day War of 1967. In the following viewpoint, Laura Drake argues that the Golan Heights rightfully belongs to Syria and that the United Nations (UN) recognizes this. Drake maintains that for nearly two decades Israel illegally confiscated land on the Golan Heights and ultimately provoked Syria into war. Drake concludes that Israel must abide by international law and return the Golan Heights to Syria. Drake is director of research at the Council for the National Interest, a Middle East policy organization in Washington, D.C.

As you read, consider the following questions:

1. How has Israel confiscated Syrian land, according to Drake?
2. In Drake's opinion, why was Egypt compelled to attack Israel in 1967?
3. Why does the author believe that Israel is more inclined to aggression than Syria?

"The Golan Belongs to Syria" by Laura Drake. This article first appeared in the September 11, 1992, issue of *Middle East International*, 21 Collingham Road, London SW5, and is reprinted with permission.

Syria has repeatedly affirmed its adherence to UN Security Council Resolutions 242 and 338 [calling for withdrawal of Israeli forces from occupied territories] and its support for the exchange of land for peace on all Arab fronts as part of a comprehensive settlement to the Arab-Israeli conflict. If Syria is to be a party to such a settlement, then this must of necessity include the Golan Heights, seized by Israel in the 1967 war and effectively annexed in 1981, a move which the UN Security Council has declared to be "null and void and without international legal effect" (Resolution 497, 1981).

Israel refuses to seriously discuss the land component of the land-for-peace formula with respect to Syria. The Knesset [Israel's parliament] affirmed this rejection through its passage of a resolution declaring that the Golan should be non-negotiable. There are currently 12,000 Israeli settlers living in the Golan and their numbers have been increasing at an accelerated pace, due to the zeal of the [former] Likud government's housing minister, Ariel Sharon. Unrestrained and actually encouraged by [then Prime Minister] Yitzhak Shamir, Sharon went so far as to establish a new Israeli settlement, Kela, in the Golan the very day after the Madrid [peace] conference, as if to ridicule the entire peace process.

Israel's arguments in defence of its continued occupation of the Golan are largely based on the following assumptions:

1. Israeli farmers in the Hula valley were the victims of constant "unprovoked" Syrian shelling from the Golan Heights prior to the 1967 war;

2. Israel seized the Golan in a "defensive" war;

3. the extra territory is essential to Israeli security.

Border Encroachments

The major point of contention along the Syrian-Israeli border which obtained before the 1967 war arose from Israel's illegal assertion of sovereignty over the entirety of the demilitarised zone created as a result of the 1949 armistice. According to the UN Truce Supervision Organisation (UNTSO) and the chairman of the Mixed Armistice Commission (MAC), which were responsible for investigating and reporting on border incidents, many such resulted from the "progressive extension of Israeli cultivation towards the east" in the demilitarised zone. This involved repeated encroachments onto disputed and Arab-owned lands in violation of the rules of the armistice agreement.

Often backed by armed Israeli units illegally brought into the zone, Israeli settlers repeatedly moved their tractors onto Arab-owned lands which they began to cultivate, despite warnings by the MAC chairman that their actions constituted a violation of the armistice and would, in addition, provoke a strong Arab reaction. Indeed, the Arabs sitting atop the Golan, now bitter refugees who could see their confiscated lands below being ploughed by intruders in plain view, vented their anger and frustration by firing at the tractors. Israel consistently interfered with the movements of the UN observers whose job it was to prevent Israeli settlers from forcibly encroaching on Arab lands.

Beginning in 1951 armed Israeli units entered a number of Arab villages in the zone, destroyed Arab houses and other civilian property and forced hundreds of residents to flee. Israel initially ignored UNTSO protests and refused to allow the return of the residents, but after Security Council Resolution 93 was passed calling on it to do so, it finally relented, although it refused to pay the residents the stipulated compensation for the property it destroyed.

Exercising Complete Control

Other provocations by Israel included illegally moving heavy equipment into the zone and carrying out its various irrigation and other projects on Arab-owned lands without consulting or even giving proper warning to the UN observers or the Arab inhabitants who would be affected. In addition, Israel triggered incidents by repeatedly using "armoured landing craft with machine guns and cannons [posing as] police boats" on Lake Tiberias, in order to illegally prohibit Syrian access to the lake.

According to Lieutenant-General E.L. Burns, a former UNTSO chief of staff: "The Israelis claimed sovereignty over the . . . zone. They then proceeded, as opportunity offered, to encroach on the specific restrictions, and so eventually to free themselves, on various pretexts, from all of them. . . . The Israelis in fact exercised almost complete control over the major portion of the . . . zone through their frontier police. . . . This was directly contrary to Article V of the General Armistice Agreement".

On occasion, the Israeli army launched full-scale attacks on villages and military positions on Syrian territory beyond the demilitarised zone. One such raid on 11 December 1955 left 56 Syrians dead, 7 wounded and 32 missing. UNTSO called Israel's action completely "unjustified", and shortly thereafter the Security Council passed Resolution 111, condemning Israel's "flagrant violation" of its obligations under the armistice regime.

Another assault of a similar nature mounted by Israeli forces on 16-17 March 1962 against Syrian territory resulted in an exchange of fire that left casualties on both sides. The UNTSO chief of staff deplored Israel's action as a violation of the armistice, and on 9 April, the Security Council unanimously passed Resolution 171, which strongly condemned Israel.

Israel's supporters have for 25 years systematically repeated that the Arabs started the 1967 Arab-Israeli war. This piece of flagrant disinformation is intended to legitimise Israel's contin-ued occupation of Arab territory, including the Golan. Israel claims the right to keep the territory it captured as a result of that "defensive" war, so that "the Arabs will not be able to use those territories as a base to attack Israel again." The problem with this argument is that the Israelis themselves started the 1967 war, not with a "preemptive strike" as their apologists will say if pressed on the subject, but with designs on Arab land and resources, just as in 1956, when Israel invaded the Egyptian Sinai, and in 1982, when it invaded Lebanon.

Worthless Territory

In a process of "give and take" it is clear that the only transaction possible between [Israel and Syria] is a return of the Golan Heights to Syrian sovereignty in exchange for a contractual peace and reliable security arrangements. . . . All the talk today about the security need for holding on to a worthless strip of territory in the Golan Heights, as if our very lives depended on it, distorts reality and should be stopped.

Matti Peled, *New Outlook*, November/December 1992.

Starting in 1966, the Israelis escalated their campaign of trying to provoke Syria into war by constantly edging beyond their own borders with their bulldozers, trying to cultivate land in-side Syrian territory. Fearing Israeli-style expansionism—the "creation of facts on the ground"—Syria responded with light fire against the Israeli bulldozers whenever they veered over the border. Israel then used the cumulative effect of all such inci-dents as a pretext for starting a war.

The Egypt-Syria Treaty

The later pre-1967 war developments included Egypt as well as Syria, for the simple reason that Egypt had signed a treaty of mutual defence with Syria, obligating it to act should Syria be attacked by Israel. Therefore, when on 7 April Israel launched a major attack on Syrian border villages using tanks, artillery and warplanes and a senior military official threatened that Israel would occupy Damascus and overthrow the government, Egypt then came under intense Arab pressure to do something to help its besieged ally. On 14 May the Syrians publicised the Israeli declaration and vowed to invoke the defence agreement with Egypt if Israel attacked again. In order to prove that he was seri-ous about his promise to protect Syria, President Gamal Abdel Nasser asked the UN to redeploy its observation forces to new positions, so that Egypt would be prepared to respond quickly should Syria be attacked. Unfortunately [then UN Secretary General] U Thant insisted that the UNEF [United Nations Emergency Force] forces would have to stay positioned exactly as they were or withdraw completely. Nor would Israel accept any UNEF contingents on its own territory, claiming this would somehow violate its sovereignty (although the UN presence on Arab soil does not seem to violate Arab sovereignty). Under the circumstances, Nasser was left with no choice but to ask for UNEF's departure. At the same time, he was desperately proclaiming to U Thant and other diplomats that the Arabs were the last people who wanted war.

It was in this atmosphere that Egypt reinstated the blockade of the Straits of Tiran which had existed before the 1956 war. Some of Israel's supporters argue that this constituted an act of aggression, but they are in error for two reasons:

1. the Egyptians do not consider the Straits to be international waters but rather a part of Egyptian territorial water;

2. under international law, belligerent countries should not profit from their aggression, yet Israel was profiting because the original prohibition on Israeli shipping in this area was ended only by Israel's unprovoked invasion of the Egyptian Sinai in 1956.

On 5 June 1967 Israel started the third Arab-Israeli war. Four days later, the Israeli army invaded Syria and subjected it to a fierce aerial attack. This action had to be postponed by one day because of the existence of the American communications ship USS *Liberty* off the Mediterranean coast. According to the *Washington Post*, Israeli warplanes attacked and destroyed the American ship "because it would have picked up every word of communication between IDF [Israeli Defense Force] headquarters and Israeli units preparing to invade Syria that very day—8 June. With the *Liberty* barely afloat, its crew dead (34) and wounded (171) and its electronic spying silenced after the aerial attack, Israel invaded Syria one day later, 9 June."

No Syrian Threat

If anyone is insecure militarily, it is Syria, not Israel. Apologists for Israel have been able to turn reality on its head by claiming that Syria currently presents a military threat to Israel, which would be increased to intolerable levels if the Golan were returned. Only where Israel is concerned could such an absurd construction be elevated to the level of reasonable discourse and accepted as fact.

The Syrian strategic situation is dubious, if not catastrophic. The economy is struggling and its only superpower supporter, the USSR, its main source of aid, is gone. Unlike the Israelis, the Syrians do not have the capacity to manufacture advanced weaponry or the means to import the quantity and quality of arms necessary to defend themselves, to say nothing of initiating an attack. Nor do they receive upwards of $4 billion in military and economic aid each year from a foreign power, including all the latest state-of-the-art technology, as Israel does from the U.S. And according to Seymour Hersh's book, *The Samson Option*, Israel now has a nuclear arsenal consisting of at least 300 warheads as well as the delivery system necessary to wipe most Arab capitals off the face of the earth in less than ten minutes. Syria does not have any nuclear weapons; it does not even have an active nuclear weapons programme. In short, the Syrians hardly have the military strength necessary to deter an Israeli offensive or even to fight a serious defensive war should Israel attack, to say nothing of comprising a strategic threat to Israel's existence. This strategic inequality was made apparent most recently during the Israeli invasion of Lebanon on 6 June 1982, when the Israeli army deliberately engaged Syrian regular units in the Beqaa Valley. By 10 June, the Syrian forces had been routed, with most of their warplanes shot down and their entire anti-aircraft system in Lebanon destroyed.

Beating War Drums

Ever since the end of the Gulf crisis, Israel has been consistently beating the war drums, turning its attention from Iraq to Syria, focussing on the so-called "Syrian threat" and comparing the Syrian president to his Iraqi counterpart, Saddam Hussein. The Israeli press is full of references to "the next war" or "the coming war" with Syria in inevitable terms. They predicted a Syrian-Israeli war on the Golan front in 1993 if the peace negotiations had failed. These voices, which are growing louder and louder, are enough to make any Syrian nervous, because on the Golan front Damascus is only 22 miles away from the nearest Israeli occupation outpost, and there are no longer any natural barriers to protect the Syrian capital.

The Concept of Limits

Israel claims it needs to keep the Golan as a "strategic buffer" against the "Syrian threat", but it is apparent that even Israel itself does not believe in the existence of such a threat. This is evidenced by its routine placement of civilian settlements on the edge of its new frontier with Syria, at the far end of the so-called "military buffer" which is the Golan, leaving them unprotected in the event of the "Syrian offensive" which Israel is obviously confident cannot possibly take place, given its own military superiority. On the contrary, Syria has every right to worry that Israel will soon seek a buffer for its buffer, in order to protect those civilians, and so on.

It is essential if peace is to prevail in the region that Israel be made to understand the concept of limits. It cannot be allowed to expand every 10 or 20 years at Arab expense with no adverse consequences. Under international law, Israel is required to restore the Golan Heights, as well as the other occupied Arab territories, to their original sovereignty.

"The Golan Heights must remain permanently under Israeli sovereignty."

Israel Must Retain the Golan Heights

Eliav Shochetman

Israel has a historical and legal right to the Golan Heights, Eliav Shochetman argues in the following viewpoint. Shochetman maintains that the Bible and other religious writings define Jews' connection to the Golan, and although Jews have often been cut off from it, their ties to the region never weakened. Shochetman also contends that the creation of the state of Israel did not permanently fix the nation's borders and that Israel is entitled to demand borders that reflect its vital interests. Shochetman is a law professor and head of the Faculty of Law of the Institute for Research in Jewish Law at the Hebrew University in Jerusalem.

As you read, consider the following questions:

1. What gives Israel a legal right to the Golan Heights, according to Shochetman?
2. Why does Shochetman believe that Israel has a moral right to the Golan Heights?
3. Why would cession of the Golan lead to Arab demands for further concessions, in the author's opinion?

From "Israel's Right to the Golan Heights" by Eliav Shochetman, *Midstream*, August/ September 1993. Reprinted by permission of the Theodor Herzl Foundation, New York.

The legal status of Israel is based on the Golan Heights Law, 1981, which was passed by an absolute majority of the Members of the Knesset [Israel's parliament]. This law imposed Israeli law, jurisdiction and administration in the Golan Heights, and constituted an expression of a wide national consensus concerning the historic connection of the Jewish people with this region.

This historic connection stems from the links of thousands of years between the Jewish people and the Land of Israel (Eretz Israel), the borders of which were defined in the Bible. The Golan region fell to the portion of the half tribe of Menasseh. During the Hasmonean State the Golan Heights was reconquered by the Maccabees and remained part of Jewish Galilee until the Arab conquest of 637 CE [Common Era, or A.D.]. Jewish life thrived there over other extended periods of time.

The conception whereby the Golan Heights are an inalienable part of historic Eretz Israel is evident in the writings of the Jewish sages throughout the generations, who dealt with the question of the halachic [legal] status of the Golan in the practical context of the performance of the commandments connected with the Land, and of the commandment to settle Eretz Israel.

Zionist Claims

The historic connection served as the basis for the claims of the leaders of the Zionist Movement regarding the question of determining the northern borders of Eretz Israel when the question was discussed in negotiations between Britain and France after their conquest of the region from the Turks in World War I. These claims, relating to the Golan Heights and much more, find expression in a memorandum and map showing the borders of the Land of Israel, submitted by the Zionist delegation in 1919 to the Paris Peace Conference convened after the war. The claims and the basic concepts underlying this document continued to guide the leaders of the Zionist Movement in their later struggles and also served as the basis for the policies of the governments of Israel after the Six-Day War. Of particular note is the concept which attributes utmost importance to control by Israel of the sources of water, which are found in the region of the Golan Heights. . . .

Nonbinding Resolutions

The resolutions of the League of Nations regarding the northern borders of Eretz Israel, which totally ignored the historical links of the Jewish people with the Golan region, despite the international recognition that the same organization had accorded these links a few years before, need not bind the sovereign State of Israel as the entity responsible for the realization of the national rights of the Jewish people in its land.

Neither did the leaders of the Zionist Movement view the resolutions concerning Palestine that had been passed in opposition to the opinion of the representatives of the Jewish people as binding the Jewish people. David Ben-Gurion, for example, considered the Jordan River as a temporary border only, and said that "no just solution is possible if it does not consider the entire territory of the Mandate and does not consider all the possibilities held by the Land, both west and east of the Jordan, as well as south."

According to the experts, Syria did not recognize the international border between itself and Israel; consequently, those borders which were approved by the League of Nations do not bind Israel, and Israel is entitled to demand borders which reflect its vital interests.

Whatever the stand international law takes on the question of the borders between Israel and Syria, one thing is clear: in the case of a clash between the laws of the state and the rules of international law, the laws of the State of Israel—and in this case, the Golan Heights Law—shall prevail.

An Open Question of Borders

Historical circumstances such as persecutions, decrees, etc., dictated that the Jewish people be cut off from the Golan and other parts of Eretz Israel for an extended period. Jewish settlement disappeared from Jerusalem, too, for long periods, but the ties of the Jewish people to this city, like their ties to Eretz Israel as a whole, including the Golan, never weakened. Not all parts of Eretz Israel were liberated in the War of Independence, and Israeli sovereignty was imposed only upon those territories actually liberated. At the time of the establishment of the state, its future borders were not clear (in view of the objection of the Arab nations to a Jewish state, and their instigation of a war against it). The question of the borders of the state thus remained open, on the assumption that "if a state has to be declared by force, then by force the future borders of the state will be fixed," as said by David Ben-Gurion. Each of the four armistice agreements concluded in 1949 with Lebanon, Syria, Jordan and Egypt had a clause stating that the borders were not final.

After the Six-Day War was forced upon Israel in 1967, Israel did not impose sovereignty upon all parts of Eretz Israel taken in this war, but subsequently enacted legislation which constituted annexation of only two areas:

East Jerusalem (immediately following the Six-Day War) and the Golan Heights, thus completing a process which had not been completed in the War of Independence, and justifying the approach of David Ben-Gurion, who objected to the inclusion of the subject of borders in the Declaration of Independence on the grounds that "the matter should be left open for further developments."

What is the legal significance of this legislation relating to Jerusalem and the Golan Heights? Does the Golan Heights Law

"Keep your eye on the birdy, Yitzhak, and kindly move one small step backwards."

Lurie/Cartoonews, Inc., © 1992. Reprinted with permission.

constitute imposition of Israeli sovereignty on the Golan Heights? The answer is yes. Article 1 of the Golan Heights Law states: "The Law, jurisdiction and administration of the state will apply in the territory of the Golan Heights." The law does not mention the word "sovereignty," but there is no doubt that its legal and practical import is the imposition of sovereignty.

Golan Annexation

This conclusion emerges from the statements of the Members of the Knesset in the debates preceding passage of the law, including then Prime Minister Menahem Begin, who brought the law to a vote 14 December 1981, and also from the case law of the Supreme Court of Israel. According to the Supreme Court, the significance of the legislation applying Israeli law and administration in Jerusalem is the imposition on the city of state sovereignty. The formulation of the Golan Heights Law is similar to the formulation of the legislation regarding the annexation of East Jerusalem, and its import is therefore the application of Israeli sovereignty also to this region.

The argument that the Golan Heights Law did not actually *annex* the Golan Heights has already been raised in the Supreme Court, but dismissed unanimously:

> The language of the Law as well as its legislative purpose lead to the conclusion, that wherever the word "Israel," or another expression denoting the state, appears in Israeli legislation, the Golan Heights are included.

The approach according to which Israeli sovereignty applies in the Golan Heights is also accepted by jurists such as Professor Amnon Rubinstein, now a government minister, who in his book *The Constitutional Law of the State of Israel* writes: "This law annexed the Golan Heights to the state of Israel."

Whoever doubts the moral right of Israel to sovereignty in the Golan Heights in fact negates the basis of the moral right of Israel to sovereignty in any other part of the historic Land of Israel at present ruled by Israel. The Golan Heights, as an inalienable part of Israel, does not differ in this respect from any other part of the sovereign State of Israel, and a decision concerning the ceding of territory in the Golan Heights to Syria is the same as a decision to hand over part of the Galilee.

Israel's Moral Right

Is the government of Israel entitled to decide to cede any territory in the Golan Heights to a foreign state? This question must be examined on two levels: the level of moral authority, in view of the historic ties, and that which is legal, with regard to the law of the state of Israel. The moral authority for the imposition of Israeli sovereignty in territories of Eretz Israel lies in the natural and historic right of the Jewish people to its land. Concerning the rights of the Jewish people to the Western Wall, the then President of the Supreme Court J. Agranat once said:

> The rights of the Jewish people to the Western Wall are natural and historic rights, which prevail over every law and which no law can negate or diminish.

Does this mean that the Knesset is powerless to enact a law negating or diminishing the rights of the Jews to the Western Wall? Clearly, the Knesset has the formal power to enact any law, including a law preventing Jews from approaching the Western Wall. Justice Agranat meant that it is inconceivable that such a law could invalidate the natural and historic rights of the Jewish people in dealing with the Western Wall.

From the perspective of the historic rights of the Jewish people in its land, there is no difference between certain areas of Eretz Israel. Therefore, it is difficult to imagine how any Zionist government would voluntarily renunciate Israeli sovereignty over any part of Eretz Israel, including the Golan Heights.

The Defense of Settlements

It must be recalled that the borders of the state were determined to a large extent on the basis of the map of Jewish settlement in Eretz Israel. Suffice it to mention the example of the heroism of Joseph Trumpeldor and his friends, defenders of Tel Hai, who laid down the principle whereby no Jewish settlement in Eretz Israel would be evacuated. The refusal of the defenders of Tel Hai to evacuate their settlement, for which they laid down their lives, played a major role in the inclusion of the area of the Galilee panhandle in the region of the 1922 British Mandate [Palestine], and later in the borders of the State of Israel. While any decision involving cession of sovereignty would necessarily lead to the evacuation of existing settlements—settlements which were established on the conception, namely that they would be determining the borders of the state. The concept of nonevacuation, which has underlain the Zionist enterprise for over a century of settlement, should not be dismissed by any Zionist government. Any expression of a readiness to evacuate existing settlements in a region which the Zionist Movement has demanded be included within the borders of the Jewish State is a clear signal to the Arab world, embracing 21 states and territories of over 5 million square miles, that by applying pressure, Israel can be made to retreat from its most hallowed principles; it also plants in the hearts of the leaders of the Arab world the hope that what Israel has agreed to do today in the Golan Heights, it might agree to do tomorrow in Judea, Samaria, and Gaza. The Arab world will interpret any readiness on the part of Israel to evacuate settlements as a retreat from Zionist principles in general, as the beginning of the end of the Jewish State, and as the beginning of the realization of the Arab dream—to bring about the eradication of the Zionist entity in Eretz Israel.

What Israel Gave to Syria

Prima facie, therefore, the announcements of the government that it recognizes that the UN resolutions that talk about withdrawal from territories conquered by Israel in the Six-Day War apply to the Golan Heights as well would constitute a violation of the law, even before any decision has been taken on the operative level. As for implementation of the UN resolutions concerning the border with Syria, it must be recalled, apart from the fact that these resolutions are not binding, that Israel has already handed over to Syria areas in the Golan Heights in the framework of the Disengagement Agreement following the Yom Kippur War, thus fulfilling the resolutions. The borders to which the Israel Defense Forces withdrew in the framework of this agreement reflected the minimal needs of Israel for secure borders: any additional movement of forces is contrary to the conception of security accepted by Israel since the Six-Day War.

Indeed, in the absence of a constitution, the Knesset is sovereign to change any law, and from a formal point of view no special majority is required in order to amend or repeal the Golan Heights Law. Accordingly, if the law should be amended to allow the government to cede territory under sovereignty of the state, no criminal offense will have been committed, since sec. 91 of the Penal Law refers only to an act done to transfer territory to another state "without lawful authority."

Despite the power of the Knesset to amend the Golan Heights Law with a regular majority, it would seem that cession of sovereignty should not be treated as a question to be decided by the Knesset with a regular majority.

There are some states in which the constitution rules out the possibility of cession of sovereignty in part of the territory. For instance: article 1 of the Syrian Constitution states: "No part of [its] territory may be ceded. . . ."

Knesset Approval Is Required

In other states the constitution allows for cession of sovereignty, but attaches serious constraints, e.g., the French Constitution, under which territory may be ceded by special statute, but on condition that the population involved gives its consent (article 53 of the Constitution): "No cession . . . shall be valid without the consent of the populations concerned."

On a matter as fateful for the future of the Jewish people and the State of Israel as amending the Golan Heights Law, the government should be expected to refrain from making such change unless decided by a majority of at least two-thirds of the Members of the Knesset, recognizing in particular the opinion of the residents of the Golan Heights, who settled the area with the blessing and encouragement of all past Israeli governments. All the settlements in the Golan were established on the basis of the political conception, accepted by the decisive majority of the state's Jewish population, as well as the current ruling party, whereby any peace treaty must be founded on secure borders for Israel. In the north, this means that the Golan Heights must remain permanently under Israeli sovereignty.

Periodical Bibliography

The following articles have been selected to supplement the diverse views presented in this chapter.

David Aviel	"The Land for Peace Mirage," *Midstream*, February/March 1993. Available from the Theodor Herzl Foundation, 110 E. 59th St., Fourth Fl., New York, NY 10022.
David Bar-Illan	"Why a Palestinian State Is Still a Mortal Threat," *Commentary*, November 1993.
David Bowen and Laura Drake	"The Syrian-Israeli Border Conflict, 1949-1967," *Middle East Policy*, vol. 1, no. 4, 1992. Available from the Middle East Policy Council, 1730 M St. NW, Suite 512, Washington, DC 20036.
William Claiborne	"For Israeli Settlers, a Determination to Stay," *The Washington Post National Weekly Edition*, September 20-26, 1993.
Eugene Cotran	"Why There Is Now a State of Palestine," *Middle East International*, October 22, 1993. Available from 1700 17th St. NW, Suite 306, Washington, DC 20009.
Rael Jean Isaac	"Israel in the Borders of 1949: Then and Now," *Outpost*, October 1993. Available from Americans for a Safe Israel, 147 E. 76th St., New York, NY 10021.
Middle East Report	Special issue on Jerusalem, May/June 1993.
Benjamin Netanyahu	"The West Pushes the Wrong Kind of Mideast Peace," *The Wall Street Journal*, May 26, 1993.
Suliman S. Olayan	"No Statehood, No Peace," *The Wall Street Journal*, November 5, 1993.
Amos Perlmutter	"The Next Step for Mideast: Confederation," *Insight*, October 25, 1993. Available from 3600 New York Ave. NE, Washington, DC 20002.
Time	Interviews with PLO chairman Yasir Arafat and Yitzhak Rabin, September 27, 1993.
Time	Interviews with Syrian president Hafez al-Assad and Israeli prime minister Yitzhak Rabin, November 30, 1992.

Are Palestinian Rights
Being Violated?

Chapter Preface

Since Israel's occupation of the West Bank and Gaza Strip in 1967, Palestinians have struggled to protect their civil, economic, and human rights. In 1987, their struggle erupted into violence as the Palestinian uprising (the *intifada*) broke out and spread throughout the occupied territories.

In the tense environment of these occupied territories, Israel has frequently restricted the rights of many Palestinians. For example, thousands of students and workers have been cut off from classes and laborer jobs by occasional closures of Arab universities and border crossings into Israel. Furthermore, according to an *Atlanta Constitution* editorial, "Soldiers are permitted to shoot at fleeing Palestinians for such dangerous offenses as painting graffiti, fire into a crowd during the course of a chase, and destroy a whole block of houses in Gaza to flush out a single suspected terrorist." Such acts, writes American University law professor Tom Farer, "constitute punishment without due process of law and are affronts to the very idea of individual autonomy"—forms of collective punishment that only heighten Palestinian animosity, he argues.

But many Israeli officials and others point out that the warlike conditions of the *intifada* necessitate certain limitations on individual rights, as international law allows. According to Israel's Ministry of Foreign Affairs, "Israel's measures, in keeping with international standards, have not differed from those of other democratic countries when facing violence in the form of riots, armed assaults, murder, and terror." Proponents of these measures argue that without them, Jews in both Israel and the territories would be vulnerable to extremists' attacks.

The following viewpoints examine allegations of Israeli civil and human rights abuses and debate whether the rights of Palestinians are being violated.

"The Palestinian national minority faces discrimination in all walks of life."

Israel Violates Palestinian Civil Rights

Arab Association for Human Rights

The basic laws of Israel define the nation as a Jewish state. In the following viewpoint, the Arab Association for Human Rights argues that this definition officially makes Palestinians (predominantly Arabs) less equal citizens than Jews and denies them the civil rights that Jews enjoy. The association maintains that Arabs suffer from institutional discrimination in all areas of life, including citizenship, education, employment, and housing. The Arab Association for Human Rights (AAHR) is located in Nazareth, Israel.

As you read, consider the following questions:

1. How has Israel restricted the freedom of Palestinians, according to the AAHR?
2. According to the AAHR, how has Israel violated Arab land rights?
3. Why are army service benefits important to Israelis, according to the AAHR?

"Palestinians in Israel" by the Arab Association for Human Rights, *Al-Fajr*, August 2, 1993. Reprinted by permission.

In 1947, Palestinian Arabs comprised 67 percent of the population of Palestine. When the Israeli state was founded in 1948, the vast majority of the indigenous Palestinian residents were made refugees. Only a small portion remained behind on their land and were forcibly included in the Jewish state.

Currently, Palestinians within the 1948 borders of Israel make up 18 percent of the total population. Living as citizens in the self-declared Jewish state, the Palestinian national minority faces discrimination in all walks of life. While Israel claims that "her" Arab citizens enjoy full and equal rights—carrying Israeli citizenship and having the right to vote—in actuality, there are numerous laws and institutional policies that designate them as less than equal citizens.

Until 1966, Palestinians in Israel lived under a military administration that was applied only to the Arab population. This affected all aspects of their lives, restricting [everything from] their ability to travel and farm their fields to gathering together for special events. Among other policies, the administration restricted the movement of individuals—traveling from one village to another required a permit—and people without the proper documents or who resisted the oppressive policies of the government were often exiled or deported.

These repressive policies allowed the Israeli state to confiscate massive amounts of Palestinian agricultural and pasture lands under laws that were applied only to the Arab population. Whereas in 1947, Jewish land ownership in Palestine totalled less than 7 percent, by 1993 Palestinian land ownership in Israel had been reduced to 4.5 percent. For these Palestinians, living in Israel has meant their national, political and economic marginalization and their transformation into an impoverished landless minority in the midst of "the state of the Jewish people."

Israel: An Unequal State

In its Declaration of Independence, Israel defines itself as "a Jewish state in Eretz-Israel" which "would open its doors to every Jew. . . ." In this way, Israel does not define itself as the state of all its citizens but rather as the state of one specific religious group, thereby denying the rights of the indigenous inhabitants to live in their land and to be part of the state.

The exclusivity of Israel as a Jewish state also appears in an amendment added to the "Basic Law: Knesset" in 1984, which stipulated that the "denial of the existence of the State of Israel as the state of the Jewish people" was grounds for banning a political party from participating in the parliamentary elections. This law does not refer to those who deny the existence of Israel, rather to those who deny the Jewish nature of Israel.

Although not explicitly stated in the law, but by extension, anyone who calls for the equality of Jews and Arabs as citizens of the state denies the special and exclusive nature of the state. Tawfik Toubi, as an Arab member of the Knesset [Israel's parliament], argued that "to say today in the law that the State of Israel is the state of the Jewish people, means saying to 16 percent of the citizens of the State of Israel that they have no state and that they are stateless, that the State of Israel is the state only of its Jewish inhabitants, and that the Arab citizens who live in it reside and live in it on sufferance and without rights equal to those of its Jewish citizens. . . . Don't the people who drew up this version realize that by this definition they tarnish the State of Israel as an apartheid state, as a racist state?"

Wanton Destruction of Homes

Since Prime Minister Yitzhak Rabin took power in Israel in 1992, the Israel Defense Forces have initiated a new policy of attacking Arab homes in the occupied territories with rockets and grenades. Though the IDF claims it only attacks homes where armed Palestinian fighters are thought to be hiding, the most destructive operations have yielded no armed Arab fighters. They did, however, leave hundreds of men, women and children homeless.

The pattern in which the IDF has attacked the homes suggests that the motivation is wanton destruction rather than actual security. . . .

The vast majority of IDF rocket attacks have taken place in the Gaza Strip, where Palestinian resistance is stronger and foreign media access during and after the attacks easily controlled. Since the IDF first employed anti-tank rockets in July 1992, hundreds of Palestinian men, women and children have been rendered homeless.

Stephen Sosebee, *The Washington Report on Middle East Affairs*, April/May 1993.

The Law of Return of 1950 and the Nationality Law of 1952 lay down the legal basis for discrimination against indigenous Palestinians. Section One of the Law of Return states that "every Jew has the right to come to this country as an immigrant," and the Nationality Law restricts citizenship to those who immigrate to Israel, reside there or are born there. Thus, immigration is restricted to Jews throughout the world.

Palestinians (non-Jews) can only obtain citizenship by being born in, or residing in the country, or by naturalization. Because of these laws, the hundreds of thousands of Palestinians who were born in the country but no longer reside there are denied the right to return to their homeland and place of birth, while a

Jew who was not born there is automatically given citizenship by virtue of his being Jewish.

By applying different rules for acquiring nationality for Jews and non-Jews, the Nationality Law and the Law of Return, as fundamental laws making up the nature of the Israeli state, serve as a clear case of overt statutory discrimination.

A number of government bodies incorporate voluntary organizations that work on behalf of Jews throughout the world into the state structure, making their limited and exclusionary nature part of government policy. Shortly after the Israeli state was founded in 1948, international Zionist bodies—the World Zionist Organization and the Jewish Agency—were given special status within the government, allotting them representation in various government agencies, particularly the field of land and agriculture. While these organizations have become part of the government sphere, their mandates restrict their activities to only the Jewish sector. The role of these organizations in formulating land and agricultural policy is so large that, for example, Arabs may not establish any new villages or agricultural settlements.

In fact, over 90 percent of the land in the state is defined as "Israel lands"—property of the Jewish people and administered by the Israel Lands Administration. This government body is comprised of government officials and members of the Jewish National Fund (JNF), a voluntary organization which signed a cooperation treaty with the Israeli government in 1961. The JNF owns some 13 percent of the land which is dedicated "for the purpose of settling Jews on the said lands and property" and which according to their charter may not be leased to non-Jews.

Military Service

The Defense Service Law (1986) stipulates that every citizen of Israel must serve in the Israel Defense Forces. However, the Palestinian Arab citizens of Israel are not recruited into the military (with the exception of the male Druze and Circassian populations).

In Israel, the completion of army service is used in determining where one can live, amounts received for housing loans, children's allowances, taxes and university fees. Newly discharged soldiers are given preference for work, acceptance for occupational training courses and subsidized educational fees, among other things. Private companies and housing also use the completion of army service as a determining criterion. As it is only Arabs who do not serve in the army and therefore do not receive the benefits, the practice of creating a criterion of army service in essence serves as a covert method of discrimination against the Palestinian population.

Interestingly, no alternative service is available to those who are not recruited into the army, thereby allowing them to obtain the services provided. However, in the case of *yeshiva* (Jewish religious school) students who are also not recruited into military service, they receive soldiers' benefits because they are students in religious institutions. No such benefits are granted to Palestinian students of Christian or Muslim religious institutions. In the context of how this law and service benefits are applied, their discriminatory nature is obvious.

Section Two of the State Education Law (1953) defines that the objectives of the state education are "to base elementary education in the State on the values of Jewish culture and the achievements of science, on love of the homeland and loyalty to the state and the Jewish people. . . ."

What this implies for the non-Jewish population is not clear. A case heard before the Israeli Supreme Court in 1990 highlights the legal difficulties faced by Palestinians in trying to achieve equality in government services and funding. In May 1990, the minister of education announced a program to progressively implement a longer school day beginning with the most needy communities. Despite the fact that in 1988, National Insurance Institute Statistics calculated that 59.2 percent of Arab children live below the official poverty line, only six out of 564 "needy" schools were Arab.

When representatives of the Palestinian community in Israel brought a case to the Supreme Court, claiming that the regulation used to decide what constitutes a needy community discriminated against Arab pupils, the case was rejected. The second year of implementation of the program resulted in the same low numbers of Arab schools. A case was again raised in the Supreme Court, and it was again rejected.

Lack of Services

Government funding discrimination is widespread in the fields of local services, agriculture, education, and health services. For example, government funding of Arab local councils represents only 25 to 30 percent of that allocated to Jewish local councils. In addition, the Arab population is excluded from special development projects (both governmental and non-governmental) that are funded by such organizations as the Jewish Agency or the World Zionist Organization, as they only fund projects for Jews, not for Israelis.

In terms of other government services, sewage systems exist in only 19 of the over 140 Arab towns and villages. Some 50,000 of the Palestinian Arabs live in villages which are unrecognized by the Israeli government and as such cannot be connected to the electricity and water grids, nor are they provided with schools or health care services.

Israel is divided geographically into graded Development Areas where investors receive tax breaks and other incentives to establish firms and factories and residents receive special housing and educational assistance. Despite the fact that Arab villages fall within the geographical boundaries of the Development Areas, not one Arab town or village is classified as a development settlement.

The numerous types of legal and institutionalized discrimination faced by the Palestinian Arab citizens of Israel affect their lives on a day-to-day basis. As a national minority in the self-defined Jewish state, they are less than equal citizens in a system that does not include them in the definition of the state, let alone acknowledge their rights and aspirations. As defenders of the human rights of the indigenous Palestinian minority in Israel, the Arab Association of Human Rights calls upon the state of Israel, as a member of the United Nations, to uphold the principles in the U.N. charter of respect for human rights, freedom and equality.

"It is Israel that is the innocent victim fighting to maintain its freedom; it is the Palestinians who are the brutal oppressors."

Israel Does Not Violate Palestinian Civil Rights

Peter Schwartz

Peter Schwartz, the author of the following viewpoint, is the consulting editor of *The Intellectual Activist*, a conservative newsletter that supports capitalism and individual rights. According to Schwartz, the media portrayal of Palestinian victims and Israeli oppressors should be reversed. Israel upholds the Western values of individual liberty and free enterprise, the author argues, while the Palestinians are part of an Arab culture in which despotic governments and collectivist societies are the norm. Schwartz concludes that the Israeli state is threatened by Palestinian rioters; hence it is justified in using the force necessary to quell disputes.

As you read, consider the following questions:

1. Why does Schwartz believe that Israel is the real victim of unrest in the occupied territories?
2. What sort of state would the Palestinians set up in the West Bank if they were allowed to do so, according to the author?
3. Why does the author believe Israel must continue to use as much force as necessary to subdue Palestinian resistance?

"The Middle East Victim" by Peter Schwartz, *The Intellectual Activist*, May 31, 1988. Used by permission of the author.

The news accounts of the Palestinian unrest in the West Bank and Gaza present the story exactly backward. They generally depict the Palestinians as long-suffering victims of oppression, refusing to tolerate their lack of freedom any longer and fighting a desperate battle to gain the rights being unjustly denied them. The accounts suggest that the Palestinians are being deprived of their "homeland," and that Israel has become an aggressive, imperialistic conqueror unwilling to relinquish to the Palestinians what is rightfully theirs. An accurate description of these events, however, requires a transposition of the names: it is Israel that is the innocent victim fighting to maintain its freedom; it is the Palestinians who are the brutal oppressors.

The Real Oppressors

The Arabs who are rioting against Israel do not seek freedom. Theirs is a tribalist, collectivist society which disavows individualism and political liberty. They are in fact far freer even under the so-called occupation by Israel than they would be under any type of Arab government now in existence. A population that actually valued individual rights would *welcome* the opportunity of living under an Israeli government rather than under the various theocracies, feudalist monarchies and socialist dictatorships that make up all the Arab states in the Middle East. But the Palestinians in the occupied territories choose instead to embrace the philosophy and the politics of the Palestine Liberation Organization. They fly the PLO's flag, they eulogize its dead leaders, they acknowledge it—and only it—as their spokesman, they obey its orders regarding what hours to close their shops and what time and place to stage their riots—and they murder any Arab who voices support for genuine peace with Israel. It is the barbarous PLO that the Palestinians wish to enshrine as the dictator of their future "independent" state.

What they desire, in other words, is not freedom, but the primitive, despotic statism of "self-determination." They are hostile to Western values—to liberty, capitalism, individualism, industrialization, reason—of which Israel, in the context of Middle East mysticism, is the embodiment. That is why, although there is constant in-fighting among Arab groups and nations—as there always is among tribalist mentalities—they are quick to unite in attacking Israel. That is also why they are just as quick to prefer living under Arab tyranny rather than Israeli freedom.

How Israel Acquired the Territories

The Palestinians' antagonism toward freedom is the very reason these territories are under occupation in the first place. Prior to 1967, the West Bank and Gaza Strip were under the rule of Jordan and Egypt. Due to their close proximity to Israel, these areas were used effectively in launching wars against Israel. After successfully defending itself in the Six-Day War of 1967, Israel held on to the territories it captured. It sought a means of preventing their being used again in the initiation of physical attacks on its citizens.

THE STONE AGE

This action was similar to the occupation of Germany and Japan undertaken by the U.S. and its allies after World War II, with the aim of establishing a governmental structure in those two nations to ensure that they would no longer become the launching grounds for military aggression. Like Israel today, America then had no interest in retaining control of its enemies' land (although in both cases there is every moral *right* to do so, since dictatorship is being replaced by freedom). The only difference is that then America's foes had been so thoroughly beaten into submission, and the goals of Nazi Germany and Imperial Japan so morally discredited, that a new political system could be imposed and could gradually take hold. In the Middle East, however, the goal of a Palestinian state—which means the goal of entrenching a regime hostile to rational values—is still a widely approved objective.

There is no collective right to a "homeland." There is only the individual right to live in a free society. The proper justification for the establishment of the state of Israel is not "Biblical heritage" or ethnic tradition, but the objective fact that it is Israel alone in that region which upholds the political value of liberty. Were the Palestinians to share that value, there would be no cause for any basic conflict with Israel. There would be no concern over whether the ruling government was run by Arabs or by Jews, but only over whether the laws recognized individual rights. There would be no concern over whether particular settlements were populated by Arabs or by Jews, but only over whether an individual's property was inviolately his. Arabs and Jews would have the same rights—as they now do in Israel. Arabs and Jews would be equally able to hold political office— as they do now in Israel. It is only because the Palestinians are fundamentally collectivists and statists that clashes with Israel are inevitable.

It is preposterous enough to describe as "refugees" the Palestinians who willingly abandoned their homes in Israel in 1948 (at the behest of the Arab leaders who were initiating the first of their several wars against Israel), and who are now scattered throughout the Middle East, prevented by their leaders from leaving the "refugee camps" and resuming normal lives. But it is the height of absurdity to refer to those who are living in the West Bank and Gaza as "homeless refugees" seeking their rightful home—when the only change in status they desire is to replace Israeli occupation with a PLO state.

Israel Must Not Compromise

Until and unless the Palestinians change their views, Israel cannot make any concessions. Whether stones and gasoline bombs are being thrown by a 12-year-old or an adult, the actions are a genuine danger and must be unhesitatingly terminated. Israel must use as much force as is needed to quash any assault, to deter future ones and to punish the assailants and their abettors. What is definitely *not* a solution is the pernicious "land for peace" compromise, which urges Israel to negotiate a "trade" with the PLO, in which the occupied territories are exchanged for a promise of peace. In saner times, this formula was stated more clearly by highwaymen as: "Your money or your life." The proposal of "Your *land* or your life" represents the same fraudulent attempt to treat the withdrawal of a threat of force as a tradeable commodity. But extortion is not a means of effecting an equal exchange. A promise of peace from the PLO or from any group that lives by force and makes the promise only to be able to assume autocratic powers once Israel moves out, is meaningless. There is one action on the part of the Palestinians that is both the prerequisite for any resolution and the clearest sign of their sincerity when they claim to favor peace. And that is for them to reject the PLO unequivocally. If and when that happens, there will no longer be any reason for Israeli occupation, any more than there is a need now for America to occupy Canada. To put this differently: if Palestinians do not renounce aggression, no compromise is possible; if they do, none is necessary.

Peace-Loving Palestinian Murderers

The media dwell lovingly on scenes of so-called Israeli brutality: security forces charging Arab crowds, teens in custody being beaten, soldiers kicking in the doors of shops on the West Bank. . . .

For a public accustomed to having complex issues offered up in soothing ethical blacks and whites, it's all quite reassuring. It is also a complete distortion of the political situation in the Israeli-administered territories. . . .

Not a week goes by that an Israeli civilian isn't assaulted (knifed, shot, stoned, or burned to death) by peace-loving Palestinians seeking self-determination. The victims weren't rabble with rocks and iron bars in their hands, but innocents peaceably going about their daily business.

Don Feder, *Human Events*, April 30, 1988.

The moral perversity here is that Israel is being widely denounced because of its virtues, while the Palestinians are being praised for their vices. One observes the nauseating spectacle of children throwing rocks to tease and provoke Israeli troops, of grandmothers feeling safe in wrestling with armed soldiers, of parents smugly confident that the Air Force will not obliterate their villages in reprisal—while Israel is accused of totalitarian brutality. One observes that the press in Israel is free to interview Palestinians, to cover the rioting and the retaliatory shootings (which are rarely shown in the press as being retaliatory), to print editorials anathematizing the government—while Israel is accused of dictatorial censorship. One observes isolated instances of unwarranted force being used by Israeli soldiers against Palestinians, instances that are reported by the Israeli press, investigated by the Israeli authorities, and concluded by the imposition of prison sentences against the guilty individuals—while Israel is accused of callous indifference to human life. In Israel, as distinct from countries (such as the Arab states) that thoroughly suppress freedom, the opponents of the government readily engage in mass demonstrations because they know that soldiers will not shoot at them except in self-defense. It is only because Israel is cognizant of individual rights—and because its enemies *count on this*—that it has been facing the hit-and-run rioting for so long.

The Palestinians, on the other hand, have no concern for rights and recognize no moral restrictions upon their use of force. They do not care that they threaten and often injure innocent people with their rock- and bomb-throwing. They have no compunction about embracing the PLO, whose avowed policy it is to blow up schoolbuses, to machine-gun airport lobbies, to hijack planes and ocean liners, to butcher the innocent and the defenseless. Yet the Palestinians are considered the aggrieved party in the Middle East conflict, and the Israelis the villains. What accounts for this moral inversion, whereby those who endorse authoritarianism and wanton destruction are hailed, while those who support freedom and productivity are excoriated? What explains the view that the rights of the latter must be subordinated to the demands of the former? Only a philosophy that preaches *sacrifice* as a moral virtue.

This philosophy insists that someone's *need* creates a moral claim upon anyone able to satisfy it. Since the Palestinians are "homeless," in need of a homeland that Israel can provide, the doctrine of altruism declares that they are being denied what is morally theirs. They are being oppressed. Their rights are being violated. It does not matter that the Palestinians are to blame for their own misery. In fact, the more at fault the needy are for their own condition—i.e., the less *deserving* they are of help—the more of an altruistic imperative it is that help be given. Israel, by seeking to protect its freedom against the Palestinian threat, is being selfish and immoral, according to this philosophy. It ought instead to sacrifice its values for the sake of those who lack them. For self-sacrifice is not the trading of one value for another, but the surrendering of a value for a *non*-value—the surrendering of Israeli security in return for Palestinian bombs, the surrendering of prosperity for desert wastelands, freedom for tyranny, civilization for terrorism.

Defending Rational Values

This is why the Israelis are under moral attack. It is pointless to argue that justice and reason are on their side. What greater act of altruism could there be than to sacrifice the just to the unjust and the rational to the irrational? In this war of ideas, it is only by upholding the principle that one has the moral right to exist for one's own sake and to live for one's own values that the Israelis can be properly defended.

"The situation in the prisons really has reached a stage where it cannot be tolerated anymore."

Israel Abuses Palestinian Prisoners

Graham Usher

In the following viewpoint, Graham Usher argues that terrible conditions in Israeli prisons and detention camps prompted thousands of Palestinian prisoners to declare a hunger strike in September 1992. Usher maintains that the strike was prompted by the cruel and brutal treatment of prisoners, including the denial of emergency health care, lengthy solitary confinement, and torture. He charges that Israel responds to protests against its inhumane treatment of Palestinian prisoners by becoming even more repressive. Usher is a correspondent in the Gaza Strip and West Bank of Israel for *Middle East International*, a pro-Palestinian and Arab affairs magazine published biweekly in London.

As you read, consider the following questions:

1. What impact did the hunger strike have on Palestinians in the West Bank and Gaza Strip, according to Usher?
2. What kinds of torture have Palestinian prisoners been subjected to, according to Usher?
3. According to the author, why does Israel resort to solitary confinement?

"Killing Souls: Palestinian Prisoners' Hunger Strike" by Graham Usher. This article first appeared in the November 6, 1992, issue of *Middle East International*, 21 Collingham Road, London SW5, and is reprinted with permission.

On 27 September 1992, 4,500 Palestinian political prisoners declared "an open-ended hunger strike" to protest conditions in eight Israeli prisons. Within a week, the action encompassed 8,000 inmates out of a total Palestinian prison population of 13,000. On 1 October, Palestinian and Israeli human rights organisations alerted consular representatives expressing concern that "the health situation of already undernourished prisoners may become critical in the coming days", while memoranda tabled by Palestinian lawyers acting for the prisoners were sent to the International Committee of the Red Cross and the United Nations demanding that they intervene "to save our lives, grant us our legitimate demands, and put an end to the policy of slowly killing bodies and souls". A further memorandum drafted by the PLO was presented to the UN secretary-general.

More disturbing to the Israeli government than the unwelcome media coverage was the impact the strike had on the smouldering fires of the *intifada*, the Palestinian uprising against Israeli rule in the occupied territories. In August 1992 an Israeli commander in the territories pronounced the *intifada* "dead". Today—as Israel reels from the sheer scale of the protest—obituaries like these sound greatly exaggerated. From day one of the strike, Palestinians from all walks of life marched, staged sit-ins, and organised solidarity strikes throughout the West Bank and Gaza Strip. Fierce clashes between Palestinian youths and the IDF [Israeli Defense Force] erupted across the territories, leaving a toll of 14 Palestinians killed by army gunfire and a further 500 injured.

Israel's Crackdown

If—in the words of Danny Rubenstein in *Ha'aretz*—"the events of the last few days in the territories are reminiscent of what took place at the start of the *intifada*", then no less reminiscent was the Israeli government's response. In a flying visit to Gaza, Prime Minister Yitzhak Rabin thundered that "Israel would use all its strength to bring the disturbances to an end". A six-day curfew was imposed on the whole Strip, schools were closed, scores of Palestinians arrested, while legal access, medical care and even salt and water for striking prisoners was "made contingent on them ending the strike". For all the new Israeli government's talk of "confidence building" amongst the Palestinians, when confronted with a genuine mass protest—in the words of one UN observer stationed in Gaza—"it reverted to force, might and beatings—to the bad old days of 1988-89".

This is not the first time Palestinian political prisoners have had to go on hunger strike to protest their treatment inside Israeli jails. "The prison strike was predictable, given the repetition of demands by prisoners over the past year for an improvement in their conditions", says al-Haq, the Palestinian human rights organisation. In June 1991, Palestinian detainees went on strike in the wake of a government report, the Adan Commission, which removed rights of movement, representation and association as "detrimental to the security of Israeli prisons". A deal was hammered out between the Gaza Bar Association and the then Israeli Director of Prisons to restore "rights of detainees secured in the past". For Salih Abd al-Jawad—professor of political science at Bir Zeit University—it is in the prison authorities' failure to honour pledges made then that the seeds of the dispute lie: "The situation in the prisons really has reached a stage where it cannot be tolerated anymore. There is overcrowding. The prisoners' health conditions are deteriorating. Many of the achievements they had previously struggled for have been taken away".

Palestinian Prisoners in Israeli Detention Facilities

Number of Prisoners 12,500-13,000
    Sentenced... 7,000
    Awaiting trial (charged) 4,000
    Under interrogation 1,000
    Administrative detention 260

Age and Sex
    Women prisoners...................................... 69
    Women aged 18 or younger...................... 22 (33%)
    Men prisoners.................................... 12,500
    Men aged 18 or younger (estimated) 3,000

Special Cases
    Mothers of young children
        (awaiting trial or sentenced two years up to life term) 9
    Unreleased prisoners who have served more than
        twenty years 7
    In prolonged isolation 59
    Seriously ill, requiring surgery (estimated) 86
    Unreleased prisoners from Lebanon, finished terms........ 30

Deaths in Detention (during *intifada*).................... 32
    Deaths during interrogation 11
    Shot in prison 7
    Deaths due to harsh conditions 14

Palestine Human Rights Information Center, *From the Field*, November 1992.

At the start of the strike, the prisoners issued a press statement detailing 28 reforms that "must be made" if the dispute was to be resolved. Most of the demands refer to articles in the

Fourth Geneva Convention which specify the rights of political prisoners to adequate medical care, which strikers allege the authorities have infringed. Al-Haq, for instance, received information in July 1992 that 50 prisoners in six detention centres were being denied "urgent surgery, and that hundreds more are not receiving the daily or intensive medical care they require". Other demands included improved recreation facilities and ventilation in cells, an end to overcrowding, regular water supply, fewer restrictions on visiting and "an end to the policy of physical violence and body searches which aims to humiliate us". However, if the reforms were mainly about welfare, "top of the list", according to the statement, "is the demand to put an end to the solitary confinement policy and to secure the closure of solitary confinement sections in Beer Sheba and Nitsan prisons".

Solitary Confinement and Death

On 30 June 1992, Muhammad Suleiman Bries hanged himself in a transit ward at Ramle prison. He was the fifth Palestinian that year to die in detention. In March, Mustafa Akawi suffered a heart attack after—in the testimony of one of his interrogators—being "hooded, beaten and handcuffed, deprived of sleep and held in freezing temperatures". Samir Omar suffered a like fate in May after spending nine days in Hebron central prison. Hazim Id committed suicide in the interrogation wing of the same prison, while Mustafa Barakat died in Tulkarm prison in August from an asthma attack brought on after being "hooded for several hours to extract a confession".

Israel's use of torture against Palestinian prisoners is both long-standing and amply documented. As early as 1977, the London *Sunday Times* published a survey of Israeli prisons which concluded that "torture against Palestinian inmates appears to be sanctioned as official policy". Since then, reports by organisations like Amnesty International have repeatedly confirmed that "Palestinian prisoners are subject to torture in Israeli jails". What marked out Muhammad Bries' death, however, were the circumstances that led to it. Prior to the transit ward, Bries had been confined to the isolation wing of Nitsan prison in Ramle. Fellow prisoners call the wing "the ward of slow death". Bries' lawyer, Abd al-Malik Dahamsha, describes the conditions:

> The men are kept in narrow, closed, underground cells. They sometimes do not see the sun for a month. They are not able to shower or shave or even cut their nails. They have also been prevented a change of clothes, including underclothes. Furthermore, they cannot leave their cells, move within the ward or even see their lawyers, unless they are bound in handcuffs; this is not the case for other prisoners.

Since the Gulf war, the Israeli prison authorities have greatly increased the use of solitary confinement as a punitive measure.

In 1990, there were no "isolated" prisoners in Nitsan; today there are 45. In 1992, Beer Sheba prison has seen its prisoners in solitary increase to include 70 adult inmates and all minors, while Ketziot in the Negev [southern Israel] has opened a section for "separated" detainees. It was prisoners and families of prisoners from these jails who were in the [forefront] of the hunger strike.

"Solitary confinement in Nitsan is the result of a political decision", says Dahamsha. "It functions basically as a punishment. The authorities want to see how it works out, how to break people, how to transform political prisoners and leaders into obedient, docile vessels".

On 9 September—three weeks before the strike—the Association of Israeli-Palestinian Physicians for Human Rights called on Israeli Justice Minister David Libai and Police Minister Moshe Shahal "to investigate immediately the conditions in Section 8 of Nitsan prison". Their statement continued, "imprisonment in premises without daylight and extended solitary confinement are forms of torture under international standards. They are prohibited regardless of the offence committed by the victim of such procedures". Israel's own prison regulations state that "isolation is a penalty that may be imposed for a period not exceeding 14 days", and that where "separation is used as a preventative measure" for a longer period "the rights of separated prisoners will be the same as the rights of any inmate".

Muhammad Bries took his life after 16 consecutive weeks of solitary confinement.

On 11 October 1992, Moshe Shahal announced that the prisoners had called off the strike "pending the setting up of a special investigative committee to look into their demands". Three days later, Hussein Ubaidat, a striker from Jabal Mukkabar in East Jerusalem, died from a heart attack. For the Israeli authorities, the death could not have been more inopportune. For Palestinians like Abd al-Jawad, Ubaidat's martyrdom encapsulated "the whole problem": "he had been suffering from his ailment for six hours before he was finally transferred to a hospital. This summarises the plight of the health situation of prisoners in general". On news of the death, clashes raged until late into the night in East Jerusalem, with the army using tear gas and live ammunition to disperse demonstrators. Prisoners' representatives declared the hunger strike "temporarily suspended rather than ended", while Shahal held to the line that Israel could not negotiate over issues, like isolation, "that are security-related".

Willing to Die for Rights

However it is eventually resolved—and what we have now is an armistice rather than a peace—the extent and escalation of the prisoners' strike has clearly rocked Israeli society. Given an issue as deeply felt as prisoners' rights, Palestinians inside the territories rallied to the cause in ways as creative, realistic and popular as in the early days of the uprising. The Israeli government knows this and has gone to great pains to deny the mass import of the struggle. Thus Rabin dismissed the spectacle of 8,000 striking prisoners as "a political move that came from outside elements . . . to prevent political negotiations". This is so much window-dressing. There were politics to the dispute, but it was not orchestrated by the PLO in Tunis. Rather, says Abd al-Jawad, the strike drew its strength from "the political crisis in the peace negotiations". After "a whole year without any results to show for it", many inside the territories reached "the point where they are convinced there's no use in sitting with the Israelis at a negotiating table", Israeli commentators like Ze'ev Schiff concur. Writing in *Ha'aretz*, he argued that the Rabin government is not interested in elections of any stripe in the territories because, were they to be held, "a different, more extremist, team would be lined up facing Israel". In other words—representative or not—the current, PLO-backed, Palestinian delegation is the most congenial the Israelis are going to get.

The issues thrown up by the strike—those of Palestinian human, political and national rights—are precisely the issues that Palestinians in the West Bank and Gaza are ready to mobilise, struggle and die for, but which Israel apparently cannot countenance. While elsewhere in the world releases of political detainees serve as preludes to peace negotiations, Israel responds to similar demands by turning the repressive lid tighter and tighter. [Palestinian spokeswoman] Hanan Ashrawi commented during the strike that every Palestinian death "takes further credibility away from the peace talks". For Salih Abd al-Jawad, the portents are graver still: "If the Palestinians reach a point where they lose hope in the negotiations, there will be an explosion, and the explosion will be violent".

"The prisons . . . cannot now be said to violate accepted standards for care of prisoners."

Israel Does Not Abuse Palestinian Prisoners

Judith D. Simon and Rita J. Simon

In 1990 and 1992 Judith D. Simon and Rita J. Simon visited army detention camps in Israel and observed the treatment of Palestinian prisoners. In the following viewpoint, the authors argue that these prisoners are treated well and receive adequate food and shelter, family and attorney visits, and other entitlements. The authors report that they heard no allegations of physical abuse at the camps. Judith D. Simon, a former corrections officer, is assistant general counsel at the Federal Bureau of Prisons in Washington, D.C. Rita J. Simon is a professor of public affairs and law at American University, also in Washington, D.C.

As you read, consider the following questions:

1. How do the Simons describe relations between the prisoners and soldiers?
2. In the authors' opinion, why had prison conditions improved in the two years between their visits?
3. According to the authors, how have family and attorney visits improved?

From "Prisons in Israel" by Judith D. Simon and Rita J. Simon, *Federal Prisons Journal*, Fall 1992. Reprinted with permission.

In the spring of 1990, Middle East Watch, a human rights organization, received permission from the Israeli government to send a delegation to visit prisons in Israel, the West Bank, and Gaza. In August 1990, a three-person delegation consisting of Rita Simon, a sociologist, Judith Simon, an attorney and a former corrections officer, and Eric Goldstein, a staff member of Middle East Watch, visited four prisons run by the National Prison Service . . . and five detention camps run by the Israeli Defense Forces (the Israeli army). [Middle East Watch and Eric Goldstein disagree with this report's findings.] Our objective was to inspect and report on conditions inside the facilities. We were instructed not to investigate or report on the propriety of incarcerating any particular inmates or groups of inmates (such as Palestinians being held under administrative detention). . . .

Army Detention Camps

The Israeli army operates a number of detention camps in which they hold Arab residents of the occupied territories who have been arrested for *intifada*-related activities (including printing pamphlets, building explosives, and possessing weapons) or who are being administratively detained. No Palestinian women are held in army-run facilities; rather, they are housed in a separate section of a Prison Service prison. [These prisons hold both Arabs and Israelis, but no Palestinian males in *intifada*-related cases.] The camps are governed by the "Military Policy Directive Concerning Detention Centers" and the Israeli Defense Forces' Standing Orders. In accordance with international law, administrative detainees are held separately from those who are awaiting trial or have been convicted.

The need for facilities to house large numbers of detainees and persons charged with *intifada*-related crimes arose quickly; therefore, the army was forced to convert existing buildings into appropriate holding facilities, and to construct camps similar to those set up for soldiers (with the addition of barbed-wire fencing surrounding each group of tents and surrounding the entire camp). The camps are all quite large; in 1990 the smallest held 450 prisoners, and the largest 6,200. The atmosphere at all of the camps was markedly more tense and more hostile than at the Prison Service prisons. The soldiers who guard the inmates were not specially trained in corrections, and they were forced to live in camps adjacent to the prison camps and endure the same uncomfortable conditions as the prisoners.

Most of the detainees live in large tents, each with 26 beds. They sleep on mattresses placed on top of wood pallets (as do the soldiers). In all but one of the camps, each group of tents has showers and toilet facilities accessible at all times, though hot water may only be available several times per week. Most inmates leave their tent areas only for attorney or family visits, or to see the doctor. There are few work opportunities in the camps, aside from food preparation and laundry. The areas are large enough to permit the men to exercise and to gather in small groups to pray.

The camp commanders generally leave the day-to-day living arrangements to the prisoners. Nearly all the camps employ the "shaweesh" system, whereby a group of men are selected jointly by the prison commander and the inmates to act as spokesmen for the prisoners. Prisoners other than the *shaweeshim* are generally prohibited from speaking to the soldiers, but this rule is not enforced at all facilities. The *shaweeshim* are responsible for such things as meal planning and setting portion sizes (the inmates' kitchens receive raw ingredients, the same as those given the soldiers, from which they prepare food as they see fit), for resolving problems among the inmates, and for speaking with the commanders about complaints and problems the prisoners are having. Aside from the counts taken several times a day and the weekly or monthly searches, the soldiers rarely enter the inmates' living areas, and generally have little contact with them. At several facilities the inmates offered us coffee, tea, and sweets while we spoke with them. At one facility the commander drank coffee and chatted with prisoners in the kitchen area while we wandered around and spoke with other inmates.

In 1990, all the camps had isolation cells for prisoners who violate rules, and for inmates needing protection. These cells were, in all cases, dark, small, and hot. In some camps the cells were empty, but those that were occupied were quite crowded and the occupants looked somewhat dazed.

Prison Entitlements

Inmates are entitled to three meals a day, to visit with lawyers freely and frequently, to receive and send mail, to receive medical treatment, and to be free from physical abuse. In no facilities are the prisoners permitted to make phone calls. Personal radios and televisions are prohibited, but news and music are broadcast several times a day in Hebrew and Arabic. The Red Cross provides reading materials, including newspapers and books; only titles on an "approved book list" are permitted. Inmates wear their own clothing, but in some facilities they are prohibited from wearing red, black, or green—the colors of the Palestine Liberation Organization. Also prohibited are the giving of lectures or seminars, and wearing jewelry (though we noticed that many inmates were wearing watches and necklaces).

The inmates at the military camps had many more complaints than did those at Prison Service facilities on our 1990 visit. The physical setup at the camps was more rugged and less comfortable, but this was not the source of the complaints. Rather, the men complained that their mail was often delayed weeks and sometimes never received at all; they lacked interesting reading material and suffered from boredom; they were not permitted to visit with their lawyers or their families as often as they desired; and they did not receive adequate medical care.

Prisoners Are Not Tortured

To prevent terrorism effectively while ensuring that the basic human rights of even the most dangerous of criminals are protected, the Israeli authorities have adopted strict rules for the handling of interrogations.

The use of physical moderate pressure is in accordance with international law. For example, when asked to examine certain methods of interrogation used by Northern Ireland police against IRA [Irish Republican Army] terrorists, the European Human Rights Court ruled that "ill-treatment must reach a certain severe level in order to be included in the ban of torture and cruel, inhuman or degrading punishment contained in Article 3 of the European Convention of Human Rights."

In its ruling, that court sanctioned the use of certain forms of pressure in the interrogation process, such as hooding (except during the actual questioning), sleep deprivation and reduction of food and drink supply. Strict measures were set down by the Israel Ministry of Justice to ensure that disproportionate exertion of pressure on suspects does not take place.

Arthur Avnon, *Chicago Tribune*, July 10, 1993.

All of the members of our delegation were pleasantly surprised at the conditions we saw at the 11 facilities during our 1990 visit. The National Prison Service prisons were impressive by any standards—in terms of the physical conditions, the relations between inmates and their custodians, and the policies. The camps run by the army were less impressive in those aspects, but were far better than we expected. We saw no evidence that the prisoners are subjected to physical abuse. The inmates are well fed and receive medical treatment, they are free to spend time with one another, and they receive visits from their lawyers and families.

We did see problems that needed to be addressed, including the lack of family visits at the largest army camp . . . and the lack of activities for the prisoners held in the army camps.

In the summer of 1992, the authors returned to three of the prison camps run by the Israeli Defense Forces that we visited 2 years earlier, and also visited an additional camp. The overall population of Palestinians held in prison camps under administrative detention has decreased significantly, due in part to a change in the policy of the military justice system to detain only those charged with more substantial offenses. The decrease in population has alleviated most of the overcrowding problems. As a result, living conditions have improved and there is less tension at the camps. In the past year there were only two murders, no suicides, and very little violence either on the part of inmates or staff.

During the past 2 years, the Israeli Defense Forces have been able to give additional training to the Military Police commanders in charge of the facilities, and they now have military police at nearly all facilities. These soldiers have been specifically trained to work with prisoners. These factors—the decrease in population, the additional training provided to staff, and the expertise gained from operating the prison camps for several years—have led to many changes in the prisons that render them more humane places of confinement.

Improvements have been made regarding the processing of mail, the quality of food, conditions under which family and attorney visits take place, forms of punishment for disciplinary violations, and staff-detainee relations. Two years ago, the detainees complained that they did not receive their mail in a timely fashion, they were not permitted to see their lawyers as often as needed, and that their family visits were problematic. In 1992 we heard no complaints about the mail except at Ketsiot (the largest facility), where we were told that inmates received very little mail and were not permitted to send out letters. We investigated these allegations and saw the log where all the incoming and outgoing mail is recorded—about 2,500 pieces each week. At every facility we were told by the military commanders that the censors were able to process the mail quickly and no problems existed.

Prison Visits

In 1992 we heard no complaints regarding lawyer visits. At every facility new structures have been built that provide the detainees and their attorneys a fair amount of privacy; the soldier who is monitoring the visit stands in a room with a closed door separating him from the detainees and lawyers. The prisoners' only complaint regarding family visits in 1992 was that the buildings are too crowded and noisy so that the visits are not as pleasant as if they were more private. An alternative would be to cut back on the frequency of visits for each detainee, but this is not an attractive possibility.

Every facility had new structures for family visits that provide shelter from the sun and rain. Even at Ketsiot, where there had been no family visits for several years, visits now take place twice a month. Family visits were taking place the day we were there, and we were able to see the families and detainees talking and visiting. When the detainee's family includes very young children the men are permitted to visit outside of the main structure (where two meshes separate the two groups) in an area where there is only a single fence. This way the father is able to put his hand through the holes in the fence and touch the child. We were able to see the orderly manner in which the army inspects and processes the packages of food, clothing, and personal supplies brought for the detainees.

Isolation Is Rare

The army now rarely uses isolation cells as punishment. In three of the four camps we visited, isolation cells are not used at all, and at Ketsiot, where they continue to be used, new cells are a dramatic improvement over the small, dark, hot cells we previously saw. The new cells are large (12 square meters with a maximum of four prisoners and a minimum of two), each has a big window, and, most importantly, the occupants are permitted to spend 90 minutes outside each day.

A significant number of detainees were in protective custody at Ketsiot. These men are permitted 6 hours in the yard, and they are the only prisoners held by the Israeli Defense Forces who are afforded the luxury of viewing television! To date there are still no personal radios allowed inside the facilities, but there is talk of changing this policy in the near future.

Detainees (administrative and others) are still prohibited from holding classes or giving lectures, though most of the commanders permit the inmates to sit in their tents and speak quietly about whatever they wish. The only exception to the prohibition against conducting classes is at Meggido [detention camp]. The commander of Meggido permits one of the adults to serve as a teacher for the 300 youths (aged 14-16) and hold classes in subjects such as math and history. The adults at Meggido are also permitted to hold classes (so long as the subject is not terrorism), but the detainees rarely do so.

No Staff Brutality

In none of the camps did we hear allegations of staff brutality and in only one facility did we hear allegations of staff misconduct: at Ketsiot the *shaweeshim* with whom we spoke claimed that soldiers have stolen from the families during the course of searching them before the visit. The Commander and his staff reported that such allegations had never been raised before, either to them or to the members of the Red Cross who visit Ketsiot.

In general, both detainees and staff felt that relations were much improved as compared to several years ago and that there was little hostility or animosity at the camps. At Meggido, where relations between staff and the detainees were remarkably good 2 years ago, the situation is extraordinary. Not only did both the detainees and the staff mention this in our discussions, but their actions made this eminently clear. For example, as we sat and talked with the *shaweeshim*, they welcomed the commander, his deputy, and the officer in charge of the section to sit at their table under a tent, smoke their cigarettes, drink their coffee, and eat their pastries and candies. They also provided these refreshments to the officer standing watch outside the gate! One of the *shaweeshim* explained:

> The commander has taught us how to live together in peace. My dream is for our own country, for peace, for our children, mine and his, to go to the same school.

> At the time of the Israeli elections we held a congress that met for 10 days to discuss the *intifada*, prison, and the world. This was our experience with democracy.

The detainees were not without complaints: there is not enough variety in the food, medical treatment is not as good as it should be, the rooms are hot, and visits are too short. But it was clear that the situation at the prisons run by the Israeli Defense Forces had improved dramatically in the past 2 years, and they cannot now be said to violate accepted standards for care of prisoners. . . .

Both the Israeli Defense Forces and the Ministry of Police should be commended on the significant efforts they have made to improve the facilities we visited. The Israeli army should also be commended for the extraordinary access they granted us to visit their facilities and to speak with the inmates.

Periodical Bibliography

The following articles have been selected to supplement the diverse views presented in this chapter.

Amnesty International	"Oral Statement by Amnesty International: Israeli Occupied Territories," *Middle East Policy*, vol. 1, 1992.
David Bar-Illan	"The Deportations," *Commentary*, March 1993.
Stanley Cohen	"Talking About Torture in Israel," *Tikkun*, November/December 1991.
Frank Collins	"Israel's Tainted System and the Torture of Palestinian Detainees," *Washington Report on Middle East Affairs*, September/October 1993. Available from American Educational Trust, PO Box 53062, Washington, DC 20009.
Caroline Hawley	"Working for the Enemy: Palestinian Labourers in Israel," *Middle East International*, April 30, 1993. Available from 1700 17th St. NW, Suite 306, Washington, DC 20009.
Mitchell Kaidy	"Israel's Unreported Death Squads," *Lies of Our Times*, December 1992.
Palestine Human Rights Information Center	"Human Rights Issues After the Agreement on the Declaration of Principles," PHRIC statement, September 27, 1993. Available from 4201 Connecticut Ave. NW, Suite 500, Washington, DC 20008.
Palestine Human Rights Information Center	"Israeli Anti-Tank Missiles Destroy Palestinian Homes," *From the Field*, February 1993.
Sara M. Roy	"Apartheid, Israeli-Style," *The Nation*, July 26-August 2, 1993.
Vernon Schmid	" 'You Shall Not Wrong the Stranger,' " *Christian Social Action*, July/August 1993. Available from 100 Maryland Ave. NE, Washington, DC 20002.
Rita J. Simon and Judith D. Simon	"Israel's Military Prisons: The Reality," *Near East Report*, October 26, 1992. Available from Near East Research, 440 First St. NW, Suite 607, Washington, DC 20001.
U.S. Department of State	"Human Rights in Israel," *Near East Report*, May 4, 1992.

223

Should the United States Support Israel?

Chapter Preface

Israel enjoys a close relationship with America. Not only is the nation America's most trusted ally in the Middle East, it is also the top recipient of U.S. foreign aid. Israel receives more than $3 billion annually in U.S. economic and military grants and loans—approximately 20 percent of the total foreign aid budget. Israel uses approximately 90 percent of this aid to buy American weaponry and pay the interest on military loans.

Supporters of this arrangement argue that both nations win—Israel bolsters its armed forces and protects its borders while America gains a strong ally to protect its strategic interests in the oil-rich but conflict-ridden Middle East. According to Middle East expert Steven L. Spiegel, "In terms of defense, what Israel costs us is minuscule, while what it gives us in return is invaluable."

Other experts disagree and contend that national and international events have reduced the justification for such massive aid. They cite, for example, the demise of the pro-Arab Soviet Union and its ample arms flow to nations such as Egypt and Syria. Domestically, as America struggles to reduce its budget deficit, many Americans rank foreign aid as a low priority and one deserving of cuts. Criticizing aid to Israel, Senator Robert Byrd of West Virginia told the Senate in 1992, "The U.S. economy is barely strong enough to support our own needs, let alone to take on additional burdens overseas."

The issue of aid to Israel promises to become even more complicated as Palestinians, promised limited self-rule by the Israel-PLO autonomy agreement, also seek U.S. foreign aid. Such a request could provoke debate in the U.S. Congress as legislators balance domestic and foreign policy concerns, and require America and Israel to more closely evaluate their relationship—a task undertaken by the authors of the following viewpoints.

"It is critical for both the United States and Israel to build upon [their] partnership."

The United States Should Strengthen Relations with Israel

Charles Brooks

Israel has long been America's trusted ally in the Middle East and the most democratic nation in the region; therefore, America should strengthen its relations with Israel, Charles Brooks argues in the following viewpoint. Brooks contends that America and Israel share common democratic and moral values, as well as economic and political interests. He also maintains that binational research and development partnerships in the areas of agriculture, defense, and industry benefit both nations. Brooks serves as a legislative fellow for defense and foreign affairs to Pennsylvania senator Arlen Specter and as costaff director of the Senate Caucus on U.S./Israel Security Cooperation. He is a member of the board of advisors of the Center for Security Policy, a foreign policy and national defense think tank in Washington, D.C.

As you read, consider the following questions:

1. How does aid to Israel benefit America economically, according to Brooks?
2. Why does Brooks believe that America and Israel should be concerned with ballistic missile defense?
3. According to the author, what is the Islamic threat to Israel?

"A New Framework for U.S./Israel Relations" by Charles Brooks, *Midstream*, June/July 1993. Reprinted by permission of the Theodor Herzl Foundation, New York.

Since the United States has become the sole superpower, there now exists an opportunity for the Clinton administration to make fundamental changes in the conduct of foreign affairs toward the Middle East. America's relationships in the region should not be based on expedience, balance of power doctrines or petrodollar influences, but on a shared sense of destiny based upon democratic principles and common moral and cultural values. Israel is the only ally in the Middle East that is reliable and democratic and American policy should be formulated to accommodate this reality.

While various countries from the former Soviet Union and Eastern Europe are instituting democratic forms of governments and establishing legal systems to guarantee the protection of human rights, the Middle East remains a region characterized by despotic rule, intolerance and fanaticism. Only Israel has a freely elected government. Even Kuwait, despite being saved by the United States and the allied coalition, has abandoned any promises of establishing a democratic form of government. The Kuwaiti royal family stills rules with an iron fist and conducts business as it did prior to the Iraqi invasion. Until fundamental change is demonstrated by Arab countries to adhere to Western values, American foreign policy should seek to greatly enhance Israel's military qualitative edge and limit sophisticated arms to Israel's potential foes in the region.

Upgrading Relations

Under a new framework for US/Israel bilateral relations, the Clinton administration's first priority should be to immediately upgrade the US/Israel economic, political and strategic relationship. Contrasted to the wavering support of our European allies on various foreign policy (e.g., Bosnia) and international economic issues, Israel is a special ally that America can count on.

The 1991 Gulf War provides an excellent example of Israel's reliability to the United States. During the Gulf War, Israel absorbed 39 unprovoked SCUD missile attacks and did not retaliate at our behest. Does the United States have any other ally in the world that would sacrifice its self-defense and allow itself to be attacked (causing the loss of life and billions of dollars in economically vital tourism) at our urging?

Israel should also be given the credit it deserves for destroying Iraq's Osirik nuclear reactor back in 1981 and preventing Saddam Hussein from acquiring a nuclear bomb. Israel did the Desert Storm Coalition an undeniable favor that probably ended up saving tens of thousands of lives. The importance of this act was brought to light during and since the Gulf crisis. Former Secretary of Defense Dick Cheney stated, "There were many times during the course of the buildup in the Gulf and the subsequent conflict that I gave thanks for the bold and dramatic action that had been taken [by Israel] some ten years before."

The West should be grateful for Israel's foresight and willingness to take preemptive action against Iraq. Israel should also be commended for its many unheralded contributions in intelligence, logistics and military hardware that led to our success in the Gulf War.

As Americans, we often forget that Israel is a tiny nation (about the size of New Jersey) that is constantly embroiled in a fight for its very survival. Thankfully, the United States has neighbors such as Canada and Mexico on our borders. Imagine the security dilemmas posed to Israel by being surrounded by over 20 non-democratic adversaries on a land-mass more than one-and-a-third the size of the United States bent on its destruction.

Indeed, the US/Israel relationship is unique and enduring. Culturally and politically, Israel is the only nation in the Middle East which shares the same moral foundations and common heritage as does the United States.

The Importance of US Aid

The political and economic interests of the United States and Israel have always been tightly intertwined. One reason for this linkage has been foreign aid. Although it is often referred to by politicians in pejorative terms, foreign aid cannot be characterized as a gift that bears no returns. According to the think tank the Center for Foreign Policy Options, in the fiscal year 1992, foreign aid represented only 0.9 percent of the overall federal budget. Facts about foreign aid should be put into proper perspective, especially in regard to Israel's role as an ally.

For national security reasons alone, the United States has a vested interest in keeping Israel economically viable and militarily strong. Since the late 1980s, the United States has provided Israel with around $1.8 billion in military aid, and about $1.2 billion in economic assistance on a yearly basis. Unlike Europe where the United States has had to station troops and spend upwards of $100 billion annually to ensure security interests, Israel's $3 billion in foreign and military aid is a relatively small sum and a real strategic bargain. The bulk of Israel's military aid is spent in an effort to offset the huge amounts of weapons and technology provided to Israel's Arab adversaries by the West. Moreover, virtually all of Israel's debt to the United States is a result of military aid loans used to purchase American weapons during the 1970s at an excessive interest rate of 11 percent per annum compounded. Much of this aid was necessitated by Israel's abandonment of key airfields and oil production facilities in the Sinai as a condition of the Camp David Accords. Despite the burdens of a strained economy due to massive immigrant absorption and security requirements, Israel has never defaulted on a loan payment to the United States.

Aid Dollars Spent in America

A key aspect of American military aid that is often overlooked by the American public is that the bulk of the aid is required to be spent in the United States. In a nutshell, Israeli foreign aid money spent in the US translates into contracts, jobs and a stronger domestic economy. Foreign and military aid to Israel has promoted exports and tax revenues for the US economy and created new customers for American businesses.

The facts show that of the approximately $3 billion in aid to Israel annually, only $300,000 is actually spent in Israel; 90 percent of the aid is spent in the United States for products, services and debt repayment. Israel buys twice as much per capita from the US as Great Britain and Japan and is second only to Canada in per capita imports of US products.

In macroeconomic terms, American exports to foreign aid recipients are estimated by the Commerce Department to have accounted for over 2.8 million jobs in the United States in 1990. Peter McPherson, former administrator of the Agency for International Development, estimated that every billion dollars of aid to Israel creates 60,000 to 70,000 jobs in the United States.

Our Common Interest

Israel's democracy is the bedrock on which our relationship stands. It's a shining example for people around the world who are on the front line of the struggle for democracy in their own lands. Our relationship is also based on our common interest in a more stable and peaceful Middle East—a Middle East that will finally accord Israel the recognition and acceptance that its people have yearned for [for] so long and have been too long denied; a Middle East that will know greater democracy for all its peoples.

I believe strongly in the benefit to American interests from strengthened relationships with Israel.

Bill Clinton, *U.S. Department of State Dispatch*, March 22, 1993.

The national security–related rewards the United States gains from aid to Israel are substantial. Former Director of Air Force Intelligence, Major General George Keegan (USAF), stated that in terms of intelligence and power projection the strategic importance of Israel is worth "five CIAs." It has been estimated that Israel's countermeasures employed in destroying Syria's Soviet–built air defense system during the 1982 war in Lebanon saved American military planners about $7 billion in research and development costs alone.

Military experts have estimated that it would cost American taxpayers over $125 billion per year to maintain a fighting force the size of Israel's to protect American interests in the Middle East. This allocation is even more astounding when contrasted to the return the US gets from the $130 billion spent annually to defend Europe and the $30-plus billion we spend every year to defend Japan. Even the most vehement critic of foreign assistance would have to agree that in contrast to our NATO [North Atlantic Treaty Organization] allies, US aid to Israel is a comparative bargain.

A Pro-American Bastion

In terms of America's regional security objectives, Israel serves as a bastion of pro-American interests in the Middle East. The United States has prepositioned weapons and supplies for use in an emergency or rapid deployment scenario. The Israeli and American military forces regularly train together to improve on tactics and capabilities.

Indicative of Israel's special allied relationship is the fact that American servicemen can proudly wear their uniforms when they are in Israel. In contrast, American servicemen are encouraged not to wear their uniforms in Europe because of host country attitudes and terrorist threats. The American military is accorded respect and camaraderie by their Israel hosts.

The Israeli port of Haifa serves as a port of choice for the US Sixth Fleet. The port was used extensively by American forces in route to the Gulf for refueling, maintenance, R & R [rest and relaxation] and numerous other support services. The Haifa port needs to be expanded and upgraded so it can be utilized as a comprehensive forward base for the US Sixth Fleet's operations. With cutbacks in US naval power projection capabilities, the importance of Israel to US rapid deployment forces is significantly increased. Israel has expressed an interest in accommodating the Sixth Fleet at Haifa and this offer should become a high priority on Secretary Les Aspin's defense agenda.

Another area where US/Israel strategic cooperation is paying special dividends is in the area of strategic defense against ballistic missiles. The Third World ballistic missile threat is growing and is ominous. For the past several years, Israel and the United States have been working closely to develop antitactical ballistic missile (ATBM) technologies that will enable our nations to destroy SCUDs and short-range missiles. The joint US/Israel Arrow program is indispensable and must be completed as a top priority for both countries. The Arrow has already proven successful in a test intercept and offers the best option for a deployable ATBM system in the 1990s.

The most efficient way for the United States to enhance dual US/Israel defense capabilities is to provide Israel with the same access to military technology that we provide our closest NATO allies. To maintain Israel's qualitative edge, such action is urgently needed. Moreover, such cooperation will also contribute to a reduction in Israel's dependency on foreign aid.

While foreign aid to Israel is clearly beneficial to the United States, misconceptions and extreme budget austerity may result in changes in the authorization and appropriations process. Frankly, the notion of foreign aid is not understood by most Americans, and it will be difficult to adequately communicate the case. Thus, new ideas are necessary to ensure that American security interests are not put at risk because of lack of funding.

Israel and the United States are already engaged in creating prototype ideas to reduce Israel's dependency on foreign aid. The framework for this kind of approach is exemplified in the proposed binational foundations designed to draw on the joint technological strengths of the United States and Israel. The Endowment for Defense Industrial Cooperation (EDIC) is a proven concept and an example of this kind of approach. The purpose of EDIC is to encourage cooperation between American and Israeli defense industries to further strengthen the US defense research and development base.

EDIC is based on the success of three prototype endowments that were designed to give the United States access to Israeli technologies: the Binational Industrial Research and Development Foundation (BIRD), the Binational Agricultural Research and Development Foundation (BARD), and the Binational Service Foundation (BSF). These endowments were funded jointly and equally by the United States and Israel and are now self-sustaining by operating from interest earnings on the endowments. Sales of products developed through these endowments have reached nearly $3 billion to date and have created thousands of jobs for Americans.

The Promise of Partnership

These US/Israel binational research and development partnerships permit the United States to maximize scarce resources and facilitate cheaper, faster, and lower-risk development of technologies for defense and commercial application. The promise of EDIC is unlimited and should serve to greatly assist the United States with technological innovation in maintaining the defense-industrial base and with new markets for export access.

The most recent contribution to the shared partnership approach is President Bill Clinton's creation of the US-Israel Science and Technology Commission. The commission will utilize a public panel with a private sector approach to encourage high-tech industries in the United States and Israel to link up on joint projects that will benefit both countries. The fusion of the best scientific minds in the United States and Israel should produce an innovative technological enterprise that will be able to match any other venture emanating from Asia or Europe.

While the promise of binational partnerships is exceptional, for the time being, foreign and military aid are still necessary for Israel's security. Despite optimism in the current peace process, reality dictates that Israel must be prepared for any of the worst case scenarios. Since there are no other democracies, nor a history of democracy in any other country in the Middle East, the threat of war to Israel is still very real, particularly with the growing threat of radical Islam to Egypt, Jordan and Algeria, whose governments can change overnight. With forces such as radical Islam and despotic nations like Iran, Libya and Syria, there are no guarantees of peace in the Middle East.

In conclusion, the US/Israel partnership is often misunderstood and underestimated, particularly in the area of foreign aid. Despite the end of the Cold War, Israel is and will remain a bulwark for American interests in the region. The future of the US/Israel relationship is promising, especially in the areas of binational industrial initiatives, and with enhanced security cooperation to meet the new and changing threats facing both the United States and Israel. It is critical for both the United States and Israel to build upon this partnership and embark on a path of friendship, mutual prosperity and shared destiny.

"Unqualified support for Israel has made the grandiose ideals of the United States ring hollow."

The United States Should Not Support an Oppressive Israel

Anne Marie Baylouny

Many United Nations resolutions against Israel have been vetoed by the United States or, if passed, ignored by Israel. In the following viewpoint, Anne Marie Baylouny argues that these resolutions highlight the severity of Israel's violations of international law and Palestinian rights. Baylouny contends that America, which prides itself on the principles of freedom and justice, devalues these principles by supporting a government that has stolen or destroyed Palestinian land and resources and that has waged a campaign of terror and violence against innocent Palestinians. Baylouny is the director of media and public relations for the American-Arab Anti-Discrimination Committee in Washington, D.C.

As you read, consider the following questions:

1. How has Israel prevented Palestinians from supporting themselves, in Baylouny's opinion?
2. What is collective punishment, and how has Israel enforced it, according to the author?
3. In Baylouny's opinion, how has Israel subverted American interests abroad?

"Human Rights Considerations and the United States-Israeli Relationship" by Anne Marie Baylouny was written expressly for inclusion in the present volume.

From the moment of its establishment in 1948 Israel has enjoyed a uniquely favored status in the foreign policy of the United States. U.S. political and financial support for Israel has been unprecedented in both its proportion and steadfastness, based in part upon claims of common moral and political values between the United States and Israel. However, a critical look at Israel's past and present reveals that the special nature of America's association with Israel is not in Israel's sharing of American ideals, but rather in America's seemingly inexhaustible capacity to forgive Israel for violating them. Despite persistent serious violations of human rights and international law, and indeed of fundamental American values on the part of Israel, American support continues unabated.

History of Palestine

A look at the history of Palestine is required in order to fully comprehend the injustice represented by Israel's present acts of violence against the Palestinians. During the First World War the government of Great Britain promised the Arabs that it would ensure their independence after the war, in reward for rebelling against their Turkish rulers. Turkey, which had ruled the Middle East for approximately 400 years, was then allied with Great Britain's enemy, Germany. While the Arabs kept their part of the bargain by helping to defeat the Turks, the British government not only reneged on its promise of independence for the Arab population of Palestine, it instituted a policy of support for the establishment of a foreign nation there, Israel. During the thirty year period of British rule under a League of Nations mandate, the British authorities held the Palestinians at bay while European immigration swelled a Jewish population clearly intent on displacing them. As the British prepared to leave Palestine in 1947, an all-out war ensued between the immigrant Jews and native Palestinians. The well-equipped Jewish army conquered over three-fourths of Palestine, driving 750,000 Palestinians into permanent exile in the process. Twenty years later, Israel conquered the remaining quarter of Palestine, producing a second wave of Palestinian refugees. Today, 13% of the world's 6 million Palestinians live as second-class citizens within the state of Israel, an additional 29% live under Israeli military rule in the occupied territories of the West Bank and Gaza Strip, and fully 52% of Palestinians live outside of Palestine altogether. Nearly half a century after the establishment of the state of Israel, nearly one in five Palestinians remain in refugee camps supported by international relief agencies.

Israel's occupation of the West Bank and Gaza Strip since 1967 is in contravention of international law. The United Nations has repeatedly condemned this occupation as illegal. United Nations

Security Council Resolution 242, passed shortly after the 1967 war, reiterates the international law prohibition against "the acquisition of territory by war." It specifically declares the necessity of the "withdrawal of Israeli armed forces from territories occupied in the recent conflict." Israel, however, continues to ignore United Nations rulings and international law by maintaining its occupation of the West Bank and Gaza Strip, and denying the legitimate right of self-determination to the Palestinian people living there.

Israel's Crimes

In the course of maintaining this illegal occupation against the expressed wishes of the population, Israel has committed numerous human rights violations. These violations fall within two broad categories. First, violations of the rights of individuals, and second, collective violations or violations which affect the structure of Palestinian society. Individual human rights abuses include killings; beatings; torture; shooting with live ammunition at unarmed civilians, including children; and imprisonment without being charged. Structural violations include the confiscation of land and water, Israeli settlements in the occupied territories, demolition and sealing of houses, collective punishments such as curfew and expulsions, closing of schools, prevention of economic development and employment, and taxation without representation or services.

Each year in the occupied territories, more Palestinian land is confiscated by the Israeli government. The owners are forced off their lands and deprived of their livelihoods, with no compensation. To date, 70% of the West Bank (not including East Jerusalem) and 30% of the Gaza Strip has been seized by the government of Israel. Water, a necessary and rare resource in the Middle East, is also extensively expropriated by the Israelis. Eighty-three percent of the water in the West Bank and Gaza Strip has been diverted from the Palestinians, for use by Israelis both in settlements in the occupied territories and within Israel. These water resources have literally been stolen from under the feet of the Palestinians, taken from underground aquifers. Deprived of this precious resource, Palestinians are unable to grow crops and feed their families. Further restricting Palestinian access to water, the Israeli military authorities prohibit them from digging new wells when the old ones run dry. Adding to the economic oppression of the Palestinians, the state of Israel levies heavy taxes, without furnishing the corresponding municipal services or political representation. Around-the-clock curfews, imposed on entire villages, prohibit Palestinians from earning money, buying food, and seeking medical attention. These curfews can last weeks or months at a time. Again, all of this is in violation of international law, as stated in the Fourth

Geneva Convention, and numerous United Nations rulings.

Hundreds of thousands of Palestinians have been forced to live in refugee camps. These camps are little more than shanty-towns crammed with tiny one-room shacks, which are usually unheated and without running water. Their narrow streets must double as sewers. Meanwhile, the land that was theirs for hundreds of years has been confiscated. This land was then given to Israeli settlers, many of whom are recent Jewish immigrants from such areas as the former Soviet Union and the United States. These Israeli settlements are contrary to the prohibition in international law against population transfer. Article 49 of the Fourth Geneva Convention specifically prohibits such settlements: "The Occupying Power shall not deport or transfer parts of its own civilian population into the territory it occupies."

The Palestinian Uprising

In response to these international law violations and the worsening situation in the occupied territories, the Palestinian *intifada*, or uprising, began in December 1987. To suppress this nonviolent protest movement, the Israeli army attempted to tighten its control over the Palestinian population, resulting in a dramatic increase in human rights violations against Palestinians.

One of the most prevalent Israeli human rights abuses is the practice of arbitrary arrest and detention. Under Israeli military law, Palestinians can be arrested and held in prison for periods up to six months, without trial or even charge. The Israeli authorities refer to this as "administrative detention." Imprisonment without due process of law violates both international law and the American Constitution. At any given time during the *intifada*, an average of 10,000–15,000 Palestinians were unlawfully detained by the Israeli military in the occupied territories. In 1990 when former American president Jimmy Carter visited the occupied territories, he noted in his report, "There is hardly a family that lives in the West Bank and Gaza that has not had one of its male members actually incarcerated by the military authorities." It is estimated that one in three adult male Palestinians have been detained at some time during their lives; many have been detained more than once.

The torture and beating of detainees is practiced regularly in Israeli prisons. Numerous Palestinians have died while under "interrogation." The Palestinian Human Rights Information Center, an internationally recognized human rights watch organization, reported that 35 people have died in detention from the start of the *intifada* to September 1993. The causes of these deaths include torture, medical negligence, shootings, and what is listed as "unexplained deaths." In one of these cases, a 17-year-old boy is reported to have died after being hooded and handcuffed to a chair for four days, denied food, and beaten repeatedly, especially on his spine, with hammer blows to his head and joints.

"We beat them and killed them, occupied their land and expelled them. Help us figure out what else we can do to them."

Higazi/*Al-Ahali.* By permission of MERIP/Middle East Report, 1500 Massachusetts Ave. NW, #119, Washington, DC 20005, from p. 45, *MER* no. 152, May/June 1988. MERIP's mission is to educate the public about the contemporary Middle East. Our work is especially concerned with U.S. policy, human rights, and social justice issues. MERIP's major program, *Middle East Report*, is a bimonthly magazine that provides a lively, independent look at the region and U.S. policy.

An even more atrocious fact is that during this same period 1,240 Palestinians were killed or executed by Israeli security forces. This number includes a long litany of deaths by torture, beatings, tear gas, and gunfire. Many of those killed were in their homes, on their way to work or school, or engaged in nonviolent protests, such as writing political graffiti. The victims range in age from the very young to the very old. During the raid of one home, the army beat a 75-year-old woman to death. Three hundred and twenty-five children, 16 years old or younger, were killed by Israeli forces. Indeed, infants have been shot by soldiers. One young boy, little more than a year and a half old, was killed while holding his father's hand. A 3-year-old girl was shot and killed while riding in her father's car. In another instance, two young boys, 11 and 12 years old, were shot in the head and killed while playing together. Ten-year-olds have been fatally shot, often multiple times, by Israeli army gunfire while coming home from school. Infants several months old have died from exposure to the extremely toxic elements in the tear gas used by the Israeli army.

The deaths reveal only part of the story. Approximately 130,000 Palestinians have been injured by the same means, namely, gunfire, torture, beatings, and tear gas. Again, one-third of all those injured were 16 or younger, and one-fourth were women. These injuries were of a serious nature: arms, legs, and eyes have been lost, skulls fractured, bones broken. Pregnant women have been beaten. The *Physicians for Human Rights Report*, a 1988 report by four American doctors on conditions in the territories, concluded that Israel was engaged in "an unrestrained epidemic of violence by the army and police," and that many injuries were intentionally inflicted with the aim of breaking limbs. The member states of the European Community have stated that they "deeply deplore the repressive measures taken by Israel, which are violations of international law and human rights." Findings and reports by the United States Department of State confirm these conclusions, as do Amnesty International, the International Red Cross, Middle East Watch, and the United Nations.

Collective Punishment

The Israeli military authorities also use collective punishments, targeted against entire families and villages, in an attempt to suppress dissent. Collective punishment is absolutely prohibited by the Fourth Geneva Convention, Article 33, which states, "No protected person may be punished for an offense he or she has not personally committed. Collective penalties and likewise all measures of intimidation or of terrorism are prohibited." Demolitions and sealings of the homes of suspected protesters are one form of collective punishment. From the start of the uprising, 2,500 houses have been demolished or sealed. Demolitions can take place at any hour of the day or night. Families are given as little as an hour to pack their belongings, and with no place to go are left destitute in the street. This tactic is used to suppress protest and instill fear in the community. The Palestinian school system, from kindergartens to universities, was closed by the Israeli military authorities, for several years, significantly disrupting the intellectual development of an entire generation of Palestinians. Another method of collectively oppressing the Palestinian population is the systematic uprooting of economically valuable orchards and trees. Over 160,000 such trees have been uprooted during this period, depriving the owners of their main source of livelihood.

Israel's digression from American values is not limited to the lands conquered in the 1967 war, but extends to within the boundaries of Israel itself. Israel practices a peculiar type of democracy, with no constitution. The set of "Fundamental Laws," which effectively replace a constitution, are overtly discriminatory against non-Jews. Only those of the Jewish faith are entitled to full rights within Israel, including equal access to housing, social benefits, land control, and employment. Title to 93% of the land, for example, is held for the exclusive use of Jewish people. Many job opportunities in the government, the largest employer in Israel, are restricted to veterans, precluding Arabs who are not allowed to serve in the military. In Israeli Arab municipalities, the communities pay taxes without receiving proportional services. Some villages receive no services at all for the taxes they pay. For example, dozens of villages in the Galilee, home to approximately 40,000 taxpaying Palestinians, are not officially recognized by the state. As a result, these villages are without sewage systems, electricity, health facilities, and roads. Despite the patent injustice of this situation these communities have no legal recourse, since Arabs are officially considered second-class citizens. According to a justice of Israel's High Court, "The essence of a Jewish state is to give preeminence to Jews as Jews. Anyone who asks, in the name of democracy, for equality to all its citizens—Jews and Arabs—must be rejected as one who negates the existence of the Israeli state as the state of the Jewish people."

Subverting American Interests

In areas where the United States has distinct interests, Israel has subverted these interests while pursuing its own goals. For instance, while American hostages were being held in Iran in 1979, Israel continued to supply the Iranian government with military hardware. At a time when the Iranian government was actively hostile toward the United States, America's ally helped that government develop its military arsenal. In South Africa, Israel similarly ignored American goals as well as the desires of the international community. While the United States led an international economic boycott of South Africa in order to pressure the government to end its policies of apartheid and oppression of the indigenous black population, Israel continued its substantial economic relations and military cooperation with South Africa.

Another instance where American goals have been thwarted by Israeli actions is the case of Lebanon. Stability in Lebanon was an American policy goal; however Israel has worked to create instability, through its invasions, bombing and destruction of Lebanese villages, and its continued occupation of the southern part of Lebanon. The international community ruled that the continued presence of Israeli troops on Lebanese soil violates international law, and passed United Nations Resolution 425 stating this shortly after the 1978 invasion by Israel. In its most brutal violation of the international law guarantees against targeting civilians, Israel's 1982 invasion of Lebanon was responsible for the deaths of over 16,000 innocent civilians. As recently as July 1993, an Israeli invasion displaced over a quarter of a million civilians.

Americans, steeped as they are in the tradition and belief of human rights, should find these repeated violations of human rights and international law reprehensible. Still, the United States continues to give the money, technology, military equipment, and political support that allows Israel to continue along the same path. The United States has insulated Israel from international censure, vetoing numerous United Nations resolutions critical of Israeli human rights violations. The United States also continues its massive monetary aid to Israel, more than $3 billion each year. Putting this remarkable annual gift in perspective, it amounts to three times the aid given to the entire continent of Africa, and this continued aid to Israel contradicts American laws, which prohibit foreign aid to a country that, according to the United States Foreign Assistance Act, "engages in a consistent pattern of gross violations of internationally recognized human rights."

Within the context of the blatant disregard for even the most fundamental American principles of equality and freedom, unqualified support for Israel has made the grandiose ideals of the United States ring hollow. The practice of making exceptions for Israel, regardless of international law and human rights violations, poisons the American dedication to those values. To fulfill its role as world leader, the United States needs to exhibit evenhandedness in its relationship with Israel. Only unbiased support for justice will lead to a resolution of the conflict in the Middle East, and a resumption of respect for the United States and its values. As long as the present policy endures, the country that once stood as the bastion of civil liberties, freedom, and equality will continue to bear the accusations of hypocrisy and bias without an adequate response.

"Our aid to Israel . . . is comparatively one of the most cost-effective investments that the United States makes in support of its international interests."

The United States Should Maintain Aid to Israel

Thomas A. Dine

The United States has strategic and economic interests in giving aid to its only reliable ally in the Middle East, Thomas A. Dine argues in the following viewpoint. Dine contends that military aid protects America's and Israel's mutual interests of peace and democracy in the oil-rich Middle East, where hostile nations are rapidly strengthening their armies. He maintains that American aid is increasingly vital because of the combination of austerity measures in Israeli defense spending and the strain of immigrant absorption on Israel's economy. Dine is a former executive director of the American Israel Public Affairs Committee (AIPAC), a pro-Israel lobbying organization in Washington, D.C.

As you read, consider the following questions:

1. Why does Dine believe that Syria is a threat to Israel?
2. Why is the Jewish immigrant wave, at least initially, an economic burden on Israel, in the author's opinion?
3. According to Dine, what steps is Israel taking toward economic reform?

From Thomas A. Dine's testimony before the Subcommittee on Foreign Operations of the House Appropriations Committee, May 1, 1992.

I [am] in strong support of $3 billion in economic and military aid to Israel—that nation's lifeline—of which more than 80 percent is spent in the United States, and in continued strong support for $2 billion a year for five years in loan guarantees [approved by the United States in 1992] to help Israel absorb the hundreds of thousands of Russian and other immigrants who have already come.

Indeed, the absolute amount of our aid to Israel is substantial. But it is comparatively one of the most cost-effective investments that the United States makes in support of its international interests. U.S. expenditures in support of our European allies in NATO [North Atlantic Treaty Organization], for example, are more than 40 times the size of our aid to Israel. [Former] Secretary of Defense Dick Cheney noted in 1990 that "the United States provides aid and assistance to Israel, but we also get national security benefits in return." The relationship has been cooperative in the truest sense of the word. Just after the Gulf War, Secretary Cheney said that the crisis "has been a demonstration of the value of maintaining Israel's strength, and her ability to defend herself, and also the value of the strategic cooperation between our two countries."

Israel's Importance

The United States has a particular moral and strategic interest in Israel, the one democracy and our only reliable ally in the Middle East. It is the sole country in the region with meaningful free elections, a robust free press, checks and balances to prevent and correct abuses of authority, extensive protections for the rights of individuals and minorities, basic equality for women, and other vital safeguards and rights. The Israeli Supreme Court is the only independent judiciary in the region that is prepared to listen to grievances of all citizens, Jews and Arabs alike.

Israel thus stands in sharp contrast to other countries of the region, which include monarchies like Saudi Arabia, where power is permanently concentrated in the hands of a few wealthy princes; dictatorships like Iraq, whose crimes are so well known as not to require recitation, and like Syria, whose human rights record is no better than Iraq's; or radical fundamentalist regimes like Iran.

Even at this time of growing concern over the U.S. budget deficit and other domestic problems, polls still show that a large majority of Americans strongly supports U.S. economic and security assistance programs for Israel. An ABC News/*Washington Post* poll conducted in September 1991 revealed that 65% of Americans think the U.S. should either maintain its level of assistance to Israel or increase it. And in January of 1991, a CBS News/*New York Times* poll found that the percentage of Americans saying U.S. aid to Israel should be maintained at the same level or increased reached 83%. . . .

United States assistance to Israel has a critical impact on the security of the Jewish state. While Israel will benefit in the short term from the reduction in Iraq's military capability [following its Persian Gulf War defeat], its vital margin of security nevertheless continues to erode. This results largely from the severe financial and budgetary shortfalls faced by the Government of Israel for a number of years. Indeed, the effects of recent years' defense budget cuts will continue to be felt well into the 1990s. Defense expenditures in coming years will continue to be limited, and the Israel Defense Forces [IDF] are facing the choice of cancelling important projects or stretching them out over extended periods, thus driving up their ultimate cost.

The austerity measures cut Israel's defense spending by about 20% in a two-year period—one of the largest reductions ever imposed by a democracy in so brief a time span. National defense now represents only a quarter of the budget, and faces increasing competition because of the demands of immigrant absorption.

The IDF has revised its multiyear budgetary and procurement plans in light of the continuing financial crunch, exacerbated by the costs associated with the Persian Gulf War. Among the options the Israeli military is being forced to consider are a further reduction in the size of the IDF, including retiring professional soldiers and dismissing civilian staff, cutting back on the number of annual days for reserve duty, reducing investment in day-to-day security within Israel and the territories, cancelling R&D [research and development] projects and disbanding various commands within the IDF. Indeed, in December 1991, the IDF's Chief of Staff, Ehud Barak, stated that the defense cutbacks are leading to reductions in tanks, mechanized artillery, aircraft and training of reserves.

These ongoing reductions in Israel's defense resources continue to make American FMS [Foreign Military Sales] aid to Israel a vital component of that nation's ability to defend itself and thus maintain stability in the region. . . .

The Arab Military Buildup

Syria continues to build up its army with the openly stated goal of achieving "strategic parity"—i.e., a war option—with Israel, and even its membership in the U.S.-led Gulf War coalition has not dampened its enmity toward Israel. Syrian Vice President Abdul-Halim Khaddam criticized the U.S. delivery to Israel of the Patriot batteries which successfully intercepted Iraq's Scud missiles aimed at Israel's civilian population centers. In March of 1990, the Syrian General Mustafa Tlas, deputy armed forces commander, defense minister, and deputy prime minister, went as far as stating, "[President] Hafez al-Assad alone has an outlook for the future; that is, the conflict between the Arab nation and Zionism is over existence, not borders."

U.S.-Israeli Military Cooperation

More than 90% of all aid to Israel is defense related. This aid has fostered U.S.-Israel cooperation that has proven beneficial to the U.S. A recent Pentagon study revealed that a strong and stable research and development posture is vital as cuts are made in the defense budget. "Combining resources with those of our allies through effective cooperation will not only enhance our ability to achieve technological advancements, but should do so at a reduced cost," the study said. It identified 21 critical technologies to the U.S. It explicitly identified Israel as having specific capabilities in 15 of them.

Steven Liebes, *Near East Report*, February 17, 1992.

The Arab states, joined by Iran, have resumed their previous pattern of large-scale arms procurement. They have placed orders for billions of dollars worth of new weapons each year, and have tens of billions of dollars more still in the pipeline from past years. Since the 1973 Yom Kippur War, the leading Arab nations still at war with Israel have spent about $470 billion on their armed forces. U.S. arms sales in the region are on the increase again. Even after the destruction of much Iraqi hardware, the Arab world now outnumbers Israel four-to-one in tanks and almost five-to-one in aircraft. Many of the largest arms-importing countries in the world are nations actively hostile to Israel: Iraq, Iran, Saudi Arabia, Libya, and Syria. . . .

Immigrant Absorption

As a result of the successful efforts by the U.S. Congress and [Bush] Administration in winning the freedom of Jews throughout the world, Israel will be absorbing an estimated one million immigrants over the next 3-5 years [beginning in 1992]—a remarkable population increase of more than 20%. This is an unprecedented challenge, equivalent to the United States absorbing 50 million new immigrants. Over 400,000 have arrived in Israel since late 1989, boosting its population by nearly 10%. Israel took in 200,000 immigrants in 1990 and 170,500 in 1991, despite the disruptions caused by the Gulf War.

The colossal immigration wave has presented Israel with a great blessing as well as an enormous challenge. The greatest challenge lies in their economic absorption. In the short run, the burden on the economy will be great. The new immigrant who reached Israel last night may not yet be part of its productive economy, but he quickly joins the consuming public.

The cost of absorption of these new immigrants will be high. Israel will have to expand its infrastructure to accommodate the increase in size of the population. Large investments will be needed in housing, transportation, education, job training, job creation, and many other areas in order to handle an increase in the population by at least 20%. Israel's government [spent 16.8%] of its 1992 budget on absorption, compared to 7.6% in 1990. Over the next five years, Israel will devote a staggering $60 to $70 billion toward the absorption of these new immigrants.

Most of the cost will be borne by domestic Israeli sources and contributions from world Jewry. In 1992 alone, world Jewry raised more than $3 billion to assist in immigrant absorption. However, at least $20 billion will be required in foreign capital. Israel has sought to raise one half of that amount in the United States in absorption loan guarantees. . . .

An Expanding Economy

If proper financing is forthcoming, the real power of Israel's economic potential will be realized, and immigrant absorption will be a success. The U.S., whose economy has expanded dramatically after each wave of immigration, has never had one of this magnitude, nor has any other country.

Israel's economy has also expanded with every wave of immigration. The current wave causes the need for large amounts of capital. If the proper financing is in place to expand investments in high-growth, export-oriented, high-tech fields in which many of the immigrants are trained, the economic benefits will be tremendous. Only by borrowing from her friends to finance the economic expansion will Israel be able to meet this great challenge.

Israel has an impeccable record of paying back its foreign debt. Thanks to this record, as well as the present state of the Israeli economy and the effect immigration will have, there should be no doubt about Israel's ability to repay additional loans. By conventional methods of financing, Israel will be forced to take high-interest loans, with maturities of five to seven years. While such loan terms may be suitable for corporate investment, they defy the very nature of immigrant absorption. The benefits to the Israeli economy will be realized over a period of ten years or more, and—with U.S. loan guarantees—financing from the private sector with maturity rates of up to 30 years is possible.

Immigrants are not only coming from the territories of the former Soviet Union. Israel's Ethiopian community has doubled to 40,000 in the last two years, following the heroic airlift of over

14,000 Ethiopian Jews from Addis Ababa to Israel within 30 hours in May 1991. Some 4,000 Jews remain in Ethiopia, most in extremely remote locations accessible only by foot. More than 100 Ethiopian Jews continue to arrive in Israel each week.

An estimated 3 million Jews remain in the 15 former Soviet republics. Over 1.2 million have taken the first steps toward emigration, including 90% of the Jews living in the former Muslim republics. More than 600,000 have already applied for exit visas.

Periods of general upheaval in Russia have historically been accompanied by rising anti-Semitism. As conditions in the successor states continue to deteriorate, the Jewish minority remains at risk. Ethnic violence coupled with Islamic fundamentalism in Central Asia and the Caucasus has serious implications for the more than 250,000 Jews who live in those areas. Anti-Semitic incidents have been reported in several regions, particularly in Uzbekistan, Tadzhikistan, and Azerbaijan.

Economic Reform

Over the past several years, Israel has demonstrated how U.S. foreign assistance, in combination with strong and well-conceived corrective measures in the economy, can turn economic distress into an opportunity for recovery.

Capital market reform is now progressing at an unprecedented pace and led to a 75% increase in the Tel Aviv Stock Exchange in 1991. Israel continues to move down the long road of privatizing government-owned companies. In 1991, the Israeli government sold off more than $350 million in government-controlled assets. It . . . is preparing many more companies to be put on the block as well, including additional shares of Israel Chemicals; Bezek, the national telephone company; ZIM, Israel's shipping company; and six other major government-owned firms. Also, Israel will soon liquidate government shares in the nation's major banks.

There are clear signs that these economic reforms are paying off. The Israeli economy is at the start of an era of accelerated growth. In 1991, Israel's Gross Domestic Product (GDP) grew by 5.4% and in 1990 by 4.6%, while inflation has been kept to historic lows.

The U.S. General Accounting Office stated in a report released in February 1992: "We believe that if Congress authorizes the $10 billion in loan guarantees requested by the Israeli government, the Israeli government will likely be able to fully service its external debt and to continue its past record of payment." Dr. Stanley Fischer, former Chief Economist for the World Bank, stated in February 1992 before Congress: "Israel is an excellent credit risk, with an unblemished record of servicing its debt in far more difficult conditions than it is likely to face in the future. . . . The single best predictor of the likelihood that a country will default is whether it has done so before. . . . A country that has demonstrated the willingness and ability to implement the needed measures when it experiences balance of payment problems—as Israel has—is that much more credible as a good credit risk."

Standing Strong Together

Think for a moment about our strategic relationship. It is in America's interest to have a strong Israel that works closely with the United States on behalf of peace and stability in the region.

A strong Israel and a strong America stand together in opposition to the threat posed by various forms of radicalism in the Middle East. There are those in that area of the world who pursue policies that are fundamentally hostile to our most basic values. There are also those who employ or protect terrorists. Israel is our partner—indeed, a heroic partner—in the battle against international terrorism and its agents.

Dan Quayle, *U.S. Department of State Dispatch*, April 13, 1992.

The challenge for the United States is to continue to support, reinforce, and accelerate growth in the Israeli economy while encouraging continued economic reforms. Currently, 90% of all aid to Israel is defense-related, used either to purchase military equipment or to help service debt used to purchase military equipment in the past. This aid is vital to maintaining Israel's qualitative edge and to ease the extraordinarily high economic burden of defense.

Although the level of aid to Israel has remained steady for four years, the real value of that aid has declined. There has been a steady erosion in the value of Economic Support Funds and Foreign Military Sales credits to all aid recipients. Due to inflation, our aid package to Israel has eroded in value by over $1 billion since 1986. . . .

U.S. Aid Is Crucial

In sum, our aid to Israel has been a wise investment, because Israel is our one democratic friend and most reliable ally in a critical region of the world. But aid to Israel is particularly important for four reasons.

The first is to prevent any further erosion in Israel's narrow margin of security in a situation where its forces have been cut, while those of its adversaries—despite Desert Storm—continue their rapid growth. Moreover, in this era of concern over allied burden-sharing, it is important to remember that while we devote roughly $170 billion to the defense of NATO, whose members spend an average of only 5% of GDP on defense, Israel spends almost 25% of its GDP on defense.

The second reason aid is particularly important is to stay the course on the economic recovery and growth program on which Israel has embarked. This is no time to reduce our effort.

Another reason aid is crucial is to help enable Israel to meet the challenge of absorbing hundreds of thousands of new immigrants, mostly from the former Soviet Union.

Last, but not least, aid is an important tool to advance the peace process. Israel must feel confident of American support and commitment as it takes risks for peace. Israel is aware, however, of America's budget constraints and thus has not increased its basic aid request over the past four years despite the inflationary erosion of its real value.

"The termination of America's aid . . . would greatly improve [Israel's] international political standing. "

The United States Should Eliminate Aid to Israel

George W. Ball and Douglas B. Ball

Many Americans believe that the amount of U.S. foreign aid to Israel should be drastically reduced or even eliminated. In the following viewpoint, George W. Ball and Douglas B. Ball agree and argue that Israel suffers from its dependence on billions of dollars of U.S. aid. The authors assert that the elimination of aid would force long-overdue reform of Israel's economy and help Israel become more self-sufficient. George W. Ball, a former U.S. undersecretary of state and United Nations ambassador, is a columnist and investment banker in Washington, D.C. Douglas B. Ball, his son, is a historian who holds a master's degree in history from Yale University and a doctorate from the London School of Economics.

As you read, consider the following questions:

1. What problems are caused by Israel's lack of accountability for how it spends American aid, according to the Balls?
2. What do the authors identify as drags on Israel's economy?
3. Why do the Balls believe that the United States should grant aid contingent on Israel's progress toward a market economy?

Reprinted from *The Passionate Attachment: America's Involvement with Israel, 1947 to the Present* by George W. Ball and Douglas B. Ball by permission of W.W. Norton & Company, Inc. Copyright © 1992 by George W. Ball and Dr. Douglas B. Ball.

America's foreign aid programs have, at different times, been justified on different grounds.

In the immediate postwar period, the United States Marshall Plan provided economic assistance that enabled the shattered nations of Western Europe to rebuild.

In a second phase, which began under President Harry S Truman and reached its high point during the Kennedy years, America concentrated on helping nations in the so-called Third and Fourth Worlds to attain an economic development that would enable them to achieve self-generating growth. Aid was also furnished to countries that suffered Cold War subversion and communist external pressure.

Israel's Special Aid Status

Then the politicians and lobbyists superseded the academics and restructured the foreign aid machinery to advance their own political and military objectives. One result of this pragmatic *coup d'état* was that Israel replaced India as the prime recipient of America's largess.

Although the initial justification for America's aid to Israel was compassion for the tragedy of the Holocaust, leaders of the pro-Israeli lobby veered away from relying solely on emotion. They based their appeal instead on the hardheaded calculus of security. By blocking potential Soviet penetration in the Middle East, Israel could, they contended, serve a vital American interest. That rationale has, however, now lost relevance with the end of the Cold War, the disintegration of the Soviet empire, and the Gulf War.

Taken in combination, these new developments have put the Israeli leaders in an awkward position. Israel's claim to be a vital American strategic asset is now obsolete, and its brutalities to the Palestinian people have marred America's earlier compassion.

Today, U.S. foreign aid policy is no longer guided by a coherent strategy; it reflects, instead, the aberrations of America's domestic politics. The program is so distorted that the more than $3 billion of aid annually given to Israel, plus the $2.1 billion assigned annually to Egypt, comprise more than one third of the amounts appropriated for America's entire foreign aid program. . . .

Direct Aid That Benefits Israel

Between 1948 and fiscal year 1991, Congress approved net loans and grants for Israel aggregating $53,531 billion. That aid has contained both economic and military components. It includes outlays through the Economic Support Fund (ESF) and the Foreign Military Sales (FMS) programs.

Through 1961, aggregate U.S. aid to Israel had totaled only $508.1 million, split roughly 50-50 between grants and loans. In addition, Israel has used its political leverage to persuade the American Congress to grant it a long list of exemptions to restrictions that are strictly applied to America's other foreign aid recipients.

In dealing with any matter affecting Israel, Congress responds more obediently to AIPAC [American Israel Public Affairs Committee, a government lobbying organization] than to its own budget-cutting mandate. The discipline of the Gramm-Rudman-Hollings (GRH) Act, designed to reduce America's budget deficit, required severe cuts in almost all government programs. Yet Congress passed a supplemental appropriation to compensate Israel for its mandatory reduction. . . .

Asay, by permission of the *Colorado Springs Gazette Telegraph*.

For fiscal year 1991, Congress voted a $400 million loan guaranty, ostensibly to be used to pay for the resettling of Soviet Jews. Under that proposal, member firms of the Israeli construction industry would borrow from American commercial banks at a concessionary interest rate made possible by a U.S. government guarantee of 90 percent of the principal sum.

In addition, Congress gave Israel $650 million in compensation for losses suffered during the Gulf War; ordered the transfer of $700 million of surplus American military goods assigned to NATO [North Atlantic Treaty Organization] for Israeli use; and further ordered the storage of $300 million of military supplies in Israel.

In response, Defense Minister Moshe Arens announced that because of inflation and the geometric rise of the cost of weapons systems, Israel would request an increase in arms aid from $1.8 billion to $2.5 billion a year, starting in fiscal year 1992.

America's Understated Contribution

The $3 billion of directly appropriated aid, usually taken as the totality of America's assistance to Israel, therefore severely understates America's contribution. In response to a request from Congressman Lee H. Hamilton, chairman of the Subcommittee on Europe and the Middle East of the House Foreign Affairs Committee, for a statement of "all types of direct assistance provided to Israel by the United States," the State Department (after canvassing the other relevant departments and agencies) produced figures which show that the appropriate amount for U.S. direct assistance to Israel is not the $3 billion directly appropriated for that purpose, but, according to official sources, is $3.75 billion. When one includes the saving to Israel that America makes possible by permitting it to refinance its FMS debt, the amount of Israel's effective aid is increased by $150 million a year—raising America's annual contribution for the benefit of Israel to an aggregate of $3.90 billion.

Senator Robert Dole proposed in April 1990 that America should consider a 5 percent cut in the aid provided the present recipients, including Israel and Egypt, to free funds for the pressing needs of Eastern Europe. As might have been expected, Dole's proposal evoked a storm of vitriolic protests from fellow senators and members of the House. He reportedly commented at the time that, although some of his fellow senators were publicly attacking him, they were privately as critical of Israel as he was: ". . . they won't say it out loud, but they grab you in the cloakroom and tell you, 'You're right. I can't say it because I'm running' but 'When I've been here as long as you have, I'll be able to say it.'"

On May 1, 1990, in a speech on the Senate floor, Dole discussed the extraordinary concessions and special privileges granted Israel. Counting all the extraordinary concessions, he said, the United States provides Israel with "nearly $4 billion—not the $3 + billion usually cited—in aid every year. That includes direct aid and side benefits. Some of those side benefits are not widely understood by the American public—perhaps not even by some members of Congress."

Dole's assertion that the aid approached $4 billion derived from a study made (at his request) by the Congressional Research

Service (CRS), under the direction of its Middle Eastern specialist, Clyde R. Mark. The study analyzed the value to Israel of the principal special benefits of over thirty items. The most important of these was the decision of Congress to waive completely the repayment of annual FMS aid for fiscal year 1981 and subsequent years, and the decision in 1985 to accord ESF aid the same gratis treatment. That effectively placed all U.S. aid to Israel on a gift basis.

Another concession was to treat Israel's granted funds as, in effect, an increment to its general revenues. As a result, the United States deprived itself of any viable means of ascertaining how Israel was spending its American gifts, even when it was suspected of using them to undercut U.S. interests. The lack of accountability became starkly clear in 1991 when the U.S. government determined that no U.S. aid should be used for settling Soviet immigrants in the West Bank. Yet there was no way of checking how such aid was being used.

As revised in 1979, the program further undermined the concept of accountability. It reduced the obligations of the Israeli government to keep books on our economic aid, supposedly used solely for the purchase of American goods, to simply giving a general assurance that Israel would buy an unspecified amount of civilian imports from the United States. Since there is no check on whether that assurance is being honored, Israel's "buy American" promises can be easily evaded. Indeed, the program's loose oversight may well have stimulated the excessive consumerism that has debilitated the Israeli economy. . . .

Surviving an End to U.S. Aid

Widespread attention [in 1991-92] to the question of whether Israel needed [$10 billion in U.S.] loan guarantees soon revived the larger question as to when, if ever, America might prudently discontinue its whole aid package. Although the termination of America's aid might cost Israel money, it would greatly improve the country's international political standing. Israel would cease to be a mendicant nation and would instead become a self-supporting and hence self-respecting member of the international community.

Though some sensible Israelis have long yet quietly cherished the objective of self-sufficiency, government spokesmen continue by rote to contend that the perpetuation of America's subsidy is vital to Israel's very survival.

Is that really true? Some respected economists who have studied the problem have reached the firm conclusion that, by improving its national efficiency, Israel could in a short time position itself to survive the total loss of American aid.

History illuminates that point. During the quarter century

from 1949 to 1973, America stringently limited its aid to loans, to a cumulative total of $3.2 billion. Then, beginning in 1974, the United States recklessly turned out its pockets. During the following seventeen years, our country provided Israel with aid aggregating over $53 billion. Moreover, after 1984 all America's aid took the form of gifts, while, in addition, the U.S. forgave substantial past loans.

The United States and the Zionist Entity

The United States has demonstrated that it is primarily responsible for the aggressive and expansionist policies of the Zionist entity [Israel] against the Palestinian Arab people and the Arab nation—never mind the occasional disagreement it professes with this or that stance or behavior of the Zionist entity. It would not have been possible for the Zionist entity to engage in aggression and expansion at the Arabs' expense if it did not possess the force and political cover provided by the United States—the main source of the Zionist entity's aggressive military force, and the main source of its financial resources.

Saddam Hussayn, *Saddam Speaks on the Gulf Crisis*, 1992.

One might have expected that this unprecedented expansion in aid would have materially increased the growth rate of Israel's GNP [gross national product]. But its effect was quite the contrary. In contrast to the 9 percent figure of the earlier period, the growth rate of Israel's GNP since our 1974 aid expansion never exceeded 5 percent a year, and, particularly after the Likud bloc took over in 1977, that rate, except for one year (1986), fluctuated feebly between 1 and 3 percent.

Israel's Economic Drags

The reasons for this apparently irrational result are a matter of speculation. A most likely explanation is that America's quantum increase in aid—and the implication that America would continue to play Santa Claus to the same spacious degree indefinitely—deprived Israel of the incentive needed to put its house in order. Abstractly, that operation should not be difficult. Merely by eliminating certain obvious economic drags inherent in its history, structure, and practices, the Israeli economy should be restored to its earlier growth pattern.

These economic drags are easy to identify. The state owns directly or indirectly 93 percent of the land in Israel proper, and the country derives more than 20 percent of its national income from government-controlled enterprises. Even private sector businesses are so overregulated that individual initiative—and efficiency—are smothered.

The greatest restraints on Israeli production derive from its stifling bureaucracy and the relatively low competence of its state-owned unprofitable industries, where the value of a worker's output is less than half that of his counterpart in the United States. Industries managed by bureaucrats prodigally consume vast governmental expenditures and subventions, while their top-heavy bureaucratic structures contribute to exorbitant inflation. These factors, in turn, inhibit capital formation while encouraging barter, corruption, tax evasion, and black market activities.

Added to all this are the painful costs of Israel's colonization program for its Occupied Territories. That program imposes a steady drain on capital resources to build new housing and maintain repressive control of the territories' Palestinian inhabitants.

Thomas G. Donlan, the editorial page editor of *Barron's*, wrote on February 17, 1992:

> Throughout the Israeli economy, restructuring is still mostly a matter of words.

> Thanks to borrowing and aid, the government can spend more than $40 billion a year while the economy produces only about $55 billion. Some $5.5 billion of those government outlays go for a hopeless mess of public subsidies to industry, transportation, housing, health, loans and so forth. That's almost equal to the defense budget of the tiny nation surrounded by enemies. The people that "made the desert bloom" subsidize farmers' income with one hand and food prices with the other hand. Individual income taxes average 56%. Tax evasion is correspondingly large. Some analysts guess the untaxed cash economy accounts for 25% of national output.

Overhanging these economic burdens are the formidable costs of Israel's armed forces, which absorb about 25 percent of its annual budget and GNP compared with a diminishing 6 percent for America. Israel's military expenditures drain an excessive volume of resources. They could be significantly reduced were Israel to make peace with its neighbors.

Stimulating Growth and Eliminating Aid

A sensible economic program would require Israel to concentrate on reducing all obstacles to rapid growth while the United States and Israel simultaneously reached agreement on timing the elimination of American aid.

Even though Finance Minister Yitzhak Modai and certain other political leaders have privately whispered that they would welcome a program of substantially reduced aid as an incentive to restructure its economy, Israel's cabinet has given it no support. Almost every member of the cabinet controls a ministry which he regards as his own patronage fiefdom. That fiefdom gives him both power and status, and he will defend it against every assault of economic logic. In the words of one widely read Israeli columnist, "Control over the economy translates into political domination."

Unhappily, the trend toward further government ownership still continues. The government has expanded the public payroll from 18 percent to nearly 29 percent of the total work force, and has nearly doubled its share of the gross national product from 59 percent in 1973 until, during the period 1983-91, it ran between 90 and 110 percent of GNP.

A Blueprint for Reform

But that does not necessarily call for a pessimistic prognosis. The Israeli government could largely free itself from its humiliating dependence on America's generosity by following a blueprint suggested by Professor Stanley Fischer, who served from 1984 to 1987 as consultant to the American Department of State on the Israeli economy, and Dr. Herbert Stein, who was chairman of the Council of Economic Advisers under Presidents Richard Nixon and Gerald Ford. They argued in a jointly written article that:

- Israel should move with increasing speed and determination to privatize banks and other government-owned firms and get enterprises back into non-state ownership and control where they will be subject to the discipline of the market;

- It should correct labor laws and regulations that obstruct adjustment of wage rates to market conditions, and abolish measures that impede the employment of new immigrants, impede operation of plants on second and third shifts, and weaken incentives for unemployed workers to seek work;

- It should apply stern fiscal and monetary policies to reduce inflation from the present rate of 20 percent a year to 15 percent, and thereafter to 5 percent or less;

- It should reduce to zero within three years its budget deficit, now running at about 5 percent of gross national product;

- It should abolish all protective measures that shelter Israel's industry and agriculture, and so expose them to "the discipline of foreign competition," and, at the same time, it should drastically shrink the government bureaucracy by downsizing and streamlining regulatory structures;

- It should abolish all remaining controls on foreign-exchange transactions;

- It should substantially reduce government regulation and the bureaucracy that administers it.

To promote this program, they conclude, Israel should establish an independent commission to review the regulations and recommend the elimination of those that impede the operation of the market.

This need to reform Israel's economy is expressed by both concerned Israelis and informed American visitors to the country. . . . Joel Bainerman, an Israeli economic columnist, writes in the *Jerusalem Post:*

> It's important for both pro-Israel supporters and anti-Israeli voices to understand that Israel isn't, by definition, dependent on U.S. aid. The moment that faucet is shut, Israeli leaders would be forced to cut the national budget and sell off state-owned assets. . . . But as long as the yearly overdrafts are paid for by foreigners, the politicians will never voluntarily release their control over the economy.

In watching the Soviet empire disintegrate, America has insisted that before it and other Western countries provide substantial aid, the new nations broken off from that empire must show tangible progress toward market economies. Why, then, should America not apply that same standard to Israel by curtailing its assistance until Israel takes visible steps to privatize the residue of its state-owned institutions—and employ the funds derived from their sale (estimated at $15 billion) to restructure and rebuild an efficient, profit-driven society? There is no way our country could benefit Israel more than by pressing its leaders to abandon the residue of a system based on an intellectually bankrupt concept.

Periodical Bibliography

The following articles have been selected to supplement the diverse views presented in this chapter.

Shmuel Amir — "After the Gulf War," *Monthly Review*, April 1992.

Eugene Bird — "At the Grass Roots, Westerners Say, 'Rein in Israel,'" *Washington Report on Middle East Affairs*, September/October 1993. Available from American Educational Trust, PO Box 53062, Washington, DC 20009.

Jeffrey Blankfort — "Blank Check to Israel," *Lies of Our Times*, October 1993.

Warren Christopher — "Remarks by Secretary of State Warren Christopher," *Middle East Policy*, vol. 2, no. 1, 1993. Available from the Middle East Policy Council, 1730 M St. NW, Suite 512, Washington, DC 20036.

Bill Clinton and Yitzhak Rabin — "Strengthening US-Israeli Relations to Benefit America's Interests," *U.S. Department of State Dispatch*, March 22, 1993.

Steven R. David — "Bosom of Abraham," *Policy Review*, Winter 1991.

Thomas A. Dine — "Israel's Strategic Value in 1992," *Near East Report*, April 27, 1992. Available from Near East Research, 440 First St. NW, Suite 607, Washington, DC 20001.

In These Times — "Time to Stop Paying for Israeli Apartheid," April 5, 1993.

Donald Neff — "Israel's Dependence on the US: The Full Extent of the Special Relationship," *Middle East International*, May 1, 1992. Available from 1700 17th St. NW, Suite 306, Washington, DC 20009.

Dan Quayle — "The United States and Israel: An Unshakable Alliance," *U.S. Department of State Dispatch*, April 13, 1992.

William R. Van Cleave — "U.S.-Israeli Relations: A New Crisis," *Global Affairs*, Spring 1992. Available from Subscription Services, Dept. GLA, PO Box 3000, Denville, NJ 07834-9792.

For Further Discussion

Chapter 1

1. In his viewpoint, David Ben-Gurion argues that both Arabs and Jews are entitled to their own states in the land of Palestine. Author George Antonius disagrees and contends that the only Palestinian state should be an Arab one. Which argument do you find more persuasive? Why? What concerns do the authors share toward Arab and Jewish rights?

2. Judah L. Magnes stresses that creating a Jewish homeland would benefit Jews around the world and revive Judaism. But he also argues that such a homeland should be achieved peacefully. History, though, shows that the Jewish homeland was created through violence and war. Do you believe that the end justified the means—that Jewish settlers had a right to use violence to secure a homeland? Give reasons for your answer.

Chapter 2

1. Meir Kahane and Uri Avnery disagree on how nationalism can benefit Israel and the Jewish people. While Kahane promotes religious nationalism, Avnery advocates the secular version. What are the limitations and promises of these types of nationalism, according to the authors?

2. Israeli conservative Benjamin Netanyahu argues that the lie of Zionism-as-racism reflects the lies that anti-Semites spread throughout Nazi Germany—lies that led to the Jewish Holocaust. Palestinian Sami Hadawi contends that Zionism should no longer capitalize on the past persecution of Jews. Do you believe that Netanyahu's argument is valid? Why or why not? Are the Nazi atrocities relevant to current debates about Zionism? Explain your answer.

Chapter 3

1. Yitzhak Rabin's election as Israeli prime minister in 1992 instilled much optimism among Israelis for peace between Jews and Palestinians. How does Rabin's viewpoint reflect this optimism?

2. Ze'ev Benjamin Begin is a conservative Likud Party member in Israel's parliament. Khalil Jahshan is a Palestinian activist and the director of an Arab-American association. Explain how their affiliations could influence their opinions concerning the Israel-PLO accord and peace.

3. Syrian president Hafez al-Assad and former Israeli ambassador Zalman Shoval disagree on Syria's peaceful intentions. What type of evidence does each author use to support his

argument? Compare their evidence and determine whether one author is more convincing than the other. Explain.

Chapter 4

1. Palestinian leader Haydar 'Abd al-Shafi asserts Palestinians' international right to independence. How does he appeal to readers' emotions in his viewpoint? Should the international community recognize any and all people's claims of independence, or should it refuse to recognize certain claims? What criteria should be used to consider claims of independence? Explain your reasoning.

2. What sources of information does conservative Israeli leader Benjamin Netanyahu first use to support his assertion that Jordanians and Palestinians belong to the same group of people? Is his tactic effective? Why or why not?

3. Authors Bernard I. Lindner and Adnan Abu Odeh both agree that Jerusalem is an important holy site for Christians, Jews, and Muslims. But they disagree that Jews should rule the city. Read both viewpoints and compare the historical evidence each author uses to support his argument. Do you believe that the historical record justifies Jewish rule of Jerusalem, or do more recent events justify some Arab control? Explain your answer.

Chapter 5

1. A stereotype is an oversimplified or exaggerated description of people or things. On reading the viewpoint by Peter Schwartz, do you recognize any stereotypes? If so, do you believe that they strengthen his argument? Why or why not?

2. Authors Judith D. Simon and Rita J. Simon and Graham Usher describe vastly different conditions in the Israeli prisons and detention camps holding Palestinian prisoners. What reasons can you think of for this discrepancy? Do you believe that the Israeli army could have covered-up poor conditions or that the prisoners could have exaggerated their abuse? If so, what would be their motives?

Chapter 6

1. Authors Charles Brooks and Anne Marie Baylouny base their arguments for and against U.S.-Israeli relations on completely different grounds: America's national security versus Palestinian human rights, respectively. Do you think that America's security outweighs human rights protection or vice-versa? Why or why not? Which side do you believe international opinion favors?

2. Thomas A. Dine argues that Israel remains a valuable strategic asset to America despite the demise of the Soviet Union. George W. Ball and Douglas B. Ball disagree with Dine and argue that the Soviet Union's demise reduces Israel's strategic value. Which argument do you find more convincing? What threat did the Soviet Union pose to Israel and the United States? Do you believe that an arms race among Arab nations is more dangerous to Israel than the Soviet Union was? Why or why not?

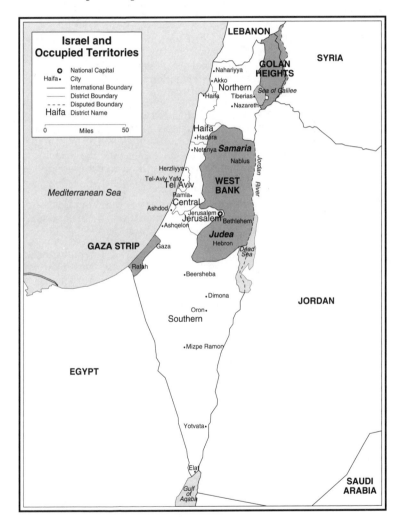

Chronology of Events

1881	Russian pogroms force thousands of Jews to move west. Leo Pinsker founds the Hibbat Zion movement which urges persecuted Jews to settle Palestine as a national homeland.
1882	A student society establishes Rishon le Zion, the first Zionist settlement in Palestine. Several other colonies are founded soon after.
1897	Theodor Herzl convenes First Zionist Congress, which designates Palestine as an appropriate Jewish homeland. Less than 10 percent of Palestine's population is Jewish.
1915	Sir Henry McMahon enlists the support of the Arabs in Britain's World War I effort against Turkey by promising British approval of a unified Arab nation. Arab nationalists later argue this promise includes Palestine; the British maintain Palestine must be an exception to Arab rule.
November 2, 1917	British foreign secretary A.J. Balfour declares Britain's support for a national homeland for the Jewish people in Palestine.
December 9, 1917	Allied forces advance into Jerusalem during World War I and force the city's surrender, ending four hundred years of Turkish rule.
1920-1948	Britain rules Palestine under agreement with the League of Nations. The British Mandate approves limited immigration for Jews.
1929-1939	Arabs rebel violently against British rule; Jews and Arabs fight each other for the right to live in Palestine.
1930	The British government, reacting to Arab riots against Jewish immigration, publishes the Passfield White Paper, which advocates restriction of Jewish immigration and land sales in Palestine.
1937	A British Royal Commission headed by Lord Peel, reports that Arab and Jewish national aspirations are irreconcilable and recommends the partition of Palestine.
1933-1939	Hitler takes power in Germany and begins segregating Jews. In these six years, he forbids

marriage between Jews and Germans, demands that Jews wear yellow stars and encourages the destruction of synagogues and Jewish property.

1939	The British tighten limits of Jewish immigration into Palestine.
1939-1945	During World War II, six million Jews are killed by Nazis. The Jewish population in Palestine reaches 608,000 by 1946.
1945-1948	Zionist organizations wage a campaign of violence to end immigration restrictions in Palestine; thousands of Jews enter Palestine illegally.
November 29, 1947	United Nations (UN) General Assembly votes to partition Palestine into Jewish and Arab states with Jerusalem being an international city. Arabs reject the plan.
May 14, 1948	David Ben-Gurion, Israel's first prime minister, proclaims the state of Israel. Five Arab League states invade Israel soon after. Israel annexes large tracts of proposed Palestinian state. Only the West Bank (under Jordanian administration) and the Gaza Strip (Egypt) remain in Arab hands.
January 1950	The new Law of Return grants every Jew the right to immigrate to Israel. Israel declares Jerusalem as its capital despite protest from Arab states and the UN.
July 1956	Egypt seizes control of the Suez Canal from its British and French owners.
October 29, 1956	Israel attacks the Sinai Peninsula and pushes toward the Suez Canal as part of an invasion coordinated with the British and French. The United States leads UN opposition to the action and persuades Israel to withdraw.
June 1964	Arab leaders convene in Jerusalem and create the Palestine Liberation Organization (PLO) nationalist movement. The Palestine National Charter calls for the PLO to engage in armed struggle to "liquidate the Zionist presence in Palestine." Yasir Arafat's Fatah group carries out its first raid on Israel the following year.
June 5-10, 1967	Six Day War. Israel attacks Egypt, Jordan, and Syria in what it calls a pre-emptive strike and captures the Sinai Peninsula and Gaza Strip from Egypt, the Golan Heights from Syria, and

	the West Bank and East Jerusalem from Jordan. One million Arabs living in the captured territories come under Israeli rule.
November 22, 1967	UN Security Council passes Resolution 242, calling for Israeli withdrawal from territory taken in the Six Day War, recognition of all states in the region, and a just settlement of the Palestinian refugee problem.
1969	Fatah faction takes control of the PLO and Arafat becomes PLO chairman.
October 6, 1973	Yom Kippur War. Egypt and Syria launch a two-front surprise attack on Israeli forces in the Sinai Peninsula and the Golan Heights on the holiest day of the Jewish calendar. Israel forces them back and negotiates cease-fire lines in the Sinai and Golan.
April 1975	Civil war in Lebanon begins.
November 1975	The UN General Assembly adopts a resolution equating Zionism with racism.
September 5-17, 1978	Camp David conference leads to the signing of a peace treaty in March 1979 by Egyptian president Anwar Sadat and Israeli prime minister Menachem Begin. Under the agreement, Israel returns all of the Sinai Peninsula to Egypt by 1982.
July 1980	Israel affirms the entire city of Jerusalem as its capital, encompassing the annexed Arab East Jerusalem.
1981	Jewish settlements on the West Bank begin.
December 14, 1981	Israel annexes the Golan Heights in Syria. The UN Security Council declares the annexation "null and void." Israel refuses to withdraw.
June 1982	Israel's ambassador to Britain is wounded by guerrillas in London. In retaliation, Israeli defense minister Ariel Sharon leads an invasion into Lebanon to dismantle Palestinian militia bases. Israeli forces advance to Beirut. Under heavy shelling, the PLO agrees to leave Lebanon and relocates in Tunis, Tunisia.
September 1984	Shimon Peres becomes prime minister of Israel.
January 1985	Israel begins withdrawal from Lebanon and declares a nine-mile-wide security zone north of Israeli-Lebanese border. Syria remains in control of most of Lebanon.

September 1986	Yitzhak Shamir of the conservative Likud Party replaces Shimon Peres as prime minister of Israel.
December 1987	Four Palestinians are killed in the northern Gaza Strip when an Israeli army truck collides with cars transporting Arab workers. Their funeral turns into a demonstration as thousands protest the killing as Israeli retaliation for the slaying of a Jewish merchant in Gaza. The demonstration marks the beginning of the uprising known as the *intifada*.
August 1988	King Hussein of Jordan announces the severing of legal and administrative ties to the West Bank. Jordan ceases to pay the salaries of the twenty-four thousand teachers, doctors, religious officials, and municipal employees it has maintained there. Responsibility for the West Bank's economic and municipal functions shifts to the PLO.
November 1988	Palestine National Council declares a Palestinian state and implicitly recognizes Israel by endorsing UN Resolution 242.
December 13-14, 1988	The Palestine National Council accepts original UN partition plan (UN General Assembly Resolution 181) and UN Security Council Resolutions 242 and 338. It also accepts Israel's right to exist and renounces terrorism. The United States immediately opens formal dialogue with the PLO.
1990	Israel airlifts most of Ethiopia's Jews to Israel.
August 1991	U.S. secretary of state James Baker III proposes Middle East peace conference. Israel, Jordan, Lebanon, and Syria agree to attend.
October 31- November 1, 1991	First round of peace negotiations take place in Madrid, Spain. It is the first peace conference ever between Israel and the Palestinians.
December 16, 1991	The UN General Assembly revokes the 1975 resolution equating Zionism with racism.
June 1992	Israel's Labor Party gains control of the government in Parliamentary elections.
July 1992	Yitzhak Rabin replaces Yitzhak Shamir as Israel's prime minister and agrees to limit construction of new Jewish settlements in the occupied territories.

September 1992	A Norwegian social science institute offers to host secret negotiations in Oslo between Israel's Labor government and the Palestinians. Both sides accept.
December 1992	Three Israeli soldiers are killed by a drive-by shooting in the worst single attack on soldiers since the beginning of the *intifada*. Hamas activists kidnap and kill an Israeli border policeman. Israel arrests more than four hundred suspected Islamic militants and deports them to southern Lebanon.
January 19, 1993	Israel's parliament lifts a 1986 ban on contacts with the PLO.
July 25, 1993	Retaliating for the killing of seven Israeli soldiers and rocket attacks on Israeli settlements by pro-Iranian Hezbollah militia attacks, Israel launches its fiercest offense on Lebanon since the establishment of the border security zone. The weeklong air and artillery assault on seventy villages in southern Lebanon kills more than one hundred Lebanese and drives more than three hundred thousand refugees northward.
August 1993	Israelis and Palestinians meeting in Oslo, Norway, reach a tentative agreement for Palestinian self-rule in the occupied territories.
September 9, 1993	Israel allows the return of nearly half of the more than four hundred suspected Islamic militants deported to Lebanon. The vast majority are arrested immediately.
September 13, 1993	Yasir Arafat and Yitzhak Rabin sign a breakthrough Declaration of Principles, the first agreement between Israel and the PLO, which calls for Palestinian self-government initially in the Gaza Strip and West Bank town of Jericho. The agreement sets deadlines for the resolution of other Israeli-Palestinian disputes.
September 13, 1993	Israel and Jordan sign an agreement that lays the foundation for a treaty to officially end the 1967 Six Day War.
October 13, 1993	Israel and the PLO open negotiations in Egypt for Palestinian self-rule.

Text of Israeli-Palestinian Declaration of Principles on Interim Self-Government Arrangements

Following is the text of the Declaration of Principles between the Government of the State of Israel and the P.L.O. team (in the Jordanian-Palestinian delegation to the Middle East Peace Conference) signed in Washington, D.C., September 13, 1993, and released by the U.S. Department of State.

The Government of the State of Israel and the P.L.O. team (in the Jordanian-Palestinian delegation to the Middle East Peace Conference) (the "Palestinian Delegation"), representing the Palestinian people, agree that it is time to put an end to decades of confrontation and conflict, recognize their mutual legitimate and political rights, and strive to live in peaceful coexistence and mutual dignity and security and achieve a just, lasting and comprehensive peace settlement and historic reconciliation through the agreed political process. Accordingly, the two sides agree to the following principles:

Article I: *Aim of the Negotiations*

The aim of the Israeli-Palestinian negotiations within the current Middle East peace process is, among other things, to establish a Palestinian Interim Self-Government Authority, the elected Council (the "Council"), for the Palestinian people in the West Bank and the Gaza Strip, for a transitional period not exceeding five years, leading to a permanent settlement based on Security Council Resolutions 242 and 338.

It is understood that the interim arrangements are an integral part of the whole peace process and that the negotiations on the permanent status will lead to the implementation of Security Council Resolutions 242 and 338.

Article II: *Framework for the Interim Period*

The agreed framework for the interim period is set forth in this Declaration of Principles.

Article III: *Elections*

1. In order that the Palestinian people in the West Bank and Gaza Strip may govern themselves according to democratic principles, direct, free and general political elections will be held for the Council under agreed supervision and international observation, while the Palestinian police will ensure public order.

2. An agreement will be concluded on the exact mode and conditions of the elections in accordance with the protocol attached as Annex I, with the goal of holding the elections not later than nine months after the entry into force of this Declaration of Principles.

3. These elections will constitute a significant interim preparatory step toward the realization of the legitimate rights of the Palestinian people and their just requirements.

Article IV: *Jurisdiction*

Jurisdiction of the Council will cover West Bank and Gaza Strip territory, except for issues that will be negotiated in the permanent status negotiations. The two sides view the West Bank and the Gaza Strip as a single territorial unit, whose integrity will be preserved during the interim period.

Article V: *Transitional Period and Permanent Status Negotiations*

1. The five-year transitional period will begin upon the withdrawal from the Gaza Strip and Jericho area.

2. Permanent status negotiations will commence as soon as possible, but not later than the beginning of the third year of the interim period, between the Government of Israel and the Palestinian people representatives.

3. It is understood that these negotiations shall cover remaining issues, including: Jerusalem, refugees, settlements, security arrangements, borders, relations and cooperation with other neighbors, and other issues of common interest.

4. The two parties agree that the outcome of the permanent status negotiations should not be prejudiced or preempted by agreements reached for the interim period.

Article VI: *Preparatory Transfer of Powers and Responsibilities*

1. Upon the entry into force of this Declaration of Principles and the withdrawal from the Gaza Strip and the Jericho area, a transfer of authority from the Israeli military government and its Civil Administration to the authorised Palestinians for this task, as detailed herein, will commence. This transfer of authority will be of a preparatory nature until the inauguration of the Council.

2. Immediately after the entry into force of this Declaration of Principles and the withdrawal from the Gaza Strip and Jericho area, with the view to promoting economic development in the West Bank and Gaza Strip, authority will be transferred to the Palestinians on the following spheres: education and culture, health, social welfare, direct taxation, and tourism. The Palestinian side will commence in building the Palestinian police force, as agreed upon. Pending the inauguration of the Council, the two parties may negotiate the transfer of additional powers and responsibilities, as agreed upon.

Article VII: *Interim Agreement*

1. The Israeli and Palestinian delegations will negotiate an agreement on the interim period (the "Interim Agreement").

2. The Interim Agreement shall specify, among other things, the structure of the Council, the number of its members, and the transfer of powers and responsibilities from the Israeli military government and its Civil Administration to the Council. The Interim Agreement shall also specify the Council's executive authority, legislative authority in accordance with Article IX below, and the independent Palestinian judicial organs.

3. The Interim Agreement shall include arrangements, to be implemented upon the inauguration of the Council, for the assumption by the Council of all of the powers and responsibilities transferred previously in accordance with Article VI above.

4. In order to enable the Council to promote economic growth, upon its inauguration, the Council will establish, among other things, a Palestinian Electricity Authority, a Gaza Sea Port Authority, a Palestinian Development Bank, a Palestinian Export Promotion Board, a Palestinian Environmental Authority, a Palestinian Land Authority and a Palestinian Water Administration Authority, and any other Authorities agreed upon, in accordance with the Interim Agreement that will specify their powers and responsibilities.

5. After the inauguration of the Council, the Civil Administration will be dissolved, and the Israeli military government will be withdrawn.

Article VIII: *Public Order and Security*

In order to guarantee public order and internal security for the Palestinians of the West Bank and the Gaza Strip, the Council will establish a strong police force, while Israel will continue to carry the responsibility for defending against external threats, as well as the responsibility for overall security of Israelis for the purpose of safeguarding their internal security and public order.

Article IX: *Laws and Military Orders*

1. The Council will be empowered to legislate, in accordance with the Interim Agreement, within all authorities transferred to it.

2. Both parties will review jointly laws and military orders presently in force in remaining spheres.

Article X: *Joint Israeli-Palestinian Liaison Committee*

In order to provide for a smooth implementation of this Declaration of Principles and any subsequent agreements pertaining to the interim period, upon the entry into force of this Declaration of Principles, a Joint Israeli-Palestinian Liaison Committee will be established in order to deal with issues requiring coordination, other issues of common interest, and disputes.

Article XI: *Israeli-Palestinian Cooperation in Economic Fields*

Recognizing the mutual benefit of cooperation in promoting the development of the West Bank, the Gaza Strip, and Israel, upon the entry into force of this Declaration of Principles, an Israeli-Palestinian Economic Cooperation Committee will be established in order to develop and implement in a cooperative manner the programs identified in the protocols attached as Annex III and Annex IV.

Article XII: *Liaison and Cooperation with Jordan and Egypt*

The two parties will invite the Governments of Jordan and Egypt to participate in establishing further liaison and cooperation arrangements between the Government of Israel and the Palestinian representatives, on the one hand, and the Governments of Jordan and Egypt, on the other hand, to promote cooperation between them. These arrangements will include the constitution of a Continuing Committee that will decide by agreement on the modalities of admission of persons displaced from the West Bank and Gaza Strip in 1967, together with necessary measures to prevent disruption and disorder. Other matters of common concern will be dealt with by this Committee.

Article XIII: *Redeployment of Israeli Forces*

1. After the entry into force of this Declaration of Principles, and not later than the eve of elections for the Council, a redeployment of Israeli military forces in the West Bank and the Gaza Strip will take place, in addition to withdrawal of Israeli forces carried out in accordance with Article XIV.

2. In redeploying its military forces, Israel will be guided by the principle that its military forces should be redeployed outside populated areas.

3. Further redeployments to specified locations will be gradually implemented commensurate with the assumption of responsibility for public order and internal security by the Palestinian police force pursuant to Article VIII above.

Article XIV: *Israeli Withdrawal from the Gaza Strip and Jericho Area*

Israel will withdraw from the Gaza Strip and Jericho area, as detailed in the protocol attached as Annex II.

Article XV: *Resolution of Disputes*

1. Disputes arising out of the application or interpretation of this Declaration of Principles, or any subsequent agreements pertaining to the interim period, shall be resolved by negotiations through the Joint Liaison Committee to be established pursuant to Article X above.

2. Disputes which cannot be settled by negotiations may be resolved by a mechanism of conciliation to be agreed upon by the parties.

3. The parties may agree to submit to arbitration disputes relating to the interim period which cannot be settled through conciliation. To this end, upon the agreement of both parties, the parties will establish an Arbitration Committee.

Article XVI: *Israeli-Palestinian Cooperation Concerning Regional Programs*

Both parties view the multilateral working groups as an appropriate instrument for promoting a "Marshall Plan," the regional programs and other programs, including special programs for the West Bank and Gaza Strip, as indicated in the protocol attached as Annex IV.

Article XVII: *Miscellaneous Provisions*

1. This Declaration of Principles will enter into force one month after its signing.

2. All protocols annexed to this Declaration of Principles and Agreed Minutes pertaining thereto shall be regarded as an integral part hereof.

Annex I: *Protocol on the Mode and Conditions of Elections*

1. Palestinians of Jerusalem who live there will have the right to participate in the election process, according to an agreement between the two sides.

2. In addition, the election agreement should cover, among other things, the following issues:

a. the system of elections;

b. the mode of the agreed supervision and international observation and their personal composition; and

c. rules and regulations regarding election campaigns, including agreed arrangements for the organizing of mass media, and the possibility of licensing a broadcasting and TV station.

3. The future status of displaced Palestinians who were registered on 4th June 1967 will not be prejudiced because they are unable to participate in the election process due to practical reasons.

Annex II: *Protocol on Withdrawal of Israeli Forces from the Gaza Strip and Jericho Area*

1. The two sides will conclude and sign within two months from the date of entry into force of this Declaration of Principles an agreement on the withdrawal of Israeli military forces from the Gaza Strip and Jericho area. This agreement will include comprehensive arrangements to apply in the Gaza Strip and the Jericho area subsequent to the Israeli withdrawal.

2. Israel will implement an accelerated and scheduled withdrawal of Israeli military forces from the Gaza Strip and Jericho area, beginning immediately with the signing of the agreement on the Gaza Strip and Jericho area and to be completed within a period not exceeding four months after the signing of this agreement.

3. The above agreement will include, among other things:

a. Arrangements for a smooth and peaceful transfer of authority from the Israeli military government and its Civil Administration to the Palestinian representatives.

b. Structure, powers and responsibilities of the Palestinian authority in these areas, except: external security, settlements, Israelis, foreign relations, and other mutually agreed matters.

c. Arrangements for the assumption of internal security and public order by the Palestinian police force consisting of police officers recruited locally and from abroad (holding Jordanian passports and Palestinian documents issued by Egypt). Those who will participate in the Palestinian police force coming from abroad should be trained as police and police officers.

d. A temporary international or foreign presence, as agreed upon.

e. Establishment of a joint Palestinian-Israeli Coordination and Cooperation Committee for mutual security purposes.

f. An economic development and stabilization program, including the establishment of an Emergency Fund, to encourage foreign investment, and financial and economic support. Both sides will coordinate and cooperate jointly and unilaterally with regional and international parties to support these aims.

g. Arrangements for a safe passage for persons and transportation between the Gaza Strip and Jericho area.

4. The above agreement will include arrangements for coordination between both parties regarding passages:

a. Gaza-Egypt; and

b. Jericho-Jordan.

5. The offices responsible for carrying out the powers and responsibilities of the Palestinian authority under this Annex II and Article VI of the Declaration of Principles will be located in the Gaza Strip and in the Jericho area pending the inauguration of the Council.

6. Other than these agreed arrangements, the status of the Gaza Strip and Jericho area will continue to be an integral part of the West Bank and Gaza Strip, and will not be changed in the interim period.

Annex III: *Protocol on Israeli-Palestinian Cooperation in Economic and Development Programs*

The two sides agree to establish an Israeli-Palestinian Continuing Committee for Economic Cooperation, focusing, among other things, on the following:

1. Cooperation in the field of water, including a Water Development Program prepared by experts from both sides, which will also specify the mode of cooperation in the management of water resources in the West Bank and Gaza Strip, and will include proposals for studies and plans on water rights of each party, as well as on the equitable utilization of joint water resources for implementation in and beyond the interim period.

2. Cooperation in the field of electricity, including an Electricity Development Program, which will also specify the mode of cooperation for the production, maintenance, purchase and sale of electricity resources.

3. Cooperation in the field of energy, including an Energy Development Program, which will provide for the exploitation of oil and gas for

industrial purposes, particularly in the Gaza Strip and in the Negev, and will encourage further joint exploitation of other energy resources. This Program may also provide for the construction of a Petrochemical industrial complex in the Gaza Strip and the construction of oil and gas pipelines.

4. Cooperation in the field of finance, including a Financial Development and Action Program for the encouragement of international investment in the West Bank and the Gaza Strip, and in Israel, as well as the establishment of a Palestinian Development Bank.

5. Cooperation in the field of transport and communications, including a Program, which will define guidelines for the establishment of a Gaza Sea Port Area, and will provide for the establishing of transport and communications lines to and from the West Bank and the Gaza Strip to Israel and to other countries. In addition, this Program will provide for carrying out the necessary construction of roads, railways, communications lines, etc.

6. Cooperation in the field of trade, including studies, and Trade Promotion Programs, which will encourage local, regional and inter-regional trade, as well as a feasibility study of creating free trade zones in the Gaza Strip and in Israel, mutual access to these zones, and cooperation in other areas related to trade and commerce.

7. Cooperation in the field of industry, including Industrial Development Programs, which will provide for the establishment of joint Israeli-Palestinian Industrial Research and Development Centers, will promote Palestinian-Israeli joint ventures, and provide guidelines for cooperation in the textile, food, pharmaceutical, electronics, diamonds, computer and science-based industries.

8. A program for cooperation in, and regulation of, labor relations and cooperation in social welfare issues.

9. A Human Resources Development and Cooperation Plan, providing for joint Israeli-Palestinian workshops and seminars, and for the establishment of joint vocational training centers, research institutes, and data banks.

10. An Environmental Protection Plan, providing for joint and/or coordinated measures in this sphere.

11. A program for developing coordination and cooperation in the field of communication and media.

12. Any other programs of mutual interest.

Annex IV: *Protocol on Israeli-Palestinian Cooperation Concerning Regional Development Programs*

1. The two sides will cooperate in the context of the multilateral peace efforts in promoting a Development Program for the region, including the West Bank and the Gaza Strip, to be initiated by the G-7. The parties will request the G-7 to seek the participation in this program of other interested states, such as members of the Organisation for Economic Cooperation and Development, regional Arab states and institutions, as well as members of the private sector.

2. The Development Program will consist of two elements:

a. an Economic Development Program for the West Bank and the Gaza Strip.

b. a Regional Economic Development Program.

A. The Economic Development Program for the West Bank and the

Gaza Strip will consist of the following elements:

(1) A Social Rehabilitation Program, including a Housing and Construction Program.

(2) A Small and Medium Business Development Plan.

(3) An Infrastructure Development Program (water, electricity, transportation and communications, etc.).

(4) A Human Resources Plan.

(5) Other programs.

B. The Regional Economic Development Program may consist of the following elements:

(1) The establishment of a Middle East Development Fund, as a first step, and a Middle East Development Bank, as a second step.

(2) The development of a joint Israeli-Palestinian-Jordanian Plan for coordinated exploitation of the Dead Sea area.

(3) The Mediterranean Sea (Gaza)-Dead Sea Canal.

(4) Regional Desalinization and other water development projects.

(5) A regional plan for agricultural development, including a coordinated regional effort for the prevention of desertification.

(6) Interconnection of electricity grids.

(7) Regional cooperation for the transfer, distribution, and industrial exploitation of gas, oil, and other energy resources.

(8) A Regional Tourism, Transportation, and Telecommunications Development Plan.

(9) Regional cooperation in other spheres.

3. The two sides will encourage the multilateral working groups, and will coordinate towards their success. The two parties will encourage intersessional activities, as well as pre-feasibility and feasibility studies, within the various multilateral working groups.

Agreed Minutes to the Declaration of Principles on Interim Self-Government Arrangements

A. *General Understandings and Agreements*

Any powers and responsibilities transferred to the Palestinians pursuant to the Declaration of Principles prior to the inauguration of the Council will be subject to the same principles pertaining to Article IV, as set out in these Agreed Minutes below.

B. *Specific Understandings and Agreements*

Article IV

It is understood that:

1. Jurisdiction of the Council will cover West Bank and Gaza Strip territory, except for issues that will be negotiated in the permanent status negotiations: Jerusalem, settlements, military locations, and Israelis.

2. The Council's jurisdiction will apply with regard to the agreed powers, responsibilities, spheres, and authorities transferred to it.

Article VI (2)

It is agreed that the transfer of authority will be as follows:

1. The Palestinian side will inform the Israeli side of the names of the authorised Palestinians who will assume the powers, authorities, and responsibilities that will be transferred to the Palestinians according to the Declaration of Principles in the following fields: education and culture, health, social welfare, direct taxation, tourism, and any other authorities agreed upon.

2. It is understood that the rights and obligations of these offices will

not be affected.

3. Each of the spheres described above will continue to enjoy existing budgetary allocations in accordance with arrangements to be mutually agreed upon. These arrangements also will provide for the necessary adjustments required in order to take into account the taxes collected by the direct taxation office.

4. Upon the execution of the Declaration of Principles, the Israeli and Palestinian delegations will immediately commence negotiations on a detailed plan for the transfer of authority on the above offices in accordance with the above understandings.

Article VII (2)

The Interim Agreement will also include arrangements for coordination and cooperation.

Article VII (5)

The withdrawal of the military government will not prevent Israel from exercising the powers and responsibilities not transferred to the Council.

Article VIII

It is understood that the Interim Agreement will include arrangements for cooperation and coordination between the two parties in this regard. It is also agreed that the transfer of powers and responsibilities to the Palestinian police will be accomplished in a phased manner, as agreed in the Interim Agreement.

Article X

It is agreed that, upon the entry into force of the Declaration of Principles, the Israeli and Palestinian delegations will exchange the names of the individuals designated by them as members of the Joint Israeli-Palestinian Liaison Committee. It is further agreed that each side will have an equal number of members in the Joint Committee. The Joint Committee will reach decisions by agreement. The Joint Committee may add other technicians and experts, as necessary. The Joint Committee will decide on the frequency and place or places of its meetings.

Annex II

It is understood that, subsequent to the Israeli withdrawal, Israel will continue to be responsible for external security, and for internal security and public order of settlements and Israelis. Israeli military forces and civilians may continue to use roads freely within the Gaza Strip and the Jericho area.

Organizations to Contact

The editors have compiled the following list of organizations concerned with the issues debated in this book. The descriptions are derived from materials provided by the organizations. All have publications or information available for interested readers. The list was compiled on the date of publication of the present volume; names, addresses, and phone numbers may change. Be aware that many organizations take several weeks or longer to respond to inquiries, so allow as much time as possible.

America-Israel Council for Israeli-Palestinian Peace (AICIPP)
4816 Cornell Ave.
Downers Grove, IL 60515
(708) 969-7584

The council is the American branch of the Israeli Council for Israeli-Palestinian Peace, which supports the Israel-PLO accord and the creation of an independent Palestinian state alongside Israel. AICIPP distributes *The Other Israel* monthly newsletter from Israel.

American-Arab Anti-Discrimination Committee (ADC)
4201 Connecticut Ave. NW, Suite 500
Washington, DC 20008
(202) 244-2990
fax: (202) 244-3196

ADC, the largest Arab-American organization in the United States, is a nonsectarian grassroots organization dedicated to the protection of the civil and legal rights of all people of Arab descent. It resists racism toward and stereotyping of Arab-Americans. ADC publishes the monthly newsletter *ADC Times*, which includes reports on U.S. Middle East policy.

The American Council for Judaism (ACJ)
PO Box 9009
Alexandria, VA 22304
(703) 836-2546

The council asserts that Judaism is a religion, not a nationality, and that Israel is not the homeland of all Jews. It believes that Jews who are not Israelis must live according to their beliefs and not necessarily according to Zionist thinking. ACJ publishes the quarterly *Issues of the American Council for Judaism.*

American Educational Trust (AET)
PO Box 53062
Washington, DC 20009
(202) 939-6050
fax: (202) 265-4574

AET seeks to disseminate unbiased and accurate information and analysis on the Middle East and on U.S. relations in the area. It supports Arab-Israeli solutions based on the United Nations charter and traditional American views on human rights, self-determination, and justice. It publishes the monthly magazine *Washington Report on Middle East Affairs* and the monthly *Translations from the Hebrew Press*.

American Israel Public Affairs Committee (AIPAC)
440 First St. NW, Suite 600
Washington, DC 20001
(202) 639-5200

AIPAC is the largest pro-Israel lobbying group in the United States and supports strong ties between the two nations. It provides information on American foreign policy in the Middle East and seeks to improve goodwill between Israel and the United States. The views of committee members are often published in the weekly publication *Near East Report*.

American Jewish Committee (AJC)
165 E. 56th St.
New York, NY 10022
(212) 751-4000

The committee conducts a program of education, research, and community services. It fights against bigotry and for civil and religious rights. AJC supports the Israel-PLO accord with cautious optimism but is opposed to a Palestinian state. AJC publishes the monthly journal *Commentary*, as well as pamphlets, and reprints.

American Jewish League for Israel (AJLI)
130 E. 59th St.
New York, NY 10022
(212) 371-1583

AJLI is a Zionist organization that seeks to rebuild the state of Israel and strengthen its ties with American Jewry. It publishes the monthly newsletter *News Bulletin of the American Jewish League for Israel*.

Americans for Middle East Understanding (AMEU)
475 Riverside Dr., Suite 241
New York, NY 10115
(212) 870-2053
fax: (212) 870-2050

AMEU's purpose is to foster a better understanding in America of the history, goals, and values of Middle Eastern cultures and peoples, the rights of Palestinians, and the forces shaping American policy in the Middle East. AMEU publishes *The Link*, a bimonthly newsletter, and books and pamphlets on the Middle East.

Americans for Progressive Israel (API)
224 W. 35th St., Suite 403
New York, NY 10001
(212) 868-0386

API is a socialist Zionist organization that provides information on Israel's labor and peace movements. API publishes the bimonthly magazine *Israel Horizons* and reprints and translations of articles from Israel.

Americans for a Safe Israel (AFSI)
147 E. 76th St.
New York, NY 10021
(212) 628-9400
fax: (212) 988-4065

AFSI provides information on the Middle East conflict "based on the belief that a strong Israel is vital to American interests." It publishes the monthly newsletter *Outpost*, books, pamphlets, and the booklet *Should America Guarantee Israel's Safety?*

American Zionist Movement (AZM)
110 E. 59th St.
New York, NY 10022
(212) 318-6100
fax: (212) 935-3578

AZM is the umbrella organization for more than twenty American Zionist organizations. AZM defends Israel and the Zionist cause and supports Israel as an ally of the United States. It promotes the travel of Jews to Israel and their investment in its economic development. AZM publishes *The Zionist Advocate* quarterly newsletter.

Anti-Defamation League of B'nai B'rith (ADL)
823 United Nations Plaza
New York, NY 10017
(212) 490-2525
fax: (212) 867-0779

The league's goal is to stop the defamation of Jewish people and to secure justice and fair treatment for all citizens. The ADL promotes better interfaith and intergroup relations and works to strengthen democratic structures and values and to counteract anti-Semitism. It publishes the newsletter *ADL on the Frontline News* ten times a year and several quarterly publications, including *Dimensions* and *Middle East Insight*.

Institute for Palestine Studies (IPS)
3501 M St. NW
Washington, DC 20007
(202) 342-3990
fax: (202) 342-3927

IPS is a pro-Arab research, documentation, and publication center specializing in the Arab-Israeli conflict and Palestinian affairs. It publishes books, papers, and the quarterly *Journal of Palestine Studies.*

The Middle East Institute (MEI)
1761 N St. NW
Washington, DC 20036-2882
(202) 785-1141
fax: (202) 331-8861

MEI is an organization of business executives, government officials, scholars, and others interested in the Middle East. It promotes interest in Middle East culture, history, and politics. MEI publishes *The Middle East Journal* quarterly.

Middle East Research and Information Project (MERIP)
1500 Massachusetts Ave. NW, Suite 119
Washington, DC 20005
(202) 223-3677

MERIP is an editorial committee of Middle East studies researchers. It provides information, research, and analysis on American involvement in the Middle East and on economic and political developments there. MERIP publishes the bimonthly *Middle East Report*, the pamphlets *Human Rights Series* and *Palestine and Israel: A Primer*, and the book *Intifada: The Palestinian Uprising Against Israeli Occupation.*

Palestine Human Rights Information Center (PHRIC)
4201 Connecticut Ave. NW, Suite 500
Washington, DC 20008
(202) 686-5116
fax: (202) 686-5140

PHRIC is an independent, nongovernmental human rights monitoring and educational organization that has worked for human rights in the West Bank and Gaza Strip. The center publishes *From the Field*, a monthly report on human rights issues, and booklets such as *The Economic Impact of the "Closure"* and *Israel's Death Squads.*

The Theodor Herzl Foundation
110 E. 59th St., 4th Fl.
New York, NY 10022
(212) 339-6037

The foundation is a pro-Israel educational agency that promotes the study and discussion of problems confronting Jews around the world. It publishes the monthly magazine *Midstream—A Monthly Jewish Review.*

Bibliography of Books

Saïd K. Aburish   *Cry Palestine: Inside the West Bank*. Boulder, CO: Westview Press, 1993.

Uri Avnery   *Israel Without Zionists: A Plea for Peace in the Middle East*. New York: Macmillan, 1968.

George W. Ball and Douglas B. Ball   *The Passionate Attachment: America's Involvement with Israel, 1947 to the Present*. New York: W.W. Norton & Co., 1992.

Mitchell G. Bard and Joel Himelfarb   *Myths and Facts: A Concise Record of the Arab-Israeli Conflict*. Washington, DC: Near East Research, 1992.

Benjamin Beit-Hallahmi   *Original Sins: Reflections on the History of Zionism and Israel*. Concord, MA: Pluto Press, 1992.

Alon Ben-Meir   *A Framework for Arab-Israeli Peace*. St. Louis: Robert Publishing, 1993.

Ian J. Bickerton and Carla L. Klausner   *A Concise History of the Arab-Israeli Conflict*. Englewood Cliffs, NJ: Prentice-Hall, 1991.

Elizabeth Warnock Fernea and Mary Evelyn Hocking, eds.   *The Struggle for Peace: Israelis and Palestinians*. Austin: University of Texas Press, 1992.

Paul Findley   *Deliberate Deceptions: Facing the Facts About the U.S.-Israeli Relationship*. Brooklyn, NY: Lawrence Hill Books, 1993.

Robert I. Friedman   *Zealots for Zion: Inside Israel's West Bank Settlement Movement*. New York: Random House, 1992.

Adam Garfinkle   *Israel and Jordan in the Shadow of War: Functional Ties and Futile Diplomacy in a Small Place*. New York: St. Martin's Press, 1992.

Dore Gold   *Israel as an American Non-NATO Ally: Parameters of Defense-Industrial Cooperation*. Boulder, CO: Westview Press, 1993.

Michael Gorkin   *Days of Honey, Days of Onion: The Story of a Palestinian Family in Israel*. Berkeley: University of California Press, 1993.

David Grossman   *Sleeping on a Wire: Conversations with Palestinians in Israel*. New York: Farrar, Straus and Giroux, 1993.

Leon T. Hadar   *Quagmire: America in the Middle East*. Washington, DC: Cato Institute, 1992.

Sami Hadawi	*Bitter Harvest: A Modern History of Palestine.* New York: Olive Branch Press, 1990.
Arthur Hertzberg	*Jewish Polemics.* New York: Columbia University Press, 1992.
Deena Hurwitz, ed.	*Walking the Red Line: Israelis in Search of Justice for Palestine.* Philadelphia: New Society Publishers, 1992.
Meir Kahane	*Our Challenge: The Chosen Land.* Radnor, PA: Chilton, 1974.
Edy Kaufman, Shukri B. Amed, and Robert L. Rothstein, eds.	*Democracy, Peace, and the Israeli-Palestinian Conflict.* Boulder, CO: Lynne Rienner, 1993.
Walid Khalidi	*Palestinians Reborn.* London: I.B. Tauris & Co., 1992.
Baruch Kimmerling and Joel S. Migdal	*Palestinians: The Making of a People.* New York: Free Press, 1993.
David A. Korn	*Stalemate: The War of Attrition and Great Power Diplomacy in the Middle East, 1967-1970.* Boulder, CO: Westview Press, 1992.
Keith Kyle and Joel Peters, eds.	*Whither Israel?: The Domestic Challenge.* London: I.B. Tauris, 1992.
David Landau	*Piety and Power: The World of Jewish Fundamentalism.* London: Seker and Warburg, 1993.
Yeshayahu Leibowitz	*Judaism, Human Values, and the Jewish State.* Cambridge, MA: Harvard University Press, 1992.
Middle East Watch	*Syria Unmasked: The Suppression of Human Rights by the Assad Regime.* New Haven, CT: Yale University Press, 1991.
Irving Moskowitz	*Should America Guarantee Israel's Safety?* New York: Americans for a Safe Israel, 1993.
Jamal R. Nassar	*The Palestinian Liberation Organization: From Armed Struggle to Declaration of Independence.* New York: Praeger, 1992.
Benjamin Netanyahu	*A Place Among the Nations: Israel and the World.* New York: Bantam Books, 1993.
A.F.K. Organski	*The $36 Billion Bargain: Strategy and Politics in U.S. Assistance to Israel.* New York: Columbia University Press, 1990.
Karen L. Puschel	*U.S.-Israeli Strategic Cooperation in the Post-Cold War Era: An American Perspective.* Boulder, CO: Westview Press, 1992.

William B. Quandt | *Peace Process: American Diplomacy and the Arab-Israeli Conflict Since 1967.* Berkeley: University of California Press, 1993.

J. Lewis Rasmussen and Robert B. Oakley | *Conflict Resolution in the Middle East: Simulating a Diplomatic Negotiation Between Israel and Syria.* Washington, DC: United States Institute of Peace Press, 1992.

Rosemary Radford Ruether and Marc H. Ellis, eds. | *Beyond Occupation: American, Jewish, Christian, and Palestinian Voices for Peace.* Boston: Beacon Press, 1990.

Edward W. Said | *The Question of Palestine.* New York: Vintage Books, 1992.

David Schoenbaum | *The United States and the State of Israel.* New York: Oxford University Press, 1993.

Harvey Sicherman | *Palestinian Autonomy, Self-Government, and Peace.* Boulder, CO: Westview Press, 1993.

Martin Sicker | *Judaism, Nationalism, and the Land of Israel.* Boulder, CO: Westview Press, 1992.

Charles D. Smith | *Palestine and the Arab-Israeli Conflict.* 2d ed. New York: St. Martin's Press, 1992.

Steven L. Spiegel, ed. | *The Arab-Israeli Search for Peace in the Middle East.* Boulder, CO: Lynne Rienner, 1992.

Ehud Sprinzak | *The Ascendance of Israel's Radical Right.* New York: Oxford University Press, 1991.

Washington Institute for Near East Policy | *Enduring Partnership: Report of the Commission on U.S.-Israeli Relations.* Washington, DC: WINEP, 1993.

Avner Yaniv, ed. | *National Security and Democracy in Israel.* Boulder, CO: Lynne Rienner, 1993.

Index

AAHR (Arab Association for Human
Rights), 198-201
Abd al-Jawad, Salih, 212, 214-15
Abd al-Malik, Dahamsha, 213-14
'Abd al-Shafi, Haydar, 139
Abdullah, king of Jordan, 151
Adan Commission, 212
administrative detention, 217, 220-
21, 236-37
Agranat, J., 192
AIPAC (American Israel Public
Affairs Committee), 241, 251
airborne warning and control system
(AWACS), 155, 158, 167
Akawi, Mustafa, 213
aliyah (immigration), 36
Allon, Yigal, 73
American-Arab Anti-Discrimination
Committee, 233
American Council for Judaism, 77
American Israel Public Affairs
Committee (AIPAC), 241, 251
Amin, Idi, 91
Amnesty International, 213, 238
Anglo-American Committee of
Inquiry, 39
An-Najar University, 119-20
anti-Semitism
Arabs and, 176, 179
as complex movement, 18
criticism of Israel is, 92-93
antitactical ballistic missiles (ATBMs),
230-31
Antonius, George, 37
Al Aqsa mosque, 170, 173
Arab Administrative Council, 113-14
Arab Association for Human Rights
(AAHR), 198
Arabs
anti-Jewish attitude of, 176, 179
countries of
arms and military advantage of,
156-57
size and population, 155-56
horrible rule of Jerusalem by,
175-76
Muslims and Jerusalem, 170-73
number of Palestinian terrorist
groups, 159
opposed British Mandate, 38-42
Pan-Arab credo, 134
promised Palestine by Great

Britain, 37
Arab Students' Congress, 41
Arafat, Yasser, 149, 150, 175
as initiator of peace, 143, 146
as target for assassins, 123
on great Arab nation, 149-50
on Israel-PLO Accord, 108-9
on Palestine independence, 143
previously denounced terrorism,
112-13
Arens, Moshe, 252
Argentina
considered for Jewish state, 23-24
Arrow (missile) program, 230-31
Ashrawi, Hanan, 215
Aspin, Les, 230
Assad, Hafez al-, 127, 131-35, 244
Association of Israeli-Palestinian
Physicians for Human Rights, 214,
238
ATBMs (antitactical ballistic
missiles), 230-31
Avnery, Uri, 60
Avnon, Arthur, 219
AWACS (airborne warning and
control system), 155, 158, 167
Ayyub, Ephraim, 125

Ba'athist, 131, 134-35
Bainerman, Joel, 257
Balfour Declaration, 33
Ball, Douglas B., 249
Ball, George W., 249
Barak, Ehud, 243
Barakat, Mustafa, 213
BARD (Binational Agricultural
Research and Development
Foundation), 231
Bar-Illan, David, 134
Bar Kochba rebellion, 177
Barnea, N., 126
Basic Law: Knesset, 199
Baum, Shlomo, 154
Baylouny, Anne Marie, 233
Begin, Menachem, 191
Begin, Ze'ev Benjamin, 111
Ben-Gurion, David, 32, 135, 189
Bergson, Peter, 77-79
Bezek (company), 246
Binational Agricultural Research and
Development Foundation (BARD),
231

Binational Industrial Research and Development Foundation (BIRD), 231
Binational Service Foundation (BSF), 231
BIRD (Binational Industrial Research and Development Foundation), 231
Bir Zeit University, 119, 120, 212
Black Panthers (Fatah), 121
blacks
Israel and, 245-46
Zionism and, 90-91
Bries, Muhammad Suleiman, 213-14
British Mandate (1922), 33-34, 149, 192
Brooks, Charles, 226
BSF (Binational Service Foundation), 231
B'tselem, 115
Burns, E.L., 182
Bush, George, 165

Camp David Accords, 100, 113, 116, 150, 159, 228
Canadian Zionist Federation, 86
Carmon, Yigal, 118-20
Carter, Jimmy, 236
Center for Foreign Policy Options, 228
Cheney, Dick, 227-28, 242
children
as Israeli prisoners, 212
killed by Israelis, 237
Christians
Jerusalem and, 170-73
Christopher, Warren, 107, 175
Church of the Holy Sepulcher, 170, 173
Circassian populations, 201
Clinton, Bill, 107-8, 150, 229, 231
Cohen, Chaim, 66
Cold War
Israel and, 80-81, 160
Columbus, Christopher, 61
Congressional Research Service (CRS), 252-53
Council for the National Interest, 180
Council of Settlements (Judea, Samaria, Gaza), 123
Cyrus (Koresh), emperor of Persia, 177

Darwish, Mahmoud, 145
David, king of Israel, 177, 179
Dayan, Moshe, 104
Declaration of Independence (Israeli), 104, 189, 199
Declaration of Principles, 108, 126

Defense Service Law (1986), 201
Democratic Front for the Liberation of Palestine (DFLP), 125
deportation of activists, 118-21, 145
de Torquemada, Tomás, 89
Developmental Areas, 203
DFLP (Democratic Front for the Liberation of Palestine), 125
Diaspora, 27, 30, 71, 74
Dine, Thomas A., 241
Disengagement Agreement (Yom Kippur War), 183
Dole, Robert, 252
Domb, Aaron, 123
Dome of the Rock, 170, 173
Donlan, Thomas G., 255
Drake, Laura, 180
Druckman, Haim, 125
Druze populations, 201
Dupuy, T.N., 155

Eban, Abba, 165
Economic Support Funds (ESF), 247, 250
Elazar, Rahamim, 90
Endowment for Defense Industrial Cooperation (EDIC), 231
European Convention of Human Rights, 219
European Human Rights Court, 219
Evron, Boas, 104

Fatah, 120-21
Feder, Don, 208
Fidel, Raya, 78
First Temple of Jerusalem, 177-78
Fischer, Stanley, 246, 256
Ford, Gerald, 256
Foreign Assistance Act (U.S.), 240
Foreign Military Sales (FMS), 243, 247, 250, 253
"Fundamental Laws" of Israel, 238-39

Galut(h) (exile) status, 29, 34-35, 57, 72
Gandhi, Mohandas K., 29, 45
Garibaldi, Giuseppe, 103
Gaza Bar Association, 212
Gazit, Shlomo, 124
Geertz, Clifford, 75
General Armistice Agreement (Six Day War), 182
General Security Service (Israel), 115
Geneva Convention(s), 83, 144, 213, 236, 238
Ginzberg, Asher Zvi (pseud. Ahad Ha'am), 25, 27, 35
Goebbels, Joseph, 89

Golan Heights
  ancient history of, 188
  Golan Heights Law (1981), 188-90
  Israel must retain, 187-94
  Israel must return, 180-86
  seized in Six Day War, 181
  Syrian capital near, 185
  Syria's claim to, 127-35
  Zionism and, 188-89, 192
Goldstein, Eric, 217
Gore, Al, 150
Goren, Shlomo, 123
Grass, Rueven, 87
Great Britain
  favorable consideration of Jewish
    state, 19
  promised Palestine to Arabs, 37
Green Line, 120, 126, 156
Grillparzer, Franz, 103
Gulf Cooperation Council (Arab), 109

Ha'am, Ahad. See Ginzberg, Asher
  Zvi
Hadar, Leon T., 76
Hadawi, Sami, 82
Hamas (Islamic Resistance
  Movement), 112-15, 125
  are threat to peace, 117-21
  Izzadin al-Kassam, 120-21
  vow to kill Israelis, 119
  women participate in, 118
Hamilton, Lee H., 252
al-Haq, 212-13
Hashemite royal family, 151-52
Hassan, crown prince of Jordan, 150
Herman, Simon N., 55-56, 69
Hersh, Seymour, 185
Herzl, Theodor, 17, 26, 61, 90
  Palestine for Jewish homeland and,
    23-24
Hibbat Zion, 27-30
Holocaust, 53, 89, 91
Holy Sepulcher, Church of, 170, 173
Hout, Chafiq el, 150
hunger strike by Palestinian
  prisoners, 211-14
Husain, Sharif, 37-39
Hussein, Faisal, 114, 126
Hussein, king of Jordan, 150-52
Hussein, Saddam, 112, 148, 227, 254

Ibrahim, 120-21
Id, Hazim, 213
IDF. See Israeli Defense Force
immigrants
  Israel's continued absorption of,
    244-45
Inquisition, 89

International Convention on the
  Elimination of All Forms of Racial
  Discrimination, 83
International Red Cross, 238
intifada
  Jewish, 125
  Palestinian, 118, 124, 140, 144, 236
Irish Republican Army (IRA), 219
Islamic Resistance Movement. See
  Hamas
Islamic Shariah College, 119
Israel
  Cold War and, 80-81, 160
  collective punishment of
    Palestinians by, 238
  crimes of, 235-36
  Declaration of Independence of,
    104, 189, 199
  defense expenditures by, 243, 248
  deportation of activists by, 118-21,
    145
  Developmental Areas, 203
  economy of
    expanding and reforming, 245-47
    in trouble, 254-55
  equality of women in, 242
  "Fundamental Laws," 238-39
  General Security Service, 115
  Golan Heights and
    must retain, 187-94
    must return, 180-86
  immigrants to
    continued absorption of, 244-45
  independent Palestine and
    would not threaten, 162-67
    would threaten, 154-61
  Jerusalem, control of
    Israel should not share, 174-79
    Israel should share, 168-73
  Law of Return (1950), 65, 78, 86-87,
    200-201
  "Movement for Separating Religion
    and State," 79
  Nationality Law (1952), 87, 200-201
  nuclear weapons and, 185
  Offek satellite launched by, 167
  Palestinian civil rights and
    violated by Israel, 198-201
    con, 204-9
  Palestinian population of, 199
  Palestinian prisoners in. See
    Palestinians, prisoners in Israel
  peace
    Israel is committed to, 97-101
    con, 102-5
  size and location of, 155-56
  threats to
    Hamas terrorists are, 117-21

Jewish settlers are, 122-26
United States aid to
  should be eliminated, 249-57
  con, 241-48
United States-Israel relations
  should be changed, 233-40
  should be strengthened, 226-32
USS *Liberty* and
  Israel's attack on, 184
Zionism and
  should be promoted, 52-59
  should be rejected, 60-68
  strengthens Israel, 69-75
    con, 76-81
  see also Israeli Defense Force (IDF);
    Israel-PLO Accord
Israel Chemicals (company), 246
Israeli, Rafi, 119-21
Israeli Defense Force (IDF), 100, 115
  destruction of Palestinian homes by,
    200
  military expenditures of, 243-48
  prison camps of, 211-22
Israel Institute of Applied Research,
  72
Israel Lands Administration, 201
Israel-PLO Accord
  Arab Administrative Council and,
    113-14
  Declaration of Principles, 108
  is prelude to peace, 106-10
  is prelude to violence, 111-16
  must fit into Madrid framework,
    107-8
  Palestinians' ulterior motives and,
    113
  U.S. role in implementing, 107-10
Izzadin al-Kassam, 120-21

Jahshan, Khalil E., 106
Jarrar, Bassm, 118
Jerusalem, 168-79
  Arab rule of, as horrible, 175-76
  control of
    Israel should share, 168-73
      con, 174-79
  First Temple of, 177-78
  history of, 175-79
  holy city for three religions, 170-73
  Jerusalem Program (1968), 70
  Old City of, 175
  other names for, 172
  Second Temple of, 177
Jerusalem Institute for Western
  Defence, 154
Jerusalem Program, 70
Jewish Agency, 201-2
Jewish Defense League, 52

Jewish National Fund (JNF), 201
Jewish Newsletter, 87
Jewish state, separate
  is necessary, 17-24
    con, 25-31
Jews
  aliyah (immigration) and, 36
  Galut(h) (exile) status, 29, 34-35
  Holocaust, 53, 89, 91
  Inquisition and, 89
  separate state for is necessary, 17-24
    con, 25-31
  values of, declining, 55-56
jihad, 118
Johnson, Samuel, 112
Jordanian National Assembly, 150
Judaism versus Zionism, 86-87
Judenrein, 20, 175, 179

Kahane, Meir, 52
Katzover, Zvi, 126
Keegan, George, 229
Kennedy, John F., 250
Khaddam, Abdul-Halim, 243
Khalidi, Walid, 129, 162
Khartoum statement (Arab), 105
kibbutzim, 67, 133
Kiryat Arba Settler Movement, 126
Kislev, Ron, 125
Konvitz, M.R., 87
Kook, Hillel, 77-79
Koresh (Cyrus), emperor of Persia,
  177

Lahoud, Lamia, 117
Law of Return (1950), 65, 78, 86-87,
  200-201
League of Arab States, 141
League of Nations, 151, 188-89, 234
Leibowitz, Yeshayahu, 102
Libai, David, 214
Liebes, Steven, 244
Lindner, Bernard I., 177

McMahon, Sir Henry, 37, 39
McPherson, Peter, 229
Madrid Conference and framework,
  98, 128, 135, 140, 146, 181
  Israel-PLO Accord and, 107-8
Magnes, Judah L., 43
Marcus, Yoel, 126
Mark, Clyde R., 253
Marshall Plan, 250
Masri, Taher, 152
Michaels, Marguerite, 122
Middle East Problem versus
  Palestinian Problem, 148-49
Middle East Watch, 217, 238

missiles in Middle East, 156, 159-60
  antitactical ballistic missiles
    (ATBMs), 230-31
  Arrow, 230-31
  Scud, 112, 134, 148, 217, 230
Mizrahi, Haim, 126
Modai, Yitzhak, 255
Mohsin, Zuhair, 149
Montefiore, Sir Mose Haim, 178
Moslem Brotherhood, 118-19
Mount of Olives, 175
"Movement for Separating Religion
  and State," 79
Moynihan, Daniel, 85
Mubarak, Hosni, 101
Murphy, Emma, 84
Muslims, 118, 119
  Jerusalem and, 170-73
  see also Arabs; Hamas

Naor, Aryeh, 91
Nasser, Gamal Abdel, 184
Natan (prophet), 179
National Association of Arab
  Americans, 106
Nationality Law (1952), 87, 200-201
National Prison Service, 217-18
National Progressive Front (Syria), 131
National Religious party, 125
Netanyahu, Benjamin, 88, 147
Nigar, Ahiram, 123
Nixon, Richard, 256
Nordau, Max, 23
nuclear weapons
  development in Middle East,
    100-101, 185

Odeh, Adnan Abu, 168
Offek satellite, 167
Old City (of Jerusalem), 175
Olmert, Ehud, 174
Omar, Samir, 213
Oslo peace package, 124

Palestine
  as early site for Jewish state, 19,
    23-24
  as holy land for three religions, 42,
    48-49
  as independent
    would threaten Israel, 113, 154-61
    con, 162-67
  is Arab birthright, 37-42
  is Jewish birthright, 32-36
  Palestinian Problem versus Middle
    East Problem, 148-49
  promised to Arabs, 37
  should be binational state, 43-49

terrorist groups in
  number of, 159
  see also Palestinians; PLO
Palestine Human Rights Information
  Center, 212, 236
Palestine Liberation Organization.
  See PLO
Palestine National Committee, 77
Palestine National Council, 141-43,
  150
Palestine Royal Commission, 38
Palestinian Council (West Bank and
  Gaza), 109
Palestinian Declaration of
  Independence, 141
Palestinians
  acknowledged PLO allegiance, 205,
    209
  as initiators of peace, 142-43
  Circassian population, 201
  civil rights of
    are violated by Israel, 198-201
    con, 204-9
  collective punishment of, 238
  destruction of homes by IDF, 200
  Druze population, 201
  population in Israel, 199
  poverty of, 202
  prisoners in Israel
    abuse of
      by Israel, 204-9
      not abused by Israel, 210-15
    administrative detention, 217,
      220-21, 236
    census of prisoners (detailed), 212
    hunger strike, 211-14
    torture, 213, 219, 236-37
    women and children, 212
  should have independent nation,
    139-46
    con, 147-53
Pan-Arab credo, 134
Paris Peace Conference (1919), 188
peace
  Israel is committed to, 97-101
    con, 102-5
  Israel-PLO Accord is prelude to,
    106-10
    con, 111-16
  PLO as initiator of, 142-43, 146
  Syria is committed to, 127-31
    con, 132-35
Peled, Matti, 183
Peres, Shimon, 115, 175-76
Petel, Michal, 123-24
Physicians for Human Rights, 214,
  238
PLO, 90

anti-Jewish attitude of, 179
as initiator of peace, 142-43
Black Panthers and, 121
Palestinians' acknowledged
    allegiance to, 205, 209
Red Eagles and, 121
see also Israel-PLO Accord
Podhoretz, Norman, 113
Popular Front for the Liberation of
    Palestine, 121
Presidents of Major American Jewish
    Organizations, 148
prisoners, Palestinian. *See under*
    Palestinians

Quayle, Dan, 247
Quds, Al, 172-73
    Radio Al Quds, 134

Rabin, Yitzhak, 55, 97-101, 104-5,
    111-12, 124, 200, 211, 215
racism
    U.N. resolutions and, 83-85
    Zionism as, 82-87
        con, 88-93
Radio Al Quds, 134
Ramati, Yohanan, 154-61
Ramon, Haim, 115
Rantisi, Ahmed, 120
Red Eagles, 121
Rifai, Zaid al-, 152
Rothschild, Lord, 19
Rubenstein, Danny, 211
Rubinstein, Amnon, 191
Ruether, Herman J., 80
Ruether, Rosemary Radford, 80

Sadat, Anwar, 101
Sawendaq, Kader, 119-20
Sayegh, Fayez, 83
Schiff, Ze'ev, 215
Schwartz, Peter, 204
Scud missiles, 112, 134, 148, 227, 230
Seale, Patrick, 127, 133
second strike capability, 159
Second Temple of Jerusalem, 177
Shahak, Israel, 65
Shahal, Moshe, 214
Shah'th, Nabil, 124, 126
Shamir, Yitzhak, 104, 181
Sharon, Ariel, 181
shaweesh system, 218, 221-22
Shazar, Zalman, 72
Shochetman, Eliav, 187
Shoval, Zalman, 132
Shur, Chaim, 102
Simon, Judith D., 216
Simon, Rita J., 216

Six Day War, 53, 63, 92, 97, 102-4,
    149
    debate on who started, 183-84, 189,
        206
    General Armistice Agreement, 182
    Golan Heights seized, 181
Solomon, king of Israel, 177-78
Sosebee, Stephen, 200
Specter, Arlen, 226
State Education Law (1953), 202
Stein, Stanley, 256
Syria
    capital near Golan Heights, 185
    Golan Heights and, 127-35
        must return to, 180-86
        con, 187-94
    is committed to peace, 127-31
        con, 132-35
    National Progressive Front, 131
    Radio Al Quds, 134

Thant, U, 184
Tlas, Mustafa, 243-44
torture of Palestinian prisoners, 213,
    219, 236-37
Toubi, Tawfik, 200
Truman, Harry S, 250

Ubaidat, Hussein, 214
Union of Bulgarian Lawyers, 92
Union of Writers (Bulgaria), 92
United Nations
    Declaration on the Elimination of
        All Forms of Racial
        Discrimination, 83
    Emergency Force (UNEF), 184
    Mixed Armistice Commission
        (MAC), 181
    Resolutions 37 & 40 (Zionism is
        racism), 83-85
    Resolution 93 (return of refugees),
        182
    Resolution 111 (flagrant violations),
        182
    Resolution 171 (condemnation of
        Israel), 182
    Resolution 181 (creation of Israel
        and Palestine), 142, 145
    Resolution 194 (Palestinian
        refugees), 145
    Resolution 242 (peace in Golan),
        134, 142, 145, 169-73, 181, 235
    Resolution 338 (troop withdrawal),
        142, 145, 181
    Resolution 425 (invasion of
        Lebanon), 239
    Resolution 497 (Golan Heights), 181
    Resolution 681 (deportation

condemned), 145
Truce Supervision Organisation (UNTSO), 181-82
Universal Declaration of Human Rights, 83, 86
United States
aid to Israel
Economic Support Funds (ESF), 247, 250
Foreign Military Sales (FMS), 243, 247, 250, 253
should be eliminated, 249-57
con, 241-48
see also BARD; BIRD; BSF
role in implementing Israel-PLO Accord, 107-10
United States-Israel relations
should be changed, 233-40
should be strengthened, 226-32
Usher, Graham
on abuse of prisoners, 210-15
on settlers as threat, 122-26
U.S.-Israel Science and Technology Commission, 231-32
USS Liberty, 184

Vitalis, Robert, 165

Wailing Wall, 53, 170, 173, 178-79, 192
Waldman, Eliezer, 123
West Bank and Gaza
Israel-PLO Accord and, 107-10
settlers are threat to peace, 122-26
size and description, 164

Western Wall. See Wailing Wall
women
as Israeli prisoners, 212
equality of in Israel, 242
in Hamas, 118
killed and maimed by Israelis, 237-38
World Zionist Congress(es), 17, 55, 70, 71
World Zionist Organization, 201-2

Yerushalaim, 172-73
Yeshiva Settler Council, 125
Yom Kippur War (1973), 72, 156, 244
Disengagement Agreement, 183

Zangwill, Israel, 48
ZIM (company), 246
Zionism, 33
denies Jewish rights, 65
early search for Jewish homeland and, 22-24
Golan Heights and, 188-89, 192
Hibbat Zion and, 27-30
is racism, 82-87
con, 88-93
Israel is strengthened by, 69-75
con, 76-81
Israel should promote, 52-59
Israel should reject, 60-68
myths of, 80
real basis of, 27-28
stated aims of, 70-71, 73
truths of, 58-59
versus Judaism, 86-87